Development and Brain Systems in Autism

This volume covers several perspectives on autism which bring together the most recent scientific views of the nature of this disorder. A number of themes organize major developments and emerging areas in autism:

- Cognitive and neural systems development: how autism arises in the behavior and thought of very young children.
- Discovering brain mechanisms underlying social and cognitive deficits in autism: how we can explain "social awkwardness" and poor language comprehension in terms of malfunctions of brain mechanisms, revealed by fMRI studies of people with autism.
- Integrating information about genes, brain, and biological mechanisms with behavioral evidence.
- Linking the science of autism with lives lived: how the new information about autism impacts people with autism and real-world considerations.

Marcel Adam Just is the D. O. Hebb Professor of Psychology at Carnegie Mellon University. His brain-imaging research investigates the biological mechanisms underlying the altered psychological processes in autism. His autism research has made several fundamental discoveries concerning differences in brain function, including findings of alterations in synchronization, in white matter communication tracts, and in the balance of frontal versus posterior activation.

Kevin A. Pelphrey is the Harris Associate Professor of Child Psychiatry at the Yale Child Study Center. His research addresses fundamental questions regarding the typical and atypical development of brain mechanisms for social cognition in children with and without autism spectrum disorders.

Carnegie Mellon Symposia on Cognition

David Klahr, Series Editor

Anderson • Cognitive Skills and Their Acquisition

Carroll/Payne • Cognition and Social Behavior

Carver/Klahr • Cognition and Instruction: Twenty-Five Years of Progress

Clark/Fiske • Affect and Cognition

Cohen/Schooler • Scientific Approaches to Consciousness

Cole • Perception and Production of Fluent Speech

Farah/Ratcliff • The Neuropsychology of High-Level Vision: Collected Tutorial Essays

Gershkoff-Stowe/Rakison • Building Object Categories in Developmental Time

Granrud • Visual Perception and Cognition in Infancy

Gregg • Knowledge and Cognition

Just/Carpenter • Cognitive Processes in Comprehension

Just/Pelphrey • Development and Brain Systems in Autism

Kimchi/Behrmann/Olson • Perceptual Organization in Vision: Behavioral and Neural Perspectives

Klahr • Cognition and Instruction

Klahr/Kotovsky • Complex Information Processing: The Impact of Herbert A. Simon

Lau/Sears • Political Cognition

Lovett/Shah • Thinking With Data

MacWhinney • The Emergence of Language

MacWhinney • Mechanisms of Language Acquisition

McClelland/Siegler • Mechanisms of Cognitive Development: Behavioral and Neural Perspectives

Reder • Implicit Memory and Metacognition

Siegler • Children's Thinking: What Develops?

Sophian • Origins of Cognitive Skills

Staszewski • Expertise and Skills Acquisition

Steier/Mitchell • Mind Matters: A Tribute to Allen Newell

VanLehn • Architectures for Intelligence

Development and Brain Systems in Autism

Edited by

Marcel Adam Just
and
Kevin A. Pelphrey

Psychology Press
Taylor & Francis Group
NEW YORK AND LONDON

First published 2013
by Psychology Press part of the Taylor and Francis Group
711 Third Avenue, New York, NY 10017

Simultaneously published in the UK
by Psychology Press
27 Church Road, Hove, East Sussex BN3 2FA

Psychology Press is an imprint of the Taylor & Francis Group, an informa business

Library of Congress Cataloging in Publication Data
A catalog record for this book has been requested

ISBN: 978-1-84872-866-0 (hbk)
ISBN: 978-1-84872-640-6 (pbk)
ISBN: 978-0-203-07335-3 (ebk)

Typeset in New Caledonia LT Std and Korinna
by Wearset Ltd, Boldon, Tyne and Wear

SFI Certified Sourcing
www.sfiprogram.org
SFI-00453

Printed and bound in the United States of America
by Edwards Brothers, Inc.

Contents

List of Figures

List of Tables

Contributors

Dr. Susan Bookheimer
Center for Cognitive Neuroscience
UCLA Department of Psychiatry and Biobehavioral Sciences
760 Westwood Plaza
Los Angeles, CA 90095

Dr. Susan E. Bryson
Autism Research Centre
IWK Health Centre
Dalhousie University
5850 University Avenue
Halifax, Nova Scotia
Canada B3K 6R8

Dr. Daniel H. Geschwind
UCLA Department of Neurology
710 Westwood Plaza
Los Angeles, CA 90095–1769

Dr. Temple Grandin
Department of Animal Sciences
Colorado State University
Fort Collins, CO 80523

Dr. Kathrin Hippler
Department of Paediatrics and Adolescent Medicine
Medical University of Vienna
Waehringer Guertel 18–20
1090 Vienna, Austria

Dr. Warren Jones
Marcus Autism Center
Emory University School of Medicine and Children's Healthcare in Atlanta
Atlanta, GA 30329

Dr. Marcel Adam Just
Carnegie Mellon University
Department of Psychology
5000 Forbes Avenue
Pittsburgh, PA 15213

Dr. Rajesh K. Kana
UAB Department of Psychology
Civitan International Research Center, CIRC 235G
1719 6th Ave S
Birmingham, AL 35294

Dr. Timothy A. Keller
Carnegie Mellon University
Department of Psychology
5000 Forbes Avenue
Pittsburgh, PA 15213

Dr. Christopher L. Klein
Marietta College
Department of Psychology
Marietta, OH 45750

Dr. Ami Klin
Emory University School of Medicine and Children's Healthcare in Atlanta
Atlanta, GA 30329

Dr. Laura Grofer Klinger
The University of Alabama
Department of Psychology
505 Hackberry Lane
Tuscaloosa, AL 35487

Dr. Mark R. Klinger
The University of Alabama
Department of Psychology
505 Hackberry Lane
Tuscaloosa, AL 35487

Dr. Carla A. Mazefsky
University of Pittsburgh School of Medicine
Department of Psychiatry
Pittsburgh, PA 15213

Dr. Nancy J. Minshew
University of Pittsburgh
Webster Hall – Suite 300
3811 O'Hara Street
Pittsburgh, PA 15213

Ms. Jennifer Moss
Carnegie Mellon University
Department of Psychology
Pittsburgh, PA 15213

Dr. Kevin A. Pelphrey
Yale Child Study Center
230 South Frontage Road
P.O. Box 207900
New Haven, CT 06520–7900

Dr. Susan B. Perlman
University of Pittsburgh Medical School
Western Psychiatric Institute and Clinic
Pittsburgh, PA 15213

Dr. Ashley A. Scott-Van Zeeland
Scripps Translational Science Institute, Scripps Health
3344 North Torrey Pines Court, Suite 300
La Jolla, CA 92037

Dr. Brittany G. Travers
University of Wisconsin-Madison
Waisman Laboratory for Brain Imaging and Behavior
Madison, WI 53705

Dr. Brent C. Vander Wyk
Yale University
Yale Child Study Center
New Haven, CT 06520

Dr. Bruno Wicker
Laboratoria de Neurosciencia Integrativa
Departamento de Fisica
Universidad de Buenos Aires
Pabellón I, Ciudad Universitaría
13009 Marseille
(1428) Capital Federal
Argentina

Section I
Lives Lived with Autism

1

My Experience with Visual Thinking and Sensory Oversensitivity

The Need for Research on Sensory Problems

TEMPLE GRANDIN
Department of Animal Sciences, Colorado State University, CO

My mind works like Google for images. When somebody asks me about something, it is the verbal equivalent of typing words into a search engine. Words serve only as the index tabs on all the visual images in my memory. People ask me, "How do you think?" I tell them that the basic way to understand my way of thinking is to give me a noun as a key word. For example, I will tell you how I access my memory for the word *ring*. The first picture that flashed into my mind triggered by the word *ring* was the ring in the movie *The Lord of the Rings*. Then I saw my aunt out at her ranch reading *The Hobbit*, which was her favorite book. (*The Hobbit* is the first book in the *The Lord of the Rings* series.) Then I saw all kinds of pictures from the good times I had when I visited my aunt's ranch as a teenager. My associative way of thinking jumped from the word *ring* to my aunt's ranch. If one were to analyze my thoughts by listing the "key word index tubs," it would seem to be disorganized, but if the pictures were displayed there would be an associative logic (Table 1.1).

My mind has the same associative logic that a search engine has. When I first started doing computer searches, I thought Google and other search

TABLE 1.1 List of Associations

Words List	Pictures List
Ring	The ring in the movie *The Lord of the Rings*
Ranch	Aunt Ann at the ranch reading her favorite book, *The Hobbit*
Gate	I built a gate on the ranch
Pickup Truck	I learned to drive on the ranch in a pickup truck
Model Rockets	I flew model rockets on the ranch

engines worked the same way as my mind. There are different associative branches. The word *ring* could have gone down a different branch: A ring can also be a riding ring. Then I would have been in the horse file in my mind. This brings up another totally different set of pictures. I see the riding ring I rode in high school, and the riding ring my assistant Mark built on the 126 acres that I own. If my mind stays in the riding ring file, I start to see images of horse shows, Grand Prix jumping, and other horse events that I have attended.

PHOTO REALISTIC PICTURES

All the images that flash into my mind are photo realistic images. They are not abstract. Pictures come into my memory sequentially like a series of slides flashed onto a screen. The images that are remembered the most clearly are the things that I really pay attention to, pictures that I use in my PowerPoint lectures (often they come up first), and the things that really interest me. I do not remember every hotel room I have visited because hotel rooms are way down low on my list of interests.

I visited the set where HBO was making a movie about me. I did not use my camera to take pictures, and I was not given pictures taken by somebody else. The clearest pictures I have in my memory are the things that grabbed my attention. I was fascinated by how they made fake stuff look real. An old airplane hangar was used as a sound stage. I have no memory of the hangar doors because I never attended to them. There was a small set of a chute at a meat plant. It looked like the wall was real concrete, but it was just painted plywood. I have a clear picture in my mind of looking at the edge of the fake wall and seeing that it was just paint on thin plywood. I was also fascinated by the lever system that operated a fake mechanical cow. I can see clear pictures of the cables that operated it.

The airplane hangar movie stage was a place I was highly interested in. I visited it for a relatively short time, about two hours. When I flip through my memories, I get clear pictures of about four things that I looked at intensely. It is like I took snapshots with the camera in my mind. The places where I remember the most accurate pictures of the entire place are places where I have spent a lot of time. To form a really accurate picture of a big place, I have to spend lots of time looking at each part of it to download a series of many snapshots.

PUTTING THE PIECES TOGETHER

When I first visited a big meat plant back in the 1970s, I thought that the place was so complicated. How did the plant manager understand how to manage something that was so complex? I visited the Swift Plant in Arizona every Tuesday for three years. After about six months of Tuesday afternoons standing and looking at the plant, I understood it. It became simple because I could replay a video of the entire plant in my mind. My mind had taken all the individual snapshots and put them together to form the whole place. It was like putting puzzle pieces together.

The first few Tuesdays, my attention zeroed in on details that most people would consider not important, such as a little cart for moving 55-gallon drums. The more pieces I downloaded into my mind, the better I understood. After 20 to 25 Tuesday afternoons, I had the entire plant downloaded into my memory, and this complicated place seemed really simple. I was then able to turn on the video camera in my imagination and walk through the entire plant from one end to the other.

The problem with my kind of thinking is that it takes time. After I get my "computer" loaded with lots of experiences, I can really think with it. My experience on the movie set was similar to an early visit to the meat plant. The movie set had lots of cool stuff I had never seen before, but I was there for such a short time that I could only get a few really clear "pictures" in my mind. When I see new things, it is like having a narrow lens camera that shoots pictures of details I am interested in.

DOING DESIGN WORK

My ability to think in pictures really helped me in my design work. When I design cattle handling facilities, I can test-run equipment in my mind like a 3-D virtual reality system. I thought that all designers were able to do this. It took me three years to learn how to do cattle handling facility design. The first step in my training was to visit lots of feedlots and handle cattle in many different facilities. I had to get detailed knowledge of design features that worked and ones that did not. One feedlot would have a wonderful loading ramp, but their sorting pens were bad. Another had efficient sorting pens, but the loading ramp was laid out wrong. I spent three years just downloading into my mind stuff that worked and stuff that did not. When I designed a new facility, I took the good bits and recombined these together into a new system. I describe how I did this in the first chapter of *Thinking in Pictures* (Grandin, 1996). In my earlier writing, I stated that my ability to do drawing sort of appeared like magic after I bought the same drafting tools that were used by a very talented draftsman that I had observed. The ability to do the drawing did appear like magic, but now I realize that it was based on three years of filling up the internet inside my head with images.

LEARNING TO READ DRAWINGS

When I first looked at an architectural drawing, I had difficulty relating the lines on the drawing with the real structure. I had to teach myself that a square on a drawing was a concrete column by walking through the meat plant with a complete layout drawing. I spent days walking through the plant with the drawings until I could relate every line on the drawing with a real piece of equipment or structural part of the building. A square drawn on the plans was a concrete column; a big circle was the water tower. At first, the lines on the drawing were too abstract to have meaning. I had to spend a great deal of time programming my brain, and when all the pieces of information came together my drawing ability magically appeared. Now I can look at drawings and see the finished structure.

FORMING CATEGORIES

How does my mind form a concept when I have all these detailed specific pictures in my mind? I sort them into categories. Neuroscience research has shown that the brain sorts sensory-based information into categories (Freedman, Riesenhuber, Poggio, & Miller, 2001). Even an insect brain can create categories (Giurfa, Zhang, Jenett, Menzel, & Srinivasan, 2001). It is like having file folders in the brain. Many times in my lectures, I have explained how I learned to differentiate a cat from a dog. I first used *size* to categorize dogs from cats. That worked well until our next-door neighbor got a Dachshund. I spent hours trying to figure out why the Dachshund could really be a dog when it was so small. After I studied the Dachshund, I found a visual feature that she shared with all the big dogs. Even though her nose was small, it looked exactly the same as the nose on our golden retriever. I had to make a new category of *nose shape*. Dogs and cats could also be separated into categories by sound or smell; dogs bark and cats meow. It was putting sensory-based information into categories.

FILLING UP MY BRAIN'S INTERNET

At the age of 65, I can think so much better than at age 20. The reason my thinking is more efficient now is because I have downloaded so much knowledge into my brain. This provides lots of information for my Google search engine to surf through the internet inside my mind. Nancy Minshew and others have hypothesized that autistic thinking is bottom-up instead of top-down (e.g., Minshew, Meyer, & Goldstein, 2002). I agree with this concept. For me to understand something, I have to compare it to an experience that I have in memory. I travel to many places and I read many books and newspapers. The more I learn, the more efficient my thinking. Dr. Tony Attwood, a specialist on Asperger syndrome, stated in one of his lectures that the "Aspie" is always looking for more and more knowledge. Several parents have also told me that their child has told them that he has to take in information so he can understand the world.

HOW I THINK ABOUT ABSTRACT CONCEPTS

Unless I can see a photo realistic picture in my mind, I have no thoughts. When I was little and learned The Lord's Prayer, it was incomprehensible. When I said "the power and the Glory," I saw a rainbow with an electric power tower at the end of it. Now at the age of 65, I have so many more pictures in the internet of my mind that I can understand more abstract things. To provide an example for this chapter, I opened up the dictionary, closed my eyes, and put my pencil on the page. It landed on the word *disqualify*. To understand this word, I have to retrieve from my memory specific examples of somebody being disqualified. I remember reading in the paper that students cannot get government scholarships if they have been arrested for doing drugs. In another article, I read about a brilliant illegal immigrant who won a scholarship but he could not get the money because he was illegal. Without specific examples, I would have no idea what *disqualify* meant. One of the reasons I have to read so much is because it would be impossible for me to understand a word like *disqualify* unless I had either experienced being disqualified from some activity or had read about specific examples.

PATTERN THINKING

My thoughts are in photo realistic pictures but I do have some ability to think in patterns. To recall the memories of the movie set, I walk around in the airplane hangar sound stage in my mind. I see some stuff very detailed, like the meat plant chute set, but often parts are vague. I did not have time to download all the new stuff in that place. However, I can make a decent map of the basic layout of the hangar, the food tent, and the office. The meat plant set was on the far right and the fake mechanical cow was in the back right-hand corner. Across the back part of the hangar was carpentry and welding equipment, and a large set of my apartment was in the middle of the hangar to the left. When I walked out the hangar door and turned left, there was a concession stand that had free chili. I can draw a fairly accurate map of the hangar and tell you where major sets and equipment were located (Figure 1.1).

I do not have a clear image in my mind of the welders or carpentry tools. I never looked at them because they were ordinary things that were not new and interesting. I was downloading the cool stuff, but I was able to tell you where most of the shop tools were located. I think the ability to make a map is

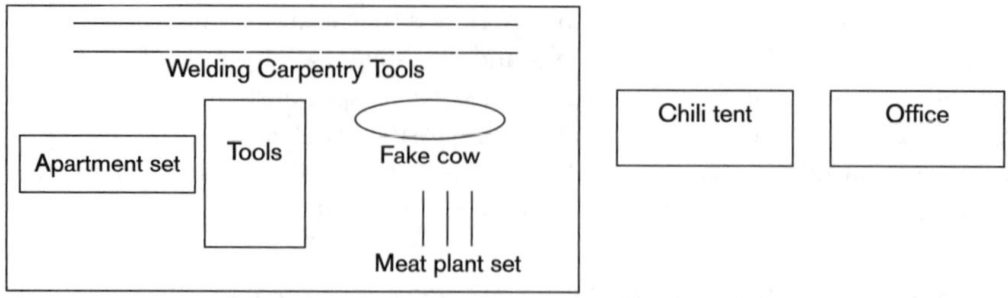

Figure 1.1 Schematic map of the movie set I toured, recalled from memory.

a separate skill compared to retrieving picture files. In fact, I have learned by reading many first-person accounts and interviewing people on the spectrum that there are three different types of specialized autistic minds.

TYPES OF SPECIALIZED THINKING

People on the spectrum have uneven skills. I am a visual thinker and doing algebra in school was impossible for me. I never got to try geometry or trigonometry because I kept failing algebra. When I have talked about my math problems at lectures, I have found five or six cases of children who failed algebra but they could do geometry really well. Some of these individuals can do the math in their heads with no written calculation. I often tell teachers that their minds work differently, and they do not need to do the step-by-step work. Based on books I have read and interviews with many people, I think there are three different autism mind types:

1. Visual Thinkers: They think in photo realistic pictures and are often terrible at algebra. I have talked to many visual thinkers who were bad at algebra. This description fits me.
2. Pattern Thinkers: They excel in math and are often musically gifted. They think in more abstract patterns instead of photo realistic pictures. Daniel Tammet and Jerry Newport are both pattern thinkers and numbers savants. To learn more about their method of specialized thinking, you can read *Born on a Blue Day* (Tammet, 2006) and *Mozart and the Whale* (Newport & Newport, 2007). Pattern thinkers are often weak in reading and English composition.
3. Word Thinkers: They are not visual thinkers and their math skills are only average. A typical word-type thinker is a person with Asperger's who loves history and knows every baseball statistic.

In all three of these cases, the person has an area of strength and an area of weakness. One trait that all the types have in common is that they attend to details and put details together to form whole concepts.

SENSORY SENSITIVITIES

Sensory oversensitivity can be extremely debilitating for many people on the autism spectrum. I know people on the spectrum who cannot tolerate a normal office or sporting event because the sound hurts their ears. There is a huge need for more research on sensory abnormalities in autism.

Sensory problems are extremely variable. When I was a child, loud noises hurt my ears like a dentist drill hitting a nerve. I hated balloons popping and the sound of the school bell was torture. As a child, when people talked directly to me, I could understand what they said. When grownups were talking fast among themselves, it sounded like gibberish. All I could hear were vowel sounds. It sounded like "oo-aa-oo-uu-a." My speech teacher slowly enunciated the hard consonant sounds. She would enunciate a word like *cup* by saying "cc u pp." Today I still have problems hearing differences between hard consonants, such as in *cat* or *bat*. I have to figure out the word by context. It is unlikely that my friend is talking about a pet bat. She would be telling me about her pet cat.

I also have problems with scratchy wool clothes. Even today I must have soft clothes against my skin. Some of my friends on the autism spectrum have even worse problems with wearing scratchy clothes. One lady told me that socks with a rough texture caused a burning sensation. Several mothers have told me that their children often take their socks or clothes off. This is probably due to sensory oversensitivity. I have found that some brands of T-shirts are rough and scratchy and others are soft. Even though all the shirts are 100% cotton, some are comfortable, and some T-shirts cannot be worn. One mother told me that her child could tolerate only one brand of very soft socks.

Some people have visual oversensitivity problems, and they cannot tolerate fluorescent lights because they can see the 60-cycle flicker. Donna Williams writes about this problem in her books *Somebody, Somewhere* and *Autism: An Inside Out Approach* (Williams, 1994, 1996). There is an old study that showed that florescent lights increased repetitive behavior in individuals with autism (Coleman, Frankel, Ritvoe, & Freeman, 1976). I had a dyslexic student who could not tolerate fluorescents. She told me that the room pulsated like a disco. She was greatly helped by the Irlen-colored lenses. Scientific studies show that they work for some people (Evans & Joseph, 2002; Lightstone, Lightstone, & Wilkins, 1999). Other interventions that helped her were using an LCD laptop computer screen and printing all her work on tan paper. She told me the print vibrated less on the laptop screen compared to a TV-type computer screen.

SENSORY RESEARCH REQUIREMENTS

When research is done on problems with sensory oversensitivity, subjects should be assigned to treatments based on their sensory problems, not just the autism diagnosis. Autism is so variable; one person will have horrible visual processing problems and another will have problems with sound sensitivity. If you had 20 subjects labeled "autistic," maybe only three would be helped by the Irlen lenses, but those three would be really helped. Irlen lenses are not going to help me. I do not have visual processing problems. People with visual processing problems are almost never photo realistic visual thinkers. Donna Williams and Tito Mukhopadhyay both use auditory representations in their thinking (Mukhopadhyay, 2008; Williams, 1994). Since their visual systems are so dysfunctional, their memories are all audio files. People with visual processing problems do not think in photo realistic pictures, but they are often pattern thinkers. My dyslexic student absolutely could not draw, but she passed the Mensa IQ test. She is definitely a pattern thinker.

Sensory oversensitivity is an area that should be a top research subject. Many people on the autism spectrum are not able to hold jobs or socialize due to sensory oversensitivity. I am pleased that researchers are now doing research on sensory oversensitivity. Why did it take so long for researchers to really start paying attention to sensory problems? I think this is due to difficulties that people may have imagining an alternate reality that they do not experience. Maybe the reason why social brain systems have been researched so much is because social interactions are the most important experience that the neurotypical person experiences. Now is the time to change the emphasis in neuroscience research in autism from looking at social mechanisms in the brain to researching sensory issues. A person on the autism spectrum can never learn to be social if social environments, such as restaurants, sound like being inside the speaker at a rock concert.

REFERENCES

Coleman, R. S., Frankel, F., Ritvoe, E., & Freeman, B. J. (1976). The effects of fluorescent and incandescent illumination upon repetitive behaviors in autistic children. *Journal of Autism and Development Disorders, 6*, 157–162.

Evans, B. J., & Joseph, F. (2002). The effect of coloured filters on the rate of reading in an adult student population. *Ophthalmic and Physiological Optics, 22*, 535–545.

Freedman, D. J., Riesenhuber, M., Poggio, T., & Miller, E. K. (2001). Categorical representation of visual stimuli in the primate prefrontal cortex. *Science, 291*, 312–315.

Giurfa, M., Zhang, S., Jenett, A., Menzel, R., & Srinivasan, M. V. (2001). The concepts of sameness and difference in an insect. *Nature, 410*, 930–932.

Grandin, T. (1996). *Thinking in pictures*. New York: Vintage Press (Div. of Random House).

Lightstone, A., Lightstone, T., & Wilkins, A. (1999). Both coloured overlays and coloured lenses can improve reading fluency, but their optimal chromaticities differ. *Ophthalmic and Physiological Optometry, 19*, 274–285.

Minshew, N., Meyer, J., & Goldstein, G. (2002). Abstract reasoning in autism: A dissociation between concept formation and concept identification. *Neuropsychology, 16*, 327–334.

Mukhopadhyay, T. R. (2008). *How can I talk if my lips don't move?* New York: Arcade Publishing.
Newport, J., & Newport, M. (2007). *Mozart and the whale*. New York: Touchstone Books.
Tammet, D. (2006). *Born on a blue day*. New York: Free Press.
Williams, D. (1994). *Somebody, somewhere*. New York: Time Books.
Williams, D. (1996). *Autism: An inside-out approach*. London: Jessica Kingsley Limited.

2

Hans Asperger and His Patients

KATHRIN HIPPLER[1]
Department of Paediatrics and Adolescent Medicine,
Medical University of Vienna, Austria

Although Hans Asperger's name has been used to describe a much-discussed syndrome, relatively little is known about his work or his person. Unlike Leo Kanner's description of early infantile autism (1943), Asperger's thesis for postdoctoral lecture qualifications on boys with *autistic psychopathy* (1944) remained unknown to the international readership until Wing's seminal paper in 1981 and Frith's translation of his original text in 1991. This may be partly due to the fact that Asperger missed or even rejected the possibility of going beyond a qualitative, phenomenological description towards a more systematic approach of conceptualizing defining features. He was not interested in conducting large studies but preferred the act of observation as a means to gain insight into the "underlying laws that govern life" (Asperger-Felder, 2000). Apart from the four cases Asperger outlined in his 1944 thesis, no information is available on the nearly 400 patients with autistic psychopathy he once said he saw during the course of his professional career. In general, few empirical studies exist on the later social adaptation of individuals with the syndrome. Ironically, especially in Austria, Asperger's home country, awareness of Asperger syndrome (AS) has only just re-developed. A large number of affected children, and even more adults, still go undiagnosed or receive a series of misdiagnoses until they finally obtain the correct diagnosis, which is often highly frustrating for individuals with AS and their parents alike.

This chapter aims to give some background information on the person, Hans Asperger, and the most important milestones of his life and career. A short section presents the literature on outcome and prognosis of individuals with AS or similar disorders (which may be identical to AS but have various other labels). Third, some selected results of a follow-up study of former patients of Hans Asperger and of his followers in Austria are outlined.

LIFE AND WORK OF HANS ASPERGER

Hans Asperger's Youth

In an article written about her father on the occasion of what would have been his 100th birthday, Asperger's daughter and renowned psychiatrist Maria Asperger-Felder recalls some memories of her father and provides insights into his life (Asperger-Felder, 2006). Johannes Friedrich Karl Asperger, called Hans, was born on February 18, 1906, the eldest of three boys. Tragically, both his brothers died early in their lives (one shortly after birth and the youngest brother during World War II). Hans Asperger grew up in a sheltered, Catholic family in Hausbrunn, Weinviertel, a village near Vienna. His father was an accountant and apparently rather strict concerning the academic education of his sons, while his mother was described as a very warm-hearted, religiously devoted, "selfless" woman (Asperger-Felder, 2006). From childhood on, little Hans was a keen reader (Asperger called himself "*ein wilder Leser*," or "a wild reader"). Apparently, he was a rather remote child who was particularly talented in language and writing (as seen later in his eloquent publications and speeches) and interested in poetry—for example, Grillparzer, Rosegger, and Waggerl. Asperger's school years from 1916 to 1928 were framed around a humanistic education—that is, with the paradigm of antique European philosophy/classicism and moral concepts, as well as Latin and Greek as major languages. When asked about Asperger, staff members of the Pediatric Clinic recalled that he would always have a quote from classic literature, poetry, or the Bible at the ready.

In early adolescence, he joined the *Bund Neuland*, a Catholic alliance of young people that was in the spirit of the German youth movement that started in the late nineteenth century (comparable to the ideology of Boy Scouts). This alliance must not be confused with Nazi youth groups (i.e., the Hitler youth), a connection that has been erroneously indicated previously. Nature, hiking, and mountaineering, confraternity and comradeship, and love of the arts, especially literature, were of high importance, as was a romantic longing for a pristine state of things.

A distinctive experience in high school led to Asperger's wish to study medicine (Asperger, 1977). He had to dissect a white mouse in a natural history lesson. When taking out the animal's liver, a little white bump was seen, and to everyone's surprise, a living parasite worm 2 cm long appeared. Asperger remembered being fascinated by the thought of one life being so closely connected to another life, and as a result, he decided to study medicine to explore the principles of nature in more depth. After completing high school, he studied medicine at the University of Vienna and was awarded his medical degree in 1931. Asperger married Hanna Kalmon in 1935, and they had four daughters and a son.

Early Years at the Vienna University Pediatric Clinic

Asperger repeatedly spoke of admirable teachers who had an immense influence on him and his career, most importantly Franz Hamburger, director of the Vienna University Pediatric Clinic (1930–1945), who employed Asperger and greatly appreciated him. Asperger (1977) wrote that Hamburger was quite open in his personality, successful in his research, fascinated by mental disorders of childhood, and showing impressive skills when communicating with children and parents; however, Hamburger was known to have National Socialist attitudes and values. Asperger wrote his thesis, *Habilitation*, under Hamburger's supervision and was grateful for his support, without actually sharing his political views, as far as we currently know. After World War II, Asperger reported that Hamburger had saved him from the Gestapo (the official secret police of Nazi Germany) on a couple of occasions.

Asperger entered the University Clinic in 1931 and was employed as an assistant doctor working in different wards. In 1932, he became the head of a special ward, the *Heilpädagogische Station* (therapeutic or remedial pedagogical ward), while still an assistant doctor. His work at the Vienna University Children's Clinic was shortly intermitted by guest positions at the psychiatric clinic in Leipzig, Germany, with Paul Schröder, and at the Vienna Psychiatric Clinic, under Otto Pötzl.

He was eager to keep a close relationship with his team (nurses, teachers, doctors, psychologists, and therapists) at the remedial pedagogical ward and to put genuine interdisciplinarity into practice. According to Asperger-Felder (2006), the time between 1931 (his entry into the University Pediatric Clinic in Vienna) and 1945 (his return to the Clinic after the war) was marked by two important experiences: Asperger became acquainted with and further developed the idea of *Heilpädagogik* and its implementation at the remedial pedagogical ward; and he was confronted with the ideology of National Socialism.

The Concept of Heilpädagogik

The concept of *Heilpädagogik* (remedial pedagogy) is situated within pediatric medicine (as opposed to psychiatry) and has a long tradition in Austria. The pediatrician Erwin Lazar (1877–1932) was a pioneer in incorporating pedagogy, psychology, and psychiatry into the pediatric discipline and was the first head of the Heilpädagogische Station, founded in 1911 (Gröger, 2008). Asperger identified five sources of remedial pedagogy: pediatrics, psychiatry, psychology, pedagogy, and social sciences. To this day, it is important to most proponents of the concept of Heilpädagogik to point out that it constitutes an independent, organically grown subject quite different from child psychiatry.

Frith (1991) explained:

> At the early 20th century the remedial ward was like any other clinical ward: The children lay in neat little rows of beds, and twice daily there was a ward round. They were treated as sick children who needed to be made well again. As the team's experience grew, their ethos changed. Soon the children were out of bed during the day and played and worked in a busy round of activities. Now the aim was to give handicapped (rather than sick) children as positive an education as possible.
>
> (p. 8)

Asperger continued Lazar's tradition of Heilpädagogik as a specialized field of pediatric care and further developed this concept (Figure 2.1). It was in this environment that he made his observations on children with autistic traits, which he first publicly spoke about in a lecture in 1938 (Asperger, 1938; Schirmer, 2002). Until his death, Asperger felt closely attached to the Heilpädagogische Station as his main endeavor and focus of interest.

Asperger: Pediatrician in the Time of National Socialism

From 1939 until the end of World War II, physicians in Nazi Austria were obliged to report any newborns or newly referred children with severe disabilities to a panel of medical "experts" in Berlin, who then decided the children's fate. Tragically, hundreds of children were murdered or suffered agonizing deaths in the *Klinik am Spiegelgrund* or the neighboring hospital, *Am Steinhof*, in Vienna.

Asperger's involvement in National Socialist ideology and its consequences concerning the fate of children with neurodevelopmental and psychiatric disorders has not been thoroughly investigated yet. A collaborative project into this topic has recently been initiated by the Medical University of Vienna and the Documentation Archives of the Austrian Resistance. Apparently, Asperger was never a member of the National Socialist party (NSDAP), which was rather unusual for professionals in leading positions at that time. It is unknown if or how Asperger reacted to the dismissal of 110 (mostly Jewish) Viennese pediatricians and university staff, including employees of the remedial ward who were very dear to him (Asperger-Felder, 2006). From the late 1930s onwards, Asperger seemed to be aware that the "law for preventing procreation of hereditary diseases" would be expanded to Austria (Schirmer, 2002).

Asperger drew attention to autistic psychopathy for the first time in 1938 during a lecture he gave at the remedial pedagogical department of the Vienna Children's Clinic (published in the Wiener Klinische Wochenzeitschrift, 1938). He presented a case study of a child with autistic psychopathy with nearly all

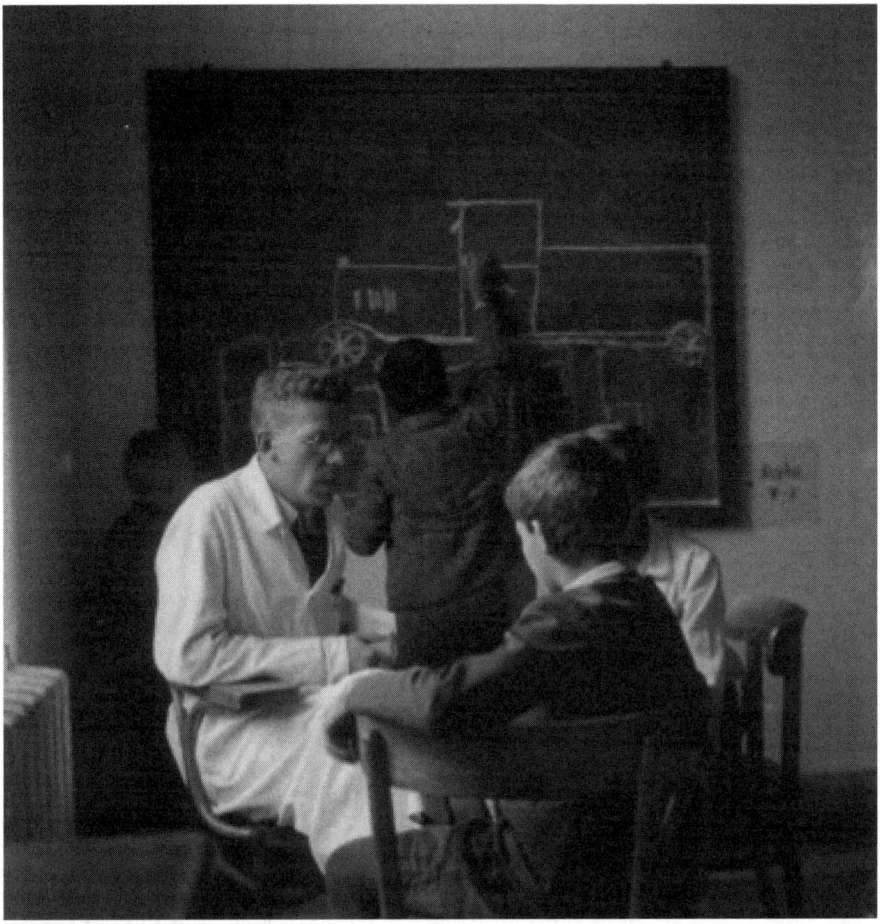

Figure 2.1 Asperger and some of his patients in the Heilpädagogik ward. Courtesy of the archive of the Heilpädagogische Station in Vienna, Austria.

the symptoms he described in his 1944 paper (Asperger, 1938; Schirmer, 2002). There was a lack of governmental support at that time for helping handicapped people. (In one illustrative instance, a schoolbook asked students to compute the answer to questions like, "The construction of a lunatic asylum costs six million marks. How many houses at 15,000 marks each could have been built for that amount?" [United States Holocaust Memorial Museum, n.d.].) Despite the prevailing lack of governmental understanding of disabilities, Asperger pleaded for his patients' needs and their rights to individualized education and treatment. Schirmer (2002) concludes that this 1938 text must have protected his patients from Nazi persecution. Similarly, Gröger (2008) reported that, strikingly, Asperger avoided racial ideology in his publications and lectures and instead stressed the positive development of the children he observed. Apparently, Asperger pointed out the possibility of problematic consequences as a result of the attitudes of his time, without openly criticizing these values (Gröger, 2008).

During World War II, Asperger served as a medical officer in Croatia from 1943–1945. He later said that he was "thankful all his life for not having to kill anyone" (Asperger-Felder, 2006).

Post-War Years

When Asperger returned from the war in 1945, he found the remedial ward destroyed by bombs and one of his closest and most valued staff members, nurse Viktorine Zak, killed in a bombing attack in 1944. Many of his former colleagues were gone; some of them had been able to emigrate, but most of their fates are unknown.

After the war, Asperger took up his clinical and university teaching position, his work at the juvenile court, and his teaching position at the nursing school. The remedial ward was carefully rebuilt. Between 1946 and 1949, he served as interim head of the Pediatric Clinic in Vienna. In 1952, Asperger's book on Heilpädagogik was published; it is not so much a textbook as it is a tutorial on how to develop a holistic approach to the child's care and make one's own individual perception the most important tool to understanding (Asperger, 1952; Asperger-Felder, 2006). In 1957, he gave a lecture on "Problems of Modern Pediatrics" to the University Clinic in Innsbruck. Asperger became chair of the University Pediatric Clinic in 1962, a post he kept until his official retirement in 1977.

Asperger was chair of several societies of remedial pedagogy, child psychiatry, and pediatric medicine, and organized several national and international conferences. His introductory lectures are vividly remembered by everyone who experienced them because of his great skill and talent "to build a bridge from the present location, its history and cultural background, to the relevant topic" (Asperger-Felder, 2006). He is said to have known how to "invite the listeners and take them on a journey with him."

Asperger is said to have enjoyed reading literature to the children in the ward. Unforgettable to many team members were the "summer camps" of the remedial ward, during which the children spent the day doing outdoor activities and Asperger would tell stories in the evening.

In 1977, Asperger gave a speech at the pediatric advanced training course, rounding off his academic career (*"Erlebtes Leben: Fünfzig Jahre Pädiatrie"* or "Lived/Experienced Life: Fifty Years of Pediatric Medicine"). He closed his speech by saying, "I still find myself standing in the middle of life with open senses, with sharpened wits – just because of my age, recognizing the gist of things, still grateful for all the miracles that lie in nature and humans."

The last topic Asperger concerned himself with was the dying child, the child's concepts of death, and the handling of a fatal diagnosis. On October 20,

1980, Asperger died very suddenly after a short illness while still actively engaged in clinical and academic work. He was a committed, compassionate, curious, and inquisitive man until the end (Asperger-Felder, 2000).

WHAT DO WE KNOW ABOUT PROGNOSIS AND OUTCOME OF INDIVIDUALS WITH ASPERGER SYNDROME?

From "Little Professors" to Exceptional Adults: Asperger's View of the Prognosis of Individuals with Autistic Psychopathy

When reading case histories and clinical files written by Hans Asperger, it becomes apparent that he was clearly intrigued by the children exhibiting what he originally named *autistic psychopathy*. The label *psychopathy* must not be confused with today's understanding—that is, a disorder characterized by intentional antisocial behavior. In those days, *psychopathy* was a synonym for a deviant variant of character or personality. Asperger did mention that spiteful and aggressive behaviors were often part of the disorder, but he did not believe that this was at the very core of the impairment he described. Characteristic of Asperger's writing style, besides his poetic, illustrative language, was the attempt to describe each child in a holistic, individualized, and vivid way, as can be seen in the extract from one of his files below:

> [He is] a very pretty and handsome prince, but not quite at home in this profane world. Often, he has his head in the clouds, but also produces independent and inventive thinking processes and shows original interests at a highly specialized level. At the same time he lacks the ability to react to the environment and its demands, the intuitive, instinctive adaptation. Being so ivory-towerish, he is at the mercy of the other children's mockery—he virtually asks for it. ... Although he likes to join in with the others' ragging and pranks, he acts so clumsily that he is always the one who gets caught—quite contrary to the other more streetwise guys. In many situations he will react with strong fear to what is an incomprehensible world to him.
>
> (Extract from a 1970 case file by Asperger, translated by the author)

Asperger was convinced that the disorder he had described was a life-long personality variant with a genetic background. The essential aspects of the impairment would remain unchanged. He reported:

> In early childhood there are the difficulties in learning simple practical skills and in social adaptation. These difficulties arise out of the same disturbance which at school age causes learning and conduct problems, in

> adolescence job and performance problems, and in adulthood social and marital conflicts.
>
> (Asperger, 1944, translated by Frith, 1991, p. 68)

Asperger always stressed the many positive traits, high intellect, and special abilities and strengths these children exhibited and had a very optimistic view concerning the prognosis of his patients:

> In the vast majority, work performance can be excellent, and with this comes social integration. Able autistic individuals can rise to eminent positions and perform with such outstanding success that one may even conclude that only such people are capable of certain achievements. It is as if they had compensatory abilities to counter-balance their deficiencies.
>
> (Asperger, 1944, translated by Frith, 1991, p. 88)

As an example, Asperger (1944) refers to a boy diagnosed with autistic psychopathy whose development he would observe over three decades. As a child, this boy showed all the characteristic symptoms of autistic psychopathy, as well as a special interest and talent in mathematics. As a young adult, he studied theoretical astronomy and, in his doctoral thesis, proved a mathematical error in Newton's work. He became a professor at the Department of Astronomy (Asperger, 1944). Asperger wrote:

> We are convinced, then, that autistic people have their place in the organism of the social community. They fulfill their role well, perhaps better than anyone else could, and we are talking of people who as children had the greatest difficulties and caused untold worries to their caregivers.
>
> (Asperger, 1944, translated by Frith, 1991, pp. 89–90)

More Recent Follow-Up Studies

What have other authors found out about the development and prognosis of individuals with AS in adulthood? The short answer is that the results vary immensely. There is still ongoing confusion concerning the validity of AS and its diagnostic criteria. Authors who have studied AS outcomes, therefore, have used different diagnostic criteria and/or concepts that may be identical with, or similar to, Asperger's autistic psychopathy but have a different conceptual background—for example, high functioning autism (HFA) (e.g., Howlin, Mawhood, & Rutter, 2000; Mawhood, Howlin, & Rutter, 2000; Rumsey, Rapoport, & Sceery, 1985) or schizoid personality disorder (Wolff, 1991; Wolff & Chick, 1980). Furthermore, in some follow-up studies, diagnoses were given retrospectively (e.g., Szatmari, Bartolucci, Bremner, Bond, & Rich, 1989).

There is no consensus among clinicians on whether AS can be diagnosed in individuals with mild intellectual impairment, as proposed by Wing (1981). As intellectual ability seems to play a crucial role in regards to outcome, this needs to be taken into account. However, even in groups with comparable intellectual functioning, outcome seems to be extremely variable. Whereas some authors studying outcome in AS, HFA, or schizoid personality disorder (Baumann, 2005; Szatmari et al., 1989; Wolff, 1991; Wolff & Chick, 1980; Wolff, Townshend, McGuire, & Weeks, 1991) have found a relatively high rate of employment and capacity for living an independent life in their samples (between 40% and 100% for both variables), other authors (e.g., Howlin et al., 2000; Mawhood et al., 2000; Rumsey et al., 1985) reported much lower levels of functioning (fewer than one third were able to live at least semi-independently). Social-emotional functioning (partnerships and family life) was severely impaired throughout all the above studies. The percentage of individuals married or in relationships varied between 0% and 34%. Psychiatric co-morbidity was high in most studies.

In a comprehensive review of follow-up studies of individuals with AS and/or HFA, Tsatsanis (2003) identified several factors that may influence later outcome—for example, age at diagnosis, intelligence profile, co-morbid psychiatric disorders, medical conditions, perinatal complications, genetic variables, and negative family dynamics, and possibly also sex, geographical influences, and socioeconomic status.

Further studies on long-term development are urgently needed not only to better understand the syndrome but also to provide for the changing needs of adolescents and adults with AS. To the author's knowledge, most outcome studies on higher functioning individuals with AS refer to adults in their late twenties, on average. Little is known about older groups of individuals with the disorder. Studies comparing childhood diagnostic symptoms with those in adulthood are valuable for clinical as well as research purposes.

SELECTED RESULTS OF A FOLLOW-UP STUDY OF HANS ASPERGER'S PATIENTS

Identification of the Sample and Methods

A study was conducted as part of a comprehensive project on the outcome of adults with AS in Austria (follow-up of Hans Asperger's patients) and in England (follow-up of a sub-sample of Lorna Wing's former patients, as well as a survey of adult volunteers with AS/HFA). Below, selected results of the follow-up study of former patients of Hans Asperger and colleagues are presented. We were interested in the life course of people who were diagnosed with autistic psychopathy as children by Asperger and colleagues. Outcome data regarding living situation and social adaptation were collected, and the question of whether today's diagnostic criteria would still be applicable for this cohort was explored.

In order to identify the former patients, we used two sources: the archives of the former remedial pedagogical ward at the University Clinic of Pediatrics and Adolescent Medicine in Vienna; and the card files of Hans Asperger's private practice. We selected all files of children diagnosed with autistic psychopathy, AS, or autism Asperger type, or distinct features of these disorders described as such on the title sheet of the case file (the presence of impaired social and communication abilities and special interests/abilities and/or restricted, ritualistic behavior were necessary for inclusion). No files could be found prior to 1950 (possibly because those files were lost during bombings in the war years). The diagnosis of autistic psychopathy seemed to be most common in the 1970s, possibly when the disorder was well-established and recognized by all staff, and Asperger's influence was still strong at the remedial ward. Interestingly, after 1980 (Asperger died in 1980), diagnoses of autistic psychopathy or similar labels decreased significantly, which gives rise to the suspicion that the use of the label was closely attached to his person and his direct followers.

To contact the now grown-up former patients, we sent letters with an invitation to take part in an interview. Of 181 case files, we were able to identify the current addresses of 133 individuals. We received 33 negative and 41 positive replies to our contact letter; 59 did not respond. Including the files found via the records search at psychiatric units in Vienna (described below), we collected adult data on 48 persons formerly diagnosed by Asperger and/or colleagues. Comparing the successfully recruited participants to the non-responsive cases, no differences could be identified in their childhood files regarding intellectual functioning, developmental milestones, reasons for referral, co-morbid diagnoses, gender, age of referral, or educational/professional qualifications of fathers.

As it was necessary to establish one diagnostic approach for comparability reasons, we included only those original patients of Asperger's who, as children, met all current criteria of AS according to ICD-10 (World Health Organization [WHO], 1993). Children with minor speech delays and rapid catch-up of language abilities in their third year of life were also included. We excluded those with more severe language delay in early childhood (which would rule out an AS diagnosis according to today's standards) or symptoms which were too mild to justify a diagnosis in childhood according to today's criteria. Information from 34 individuals was evaluated.

The contacted former patients and/or their relatives who were willing to contribute were visited at their homes and, with their agreement, either audio- or video-taped. The interviews had a semi-structured form with questions about memories of childhood, school years, and adolescence, current living situation, relationship issues, past and current employment, any other diagnoses and treatments, leisure activities, and special interests. There was a deliberately open introductory question inviting the participant to speak freely about his/her life, a personal reflection part asking about contentment with his/her life, and reflection on strengths, difficulties, and help that was considered efficient. Usually, the interviews took two to three hours. Outcome was rated using Lotter's (1974) criteria, with (1) *good outcome* signifying near normal or normal social life, (2) *fair outcome* signifying social and educational progress in spite of marked abnormalities in behavior or interpersonal relationships, (3) *poor outcome* signifying severe handicap, but some measure of social adjustment, and (4) *very poor outcome* signifying inability to lead any kind of independent life. All ratings were assessed by a second rater. The two interviewers' codes and ratings were statistically analyzed using inter-rater reliability measures and were found to be satisfactory.

Standardized assessment measures, like IQ tests or standard autism diagnostic instruments, were not used because of the sensitivity of the sample (i.e., little awareness of their own childhood diagnosis).

Furthermore, we conducted a records search in two areas: (a) the psychiatric hospitals (Vienna-wide) in order to identify any former Asperger patients with later co-morbidity and/or inpatient admissions; and (b) the Austrian Penal Register in order to find out about the rate of individuals with criminal offences.

Study Participants: Demographic Data

The study group was comprised of 33 men and one woman, with a mean age of 40 (between 23 and 62 years of age). They were interviewed on average 32 years after childhood referral/admission. Sixty-five percent had above-average intelligence according to their childhood files, 32% had average intelligence, and for one person information on intellectual ability was missing.

The control group included 102 age- and gender-matched persons recruited in waiting rooms of the general hospital. A shortened questionnaire version of the interview was used for controls. Data from the control group were mainly used for comparing more factual information or items with multiple-choice answers. Hence, for several items, information from the control group is not available.

Overall Outcome

In terms of the major variables of outcome, like employment and independent living, the former patients of Asperger and colleagues did exceptionally well compared to participants in similar studies (Baumann 2005; Howlin et al., 2000; Rumsey et al., 1985; Szatmari et al., 1989). Still, significant differences in employment rate, independent living skills, and rate of individuals with partners and families were found in comparison to the age-matched control group.

Using Lotter's criteria for outcome (as described above), we found that 42% of the follow-up sample could be described as having a good outcome. In the present study, a rating of *good* was only given if the person was able to live independently (i.e., alone or with a partner) and had a regular occupation or was regularly retired. Thirty-five percent were rated as showing a fair outcome; they may have been in some form of educational program or employment but showed marked impairments in behavior and/or interpersonal relationships. Fifteen percent had a poor outcome, having major difficulty living independently and supporting themselves (i.e., in and out of psychiatric units), while 9% had a very poor outcome of no independence at all (e.g., living in institutional care) and severe social impairment often associated with high psychiatric comorbidity. To determine predictors of outcome, three similar-sized outcome groups were created for analysis: a group of 14 participants with good outcome, a group of 12 with fair outcome, and a group of eight with poor or very poor outcome.

Observations and First Impressions

Most of the study participants appeared exceptionally intelligent, eloquent, and friendly. Remaining impairments and diagnostic symptoms were often only subtle. It was found that the majority seemed highly nervous and had difficulty relaxing even after a "warming-up phase." High tension and motor restlessness were common, which may give rise to the suspicion that features of (undiagnosed) attention deficit and hyperactivity disorder (ADHD) may have been present. It is increasingly acknowledged that ADHD is often associated with AS (Ghaziuddin, Weidmer-Mikhail, & Ghaziuddin, 1998; Green, Gilchrist, Burton, & Cox, 2000), and there is growing evidence of a genetic link between the two conditions (Ronald, Simonoff, Kuntsi, Asherson, & Plomin, 2008). Eye contact was deviant in over half of the group. Other nonverbal behavior to regulate social interaction (e.g., adequate body posture, like turning to someone when speaking to him, facial expression, and gesture) seemed clearly impaired in about a third. Only a small number, however, distinctly violated common rules of courtesy during the interview situation. In regards to communication, the majority still showed somewhat subtle peculiarities, often a failure to present an overall, coherent picture, a preference for dates and facts, or a tendency to speak bluntly about intimate topics. People with a good overall outcome and those with rather adverse outcomes differed in regards to the coherence of their free speech (i.e., the ability to present a comprehensible, overall picture of what they wanted to express), the quality of their speech (e.g., a listing character of speech was more common in those with poorer outcomes), and the capacity to report relevant autobiographical aspects and overall information in the openly posed introductory question.

Information from Childhood Files and Later Outcome

We identified childhood variables from the former patients' clinical files (for a more detailed description, see Hippler & Klicpera, 2003) and related them to later outcome. Of the cases where information on prenatal and perinatal circumstances was available, complications in pregnancy were reported for about 40%, including bleeding and infections, and complications during delivery were reported for over 20%. However, these variables had no influence on later outcome. Delays regarding motor or language development were not common in the childhood files of the follow-up group, apart from a small sub-sample with some speech delay but rapid catch-up by 36 months. Noticeably, there was a high rate of academics amongst the fathers of the former patients of Hans Asperger (60%). This may be due to the inclusion of files from Asperger's private practice, but also results from Asperger's unspoken assumption that the syndrome he described was mainly seen in (highly) intelligent children and was passed on from father to son. About a third of the fathers had professions in a technical field (mainly engineering). At first referral to the practice or ward, the dominant behavioral symptoms were difficulties at school—that is, a lack of integration into the peer group, motor clumsiness, and a tendency to "drift away" into a world of their own. Noticeably, additional ADHD-like features recorded in childhood files were associated with less favorable outcomes in adulthood. Communication and language deviancies or peculiarities (e.g., lack of appreciation of social context, adult-like speech, associative language, and a tendency to go off-topic) were seen in all of the children. Most referred children had marked special interests often associated with nature and animals, space and astronauts, or technical and scientific areas.

Education, Professional Training, and Employment

Educational qualifications were high in the study group. Over 60% finished their high school degrees (in Austria, this is commonly at age 18, after 12 years of schooling). When looking closely, however, many participants' school success must have come at a high cost: Over half of the participants and/or their parents reported that they had had to change schools, often because they had been expelled for disciplinary reasons or because of academic failure. Expectations of obeying rules were probably even more important 30 years ago, and the children's fundamental difficulties may have been mistaken for deliberate opposition. Sadly, many reported mainly negative memories of their school years, and just under half had experienced being nastily bullied.

After school, the majority completed some professional qualifications, with just under half receiving a university or college degree, a higher rate than in the control group. Subjects were often in a technical field or in natural science, but also represented disciplines such as medicine, music, and theology. About a quarter had taken some university/college courses without finishing their degrees. Another quarter completed vocational training (e.g., in merchandising, plumbing, gardening).

Concerning employment, it was found that 70% of the participants were in regular work environments (including one who was retired). Two persons worked in sheltered occupation or at a day clinic, and the rest were unemployed. Of all the participants, almost a third worked in computer programming and electronics. Strikingly, study participants were self-employed significantly more often than controls, which may reflect a preference to work on one's own, possibly with a lower demand on social or team skills.

Living and Family Situation

Most individuals of the follow-up group lived with their partners, with or without children, and over a third lived by themselves. A sub-sample resided with their parents or other relatives; three were in some form of institutional care. The majority needed no help or minimal help in their daily lives.

Those with a better outcome more often had a partner, while those with fair or poor outcomes were almost always single. Whereas the controls had partners significantly more often than study participants, a nearly equal proportion had children. This has not been found by any other follow-up study so far.

Do Individuals Still Meet ICD-10 Criteria for Asperger Syndrome at Follow-Up?

Using the information from the interviews, the interviewer ratings, and current clinical files (if available), a symptom count was conducted in order to find out whether a diagnosis of AS according to ICD-10 (WHO, 1993) still applied to the follow-up sample. In summary, 48% clearly met criteria for AS at follow-up; however, this figure includes a sub-sample who had received other psychiatric diagnoses in adult life (e.g., diagnoses of a schizophrenia spectrum or obsessive compulsive disorder), officially "ruling out" AS (12% of the total sample). In our opinion, however, underlying AS may have been overlooked in these individuals and misdiagnosis can be suspected. In addition, 12% met the overall criteria for pervasive developmental disorder but showed no clear diagnosis of AS or autism (probably fitting into the category of pervasive developmental disorder, unspecified). Thirty-nine percent could not be diagnosed with AS because they no longer met critical symptoms of the ICD-10 criteria (specifically, points B [abnormalities in social interaction] and C [circumscribed interests/stereotyped behavior]). Apparently, in these participants, an improvement of symptoms had occurred over the course of their lives. Intelligence was found to interact with outcome, and it may be concluded that, especially for individuals with high intellectual functioning, participants were able to compensate for many of their difficulties. However, some basic impairments and eccentricities persisted (especially regarding relationship issues and special interests), supporting the notion of an "autistic phenotype" blending into so-called "normality." This seems similar to Szatmari and colleagues' (1989) results that a sub-sample of people with a childhood diagnosis of HFA did not fully meet diagnostic criteria for autism at follow-up because of a true improvement of symptoms.

Not surprisingly, a significant interaction between outcome and adult diagnosis according to ICD-10 symptom count was found. Hence, most of the good outcome group did not meet criteria for AS or other developmental disorders as adults anymore; most of the fair outcome group met the criteria for AS as adults; and most of the poor/very poor outcome group had psychiatric diagnoses (mainly on the schizophrenia spectrum) and/or would meet criteria for other pervasive developmental disorders.

Adult Diagnoses and Co-Morbidity

Apart from one person, none of the participants in the follow-up group was aware of their childhood diagnosis of autistic psychopathy or AS. Seemingly, transparency concerning diagnoses was not common practice in the 1950s to the late 1970s. Only one study participant was re-diagnosed with AS/HFA as an adult; however, over 60% of the participants reported other diagnoses they had received later in life. It can be speculated that the diagnoses came from professionals who were unfamiliar with AS as it presents in adults.

The most common diagnosis was depression (over a quarter), followed by psychotic or schizophrenia spectrum disorders (SSD), which was often associated with forced psychiatric admissions due to escalating behavior (about 18%). SSD diagnoses were very probably over-estimated due to misdiagnosis and to the targeted search in psychiatric hospitals (as opposed to other outpatients' centers or individual therapists where less severe psychiatric conditions would be treated). In hindsight, the psychiatrists in charge could not clearly say whether AS had been obscured by psychotic episodes and/or acute stress disorders. It has been pointed out previously that psychotic symptoms in persons with autism spectrum diagnoses are particularly difficult to diagnose due to the risk of misinterpretation of the core syndrome (e.g., Berney, 2004; Tantam, 2000).

Other less commonly reported diagnoses included personality disorder (e.g., borderline or histrionic personality disorder), obsessive compulsive disorder, acute stress reaction, attention deficit and hyperactivity disorder, and anxiety disorder. Four persons, all in the group with poor/very poor outcome, had been suicidal (i.e., thoughts, ideas, or impulses of suicide; one man actually tried to commit suicide). All of those who had been suicidal had also received a diagnosis on the schizophrenia spectrum.

Variables Interacting with Outcome

Better outcome was associated with higher intelligence, a finding that has been reported by other authors (e.g., Helt et al., 2008). Interestingly, in our study, a significant interaction between the development of friendships in adolescence and later prognosis was found. A number of participants reported that it was not until adolescence that they started to get more interested in their peers and found this time was important for their later development. Individuals with less positive outcome often reported major difficulties in making friends and felt that they had been outsiders through most of their school years. Obviously, there may be a mutually reinforcing influence: Friendship can foster social ability and vice versa.

Summing up the results on additional diagnoses, (childhood) attention deficits, symptoms of the schizophrenia spectrum, acute stress disorders, and suicidal tendencies were connected with adverse outcome. Conversely, the rate of affective disorders (e.g., depression or anxiety disorder) was relatively high in the whole group, regardless of outcome. Interestingly, there was a tendency for depression to be associated with fewer AS symptoms in adulthood according to ICD-10 symptom count.

Satisfaction with Life

Just under half of the study participants reported that, all in all, they were happy with their lives so far. The percentage of those who said they felt unhappy or very unhappy with their lives was higher in the follow-up sample than in the control group. Work and occupation were considered most important to contributing to a feeling of happiness. No interaction between later outcome with environmental factors and support by family, friends, or caregivers could be ascertained; however, support played a major role in regards to the perceived quality of life.

Criminality in Asperger's Original Patients

Recently, a number of research articles have investigated criminality in people with AS (e.g., Schwartz-Watts, 2005; Scragg & Shah, 1994). Media reports on single offenders are often quick to suggest a link between individuals with psychiatric diagnoses, particularly AS, and crime. Maybe Asperger's own choice of the label *psychopathy* (which was never intended to propose a link with delinquency) has also led to some confusion concerning this matter. In order to find out about the rate of criminality in Asperger's original sample, we conducted a records search in the Austrian Penal Register, which is comprised of all convictions (not offences) in Austria (Hippler, Viding, Klicpera, & Happé, 2010). Registered convictions are cleared after a certain period of time if no further offences are committed by the person. We received information on 177 of Asperger's and colleagues' former patients with a childhood diagnosis of autistic psychopathy or distinct features of autistic psychopathy (i.e., showing severe social impairment, special interests and activities, and language and communication peculiarities in their childhood files). Information was retrieved anonymously and, thus, no conclusions could be drawn on the identity of those with later convictions. Results showed that the rate of convictions in Asperger's former patients was equal to the percentage of convictions in the general male population in Austria. A qualitative evaluation suggested that convictions did not differ in nature. Individuals with a clear diagnosis of autistic psychopathy in their childhood files had even fewer convictions than individuals with only a subset of the features of the condition. Possibly, patterns of rigid thinking typically linked with AS result in faithful adherence to laws, as proposed by Frith (1991).

CONCLUSION

Hans Asperger's former patients represent a very special cohort in two key ways: Intellectual functioning, as a group, was extremely high; and the participants had no awareness of their own diagnosis. As a result, it is hard to draw general conclusions from this study. With the two methods of data collection (voluntary participation and records search), we may have captured the extremes concerning outcome: high functioning individuals eager to tell their life stories at one end, and a smaller, vulnerable group with psychiatric admissions and co-morbid or super-imposed diagnoses at the other. Besides its historic implications (finding out how a diagnosis developed historically and how it may differ from today's understanding), the study may be encouraging to individuals with the syndrome, as well as their parents. Just as Asperger predicted, many of his patients succeeded in turning their special interests and talents into occupations and managed to find their niches in society. Several had partners and families. True improvement in the severity of symptoms could be seen in a high percentage of the participants.

At the same time, most of the study participants' lives have been far from easy, and a high percentage have unpleasant, even traumatic memories of their past. Though it is tempting to assume that unawareness of diagnosis (as was the case with these participants) could actually have a positive influence on outcome, we are convinced that this is true for only a very small group who today might appear eccentric rather than impaired. Understanding oneself and receiving understanding from one's environment is crucial for development and emotional well-being, and this is particularly true for individuals with AS and autism spectrum disorders. Currently, a diagnosis seems to make understanding oneself much easier for most individuals with AS. Particularly in adult services, people with AS and secondary or co-morbid disorders are often misdiagnosed. Better awareness of the syndrome by clinical professionals in adult settings would be highly desirable. With the wide range of abilities and needs of adults with AS, highly individualized, tailored support is needed. Often, minimal help with everyday life or specific job coaching is sufficient to avoid dependency on parents or caregivers. There may also be life phases where counseling, psychotherapy, or medical treatment is helpful. Therefore, I would like to finish the chapter by citing Hans Asperger (1977, p. 222) again, who stated: "*Und Verstehen … ist unsere höchste Verpflichtung, uns selber und den Menschen gegenüber*" ("And understanding … is our highest obligation, towards ourselves and all humans").

NOTE

1. Author is also corresponding author.

REFERENCES

Asperger, H. (1938). Das Psychisch Abnorme Kind. *Wiener Klinische Wochenzeitschrift, 51*, 1314–1317.

Asperger, H. (1944). Die Autistischen Psychopathen im Kindesalter. *Archiv für Psychiatrie und Nervenkrankheiten, 177*, 76–137.

Asperger, H. (1952). *Heilpädagogik*. Berlin: Springer.

Asperger, H. (1977). Erlebtes Leben: Fünfzig Jahre Pädiatrie. *Pädiatrie und Pädologie, 12*, 214–223.

Asperger-Felder, M. (2000). Foreword. In A. Klin, F. R. Volkmar, & S. S. Sparrow (Eds.), *Asperger syndrome* (pp. xi–xiii). New York: Guilford Press.

Asperger-Felder, M. (2006). Zum Sehen geboren, zum Schauen Bestellt … Hans Asperger 1906–1980, Leben und Werk. *Heilpädagogik, 49*, 2–11.

Baumann, A. (2005). *Katamnestische Untersuchungen bei Patienten mit Asperger-Syndrom und Tiefgreifenden Entwicklungsstörungen*. Marburg: Dissertation zur Erlangung des Doktorgrades der gesamten Medizin.

Berney, T. (2004). Asperger syndrome from childhood into adulthood. *Advances in Psychiatric Treatment, 10*, 341–351.

Frith, U. (1991). Asperger and his syndrome. In U. Frith (Ed.), *Autism and Asperger syndrome* (pp. 1–36). Cambridge: Cambridge University Press.

Ghaziuddin, M., Weidmer-Mikhail, E., & Ghaziuddin, N. (1998). Comorbidity of Asperger syndrome: A preliminary report. *Journal of Intellectual Disability Research, 42*, 279–283.

Green, J., Gilchrist, A., Burton, D., & Cox, A. (2000). Social and psychiatric functioning in adolescents with Asperger syndrome compared with conduct disorder. *Journal of Autism and Developmental Disorders, 30*, 279–293.

Gröger, H. (2008). Das Syndrom des "Autistischen Psychopathen" – Hans Asperger zwischen Pädiatrie, Kinderpsychiatre und Heilpädagogik. *Schriftenreihe der Deutschen Gesellschaft für Geschichte der Nervenheilkunde, 14*, 199–213.

Helt, M., Kelley, E., Kinsbourne, M., Pandey, J., Boorstein, H., Herbert, M., & Fein, D. (2008). Can children with autism recover? If so, how? *Neuropsychology Review, 18*, 339–366.

Hippler, K., & Klicpera, C. (2003). A retrospective analysis of the clinical case records of "autistic psychopaths" diagnosed by Hans Asperger and his team at the University Children's Hospital, Vienna. In U. Frith & E. L. Hill (Eds.), *Autism: Mind and brain* (pp. 21–42). Oxford/New York: Oxford University Press.

Hippler, K., Viding, E., Klicpera, C., & Happé. F. (2010). Brief report: No increase in criminal convictions in Hans Asperger's original cohort. *Journal of Autism and Developmental Disorders, 40*, 774–780.

Howlin, P., Mawhood, L., & Rutter, M. (2000). Autism and developmental receptive language disorder – A follow-up comparison in early adult life. II: Social, behavioral, and psychiatric outcomes. *Journal of Child Psychology and Psychiatry, 41*, 561–578.

Kanner, L. (1943). Autistic disturbances of affective contact. *Nervous Child, 2*, 217–250.

Lotter, V. (1974). Factors related to outcome in autistic children. *Journal of Autism and Childhood Schizophrenia, 4*, 263–277.

Mawhood, L., Howlin, P., & Rutter, M. (2000). Autism and developmental receptive language disorder – A follow-up comparison in early adult life. I: Cognitive and language outcomes. *Journal of Child Psychology and Psychiatry, 41*, 561–578.

Ronald, A., Simonoff, E., Kuntsi, J., Asherson, P., & Plomin, R. (2008). Evidence for overlapping genetic influences on autistic and ADHD behaviors in a community twin sample. *Journal of Child Psychology and Psychiatry, 49*, 535–542.

Rumsey, J. M., Rapoport, J. L., & Sceery, W. R. (1985). Autistic children as adults: Psychiatric, social, and behavioral outcomes. *Journal of the American Academy of Child Psychiatry, 24*, 465–473.

Schirmer, B. (2002). Autismus und NS-Rassengesetze in Österreich 1938: Hans Aspergers Verteidigung der 'Autistischen Psychopathen' gegen die NS-Eugenik. *Die neue Sonderschule, 6*, 460–464.

Schwartz-Watts, D. M. (2005). Asperger's disorder and murder. *Journal of the American Academy of Psychiatry and the Law, 33*, 390–393.

Scragg, P., & Shah, A. (1994). Prevalence of Asperger's syndrome in a secure hospital. *British Journal of Psychiatry, 165*, 679–682.

Szatmari, P., Bartolucci, G., Bremner, R., Bond, R., & Rich, S. (1989). A follow-up study of high-functioning autistic children. *Journal of Autism and Developmental Disorders, 19*, 213–225.

Tantam, D. (2000). Psychological disorder in adolescents and adults with Asperger syndrome. *Autism, 4*, 47–62.

Tsatsanis, K. (2003). Outcome research in Asperger syndrome and autism. *Child and Adolescent Psychiatric Clinics of North America, 12*, 47–63.

United States Holocaust Memorial Museum (n.d.). Mentally and physically handicapped: Victims of the Nazi era. Retrieved from www.ushmm.org/education/resource/handic/handicapped.php?theme=educators.

Wing, L. (1981). Asperger's syndrome: A clinical account. *Psychological Medicine, 11*, 115–129.

Wolff, S. (1991). "Schizoid" personality in childhood and adult life I: The vagaries of diagnostic labeling. *British Journal of Psychiatry, 159*, 615–620.

Wolff, S., & Chick, J. (1980). Schizoid personality disorder in childhood: A controlled follow-up study. *Psychological Medicine, 10*, 85–100.

Wolff, S., Townshend, R., McGuire, R. J., & Weeks, D. J. (1991). "Schizoid" personality in childhood and adult life II: Adult adjustment and the continuity with schizotypal personality disorder. *British Journal of Psychiatry, 159*, 620–629.

World Health Organization. (1993). *The ICD-10 classification of mental and behavioral disorders: Diagnostic criteria for research.* Geneva: World Health Organization.

Section II

Brain Mechanisms and Genetic Influences

3

A Theory of Autism Based on Frontal-Posterior Underconnectivity

MARCEL ADAM JUST[1]
TIMOTHY A. KELLER
Center for Cognitive Brain Imaging, Department of Psychology, Carnegie Mellon University, Pittsburgh, PA

RAJESH K. KANA
UAB Department of Psychology, Birmingham, AL

Although autism was first formally described many decades ago by Kanner (1943) and Asperger (1944), research on the disorder in the U.S. remained scarce until the 1990s. At that time, researchers developed new neuroscientific methods that could be applied to investigations of the psychological and biological underpinnings of autism, including genomics, eye-movement tracking, and electrophysiology. As a result, researchers and practitioners are gaining greater understanding of the disorder. The complexity and enigma of autism still remain, particularly its alterations of a wide and seemingly unrelated group of behavioral symptoms that have no obvious correspondence to a single biological function. In addition, the disorder occasionally includes perceptual advantages. To address the three elements of the enigma, we suggest that the diversity of symptoms can be understood as a consequence of a widespread neural systems disorder; the link to a biological substrate is illuminated by brain imaging; and a perturbation of the cortical system can have both negative and positive impacts on functioning.

Our focus here is on a theory of autism based on neuroimaging findings regarding cortical underconnectivity. The theory of underconnectivity proposes that the behavioral symptoms of autism result from abnormalities in the coordination of function among collaborating brain regions. This theoretical view first emerged from functional magnetic resonance imaging (fMRI) measurements of cortical activation demonstrating that the degree of synchronization (or *functional connectivity*) between frontal and posterior brain regions was lower in autism. The observation was first made in a language comprehension task (Just, Cherkassky, Keller, & Minshew, 2004), and many studies have replicated these findings in tasks that require synchronization between frontal and posterior regions of the brain (Damarla et al., 2010; Just et al., 2004; Just, Cherkassky, Keller, Kana, & Minshew, 2007; Kana, Keller, Cherkassky, Minshew, & Just, 2006, 2009; Kana, Keller, Minshew, & Just, 2007; Koshino et al., 2005, 2008; Mason, Williams, Kana, Minshew, & Just, 2008; Mizuno et al., 2011; see Schipul, Keller, & Just, 2011 for a recent review). We propose that the lower synchronization arises due to a reduction of the maximal rate of data transfer (or *bandwidth*) (Shannon, 1949) between frontal and posterior cortical areas in autism. Decreased bandwidth impacts performance of the brain system when the inter-regional communication needs are high.

To describe the implications of the theory of underconnectivity, this chapter is organized into several sections: a summary of previous findings, a description of underconnectivity theory and of its implementation as a computational model, and a discussion of its relation to other theories.

WHITE MATTER ABNORMALITIES IN AUTISM

White matter is the unsung hero of the human brain. It constitutes about 45% of the brain. Like any element of infrastructure, it allows the main work of the brain to proceed without explicitly attending to the white matter communication pathways that link various gray matter areas to each other. The main work of the brain is the thinking that gets us all through our lives. That thinking requires the collaborative activity of many gray matter brain areas whose intercommunication vitally depends on the white matter pathways. Every act of thinking requires the collaborative activity of about 20 gray matter computational centers. Human thought is a network activity. For example, reading a sentence requires at least the collaborative work of Wernicke's area in the left temporal lobe, Broca's area in the left frontal, left angular gyrus in the parietal lobe, primary and secondary visual areas in the occipital lobe, as well as the right hemisphere homologs of some of these areas.

Alterations in white matter can impair thought processes. White matter properties are key determinants of the conduction velocity and hence the bandwidth of the communication channels in the brain (Waxman, 1980), thereby impacting cortical connectivity. One such property is the degree of myelination of axons, or the formation of insulating white matter around axons.

The myelin sheath can increase the transmission speed and bandwidth of an axon by a factor of 10 or more (Hartline & Colman, 2007), so myelination and its distribution have a clear relation to cortical communication capacities, including synchronization.

In addition, several studies have reported white matter volumetric abnormalities in autism, with increased volume in some areas and decreased volume in other areas. The increased brain size observed in children with autism is largely due to volume differences in white matter, particularly in the frontal lobes (Carper, Moses, Tigue, & Courchesne, 2002, Herbert et al., 2004). One study reported overall greater white matter volume in 7- to 11-year-old children with autism (Herbert et al., 2003), and the authors found in a later study that this deviation was greatest in the radiate white matter in the frontal lobe (Herbert et al., 2004). Later in life, adolescents and adults with autism actually exhibit reduced white matter volume (Courchesne et al., 2001, Courchesne, Redcay, & Kennedy, 2004; Waiter et al., 2005), although typically developing individuals show a linear increase in white matter volume between the ages of four and 22 years (Giedd et al., 1999).

The most prominent white matter tract in the cortex, the corpus callosum, also shows abnormalities in autism. The corpus callosum enables communication among functional systems in the two hemispheres. It is usually slightly *smaller* in individuals with autism (Chung, Dalton, Alexander, & Davidson, 2004; Hardan, Minshew, & Keshavan, 2000; Manes et al., 1999; Piven, Bailey, Ranson, & Arndt, 1997; Vidal et al., 2006). As noted above, total brain size is abnormal in autism, and *larger* brain volume is correlated with *smaller* corpus callosum size (Jäncke, Preis, & Steinmetz, 1999; Jäncke, Staiger, Schlaug, Huang, & Steinmetz, 1997), suggesting multiple loci of disruption in connectivity (Ringo, 1991). The abnormalities in white matter in autism, including myelination and corpus callosum size, form a plausible neural basis for disrupted systems-level connectivity in autism.

BIOLOGICAL MECHANISMS AFFECTING CONNECTIVITY

Irregularities in a number of early neurodevelopmental processes could individually or in combination result in abnormalities in the brain's development of white matter connectivity (Bailey et al., 1998; Geschwind & Levitt, 2007). For instance, specialized glial cells, oligodendrocytes, are responsible for the production of myelin, which enhances neural transmission. Other glial cells manage waste and clean up neurotransmitters, which helps to organize the structure of the neuronal network. Postmortem samples of gray and white matter taken from individuals with autism show evidence of astroglial and microglial activation and neuroinflammation (Vargas, Nascimbene, Krishnan, Zimmerman, & Pardo, 2005).

Neuronal migration abnormalities in autism can lead to fractionated and incompletely or aberrantly formed minicolumn vertical circuitry. Abnormal minicolumn organization can result in an imbalance between excitation and inhibition within and between minicolumns (Courchesne, Redcay, Morgan, & Kennedy, 2005), or an abundance of short connective fibers relative to long ones, which may lead to a deficiency in inter-regional connectivity. More numerous and abnormally narrow minicolumns in frontal and temporal cortex have been reported in autism (Casanova et al., 2006). A recent postmortem study by Courchesne and colleagues (2011) found significantly increased numbers of neurons in the prefrontal cortex of individuals with autism relative to typically developing individuals.

Yet another possibility is that anomalies in neurochemistry could affect brain development and connectivity. Reductions in N-acetylaspartate (NAA), an amino acid that supports axon myelination (Baslow, 2003), have been demonstrated in several brain regions in autism, including cingulate gyrus, temporal gray matter, frontal and parietal white matter, hippocampal-amygdaloid complex, and cerebellum (Friedman et al., 2003; Hisaoka, Harada, Nishitani, & Mori, 2001; Levitt et al., 2003; Otsuka, Harada, Mori, Hisaoka, & Nishitani, 1999). Another amino acid, glutamate, affects neuronal migration, differentiation, axon genesis, and plasticity (Coyle, Leski, & Morrison, 2002), and several authors have proposed that autism is related to glutamatergic dysfunction (Carlsson, 1998; Polleux & Lauder, 2004; Rubenstein & Merzenich, 2003). Irregularities in these two amino acids, and potentially others, could be a factor in the abnormal development of connections and functioning in people with autism.

In summary, the disruption of cortical connectivity described in the theory of underconnectivity could plausibly stem from one or more of the biological mechanisms described above.

BRAIN-IMAGING EVIDENCE OF DISRUPTED CONNECTIVITY IN AUTISM

The lower-level biological mechanisms cited above could underpin cortical connectivity disruption. Four recent brain-imaging findings converge to more directly implicate aberrant cortical connectivity in autism.

First, the synchronization of brain activation between frontal and posterior regions of the cortex is lower in autism than in control groups across a number of different domains of thought. Poor synchronization of activation has been demonstrated in tasks such as language comprehension (Just et al., 2004; Kana et al., 2006; Mason et al., 2008; Mizuno et al., 2011), executive function (Just et al., 2007), social processing (Kana et al., 2009; Koshino et al., 2008; Schipul, Williams, Keller, Minshew, & Just, 2012), working memory (Koshino et al., 2005, 2008), high-level inhibition (Kana et al., 2007; Solomon et al., 2009), and visuospatial processing (Damarla et al., 2010). The lower synchronization, or functional connectivity, in autism measured during task performance reflects the lower degree of coordination between the two regions.

In addition to task-related functional connectivity, a number of studies have investigated task-free (or "intrinsic") functional connectivity in autism. By partialling out task-driven effects, such studies have shown evidence of both reduced (Jones et al., 2010; Villalobos, Mizuno, Dahl, Kemmotsu, & Muller, 2005) and increased (Mizuno, Villalobos, Davies, Dahl, & Muller, 2006; Noonan, Haist, & Müller, 2009; Turner, Frost, Linsenbardt, McIlroy, & Müller, 2006; Shih et al., 2010) task-free functional connectivity in autism relative to controls. Although the significance of these results remains unclear, both increases and decreases in task-free functional connectivity could plausibly reduce the available bandwidth of communication for task-relevant processing (see Schipul et al., 2011, for a discussion).

Similarly, underconnectivity is evident during a resting state in which the "task" consists of relaxed, internally generated thought. The functional connectivity between frontal and posterior areas of the default network (regions more active during rest than they are during an externally imposed task) is lower in autism than in controls (Cherkassky, Kana, Keller, & Just, 2006). This reduction in functional connectivity persists even when high-frequency fluctuations in activation are filtered out (in an effort to limit measurement to spontaneous physiological changes rather than cognitively driven modulations of activation) (Assaf et al., 2010; Kennedy & Courchesne, 2008; Monk et al., 2009; Weng et al., 2010). This finding has been replicated with EEG methods, measuring activity across cortical areas within the alpha range (8–10 Hz) (Coben, Clarke, Hudspeth, & Barry, 2008; Murias, Webb, Greenson, & Dawson, 2007). Coben et al. (2008) interpreted their EEG results as indicating "... dysfunctional integration of frontal and posterior brain regions in autistics along with a pattern of neural underconnectivity."

In sum, fMRI studies of task-relevant and task-free functional connectivity find reduced frontal-posterior synchronization of activation across many different types of thinking, but particularly in more complex tasks that involve frontal participation.

A second brain-imaging finding supporting the theory of underconnectivity is that, as described above, there are white matter volumetric abnormalities in autism that lead to cortico-cortical connection abnormalities (e.g., Carper et al., 2002; Courchesne et al., 2001; Herbert et al., 2004). These studies indicate that, for individuals with autism, there is a tendency towards excess white matter volume in some regions (such as the frontal radiate white matter) and diminished volume in other regions (such as the corpus callosum).

The third finding deals specifically with the size of the corpus callosum and how it relates to frontal-posterior connectivity. Among individuals with autism, the reduced size of their corpus callosum is correlated with the degree of impairment in functional connectivity during thinking tasks and in resting state (Cherkassky et al., 2006; Just et al., 2007; Kana et al., 2006, 2009; Schipul et al., 2011). More specifically, across a diverse set of studies, the extent of functional connectivity between frontal and posterior regions is correlated with the

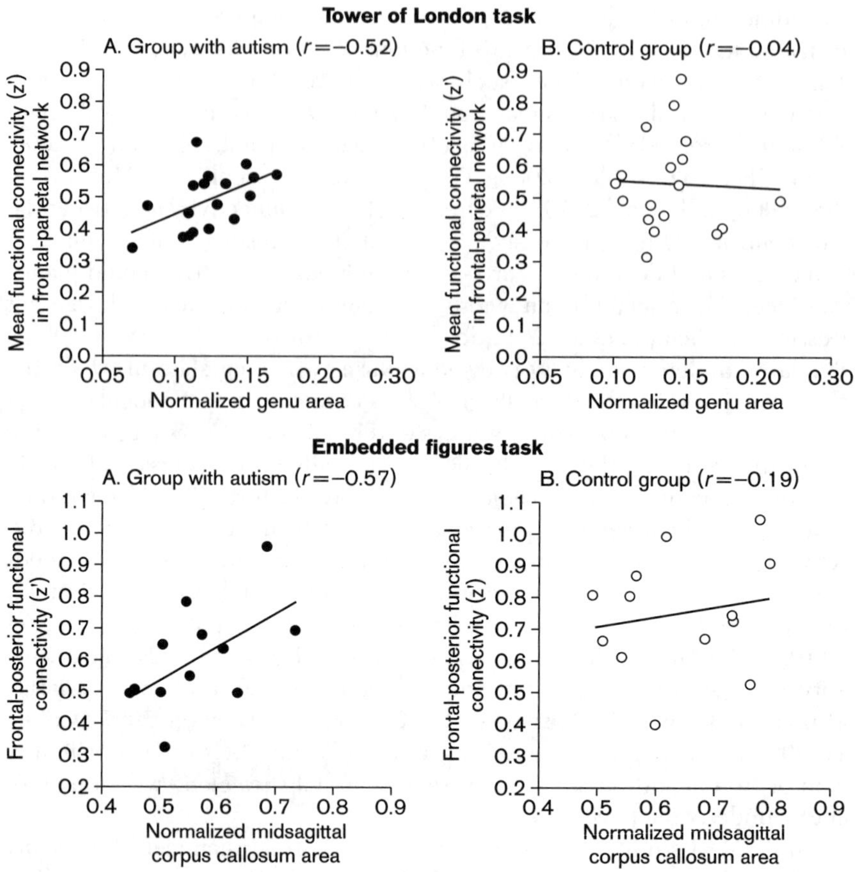

(A)

Figure 3.1 Correlation in four studies between the relevant portion of the corpus callosum and the mean functional connectivity between frontal and posterior areas for the Autism group (A) and a lack of correlation for the Control group (B).

size of the segment of the corpus callosum that connects these cortical regions, as shown in Figure 3.1. The corpus callosum size deficit is interpreted as a more general index of white matter disruption in autism that constrains the communication bandwidth between frontal and posterior brain regions and limits their synchronization. (For neurotypical participants, there is no correlation between the size of the corpus callosum or its segments with frontal-posterior functional connectivity, presumably because the white matter does not impose a constraint on bandwidth or synchronization.)

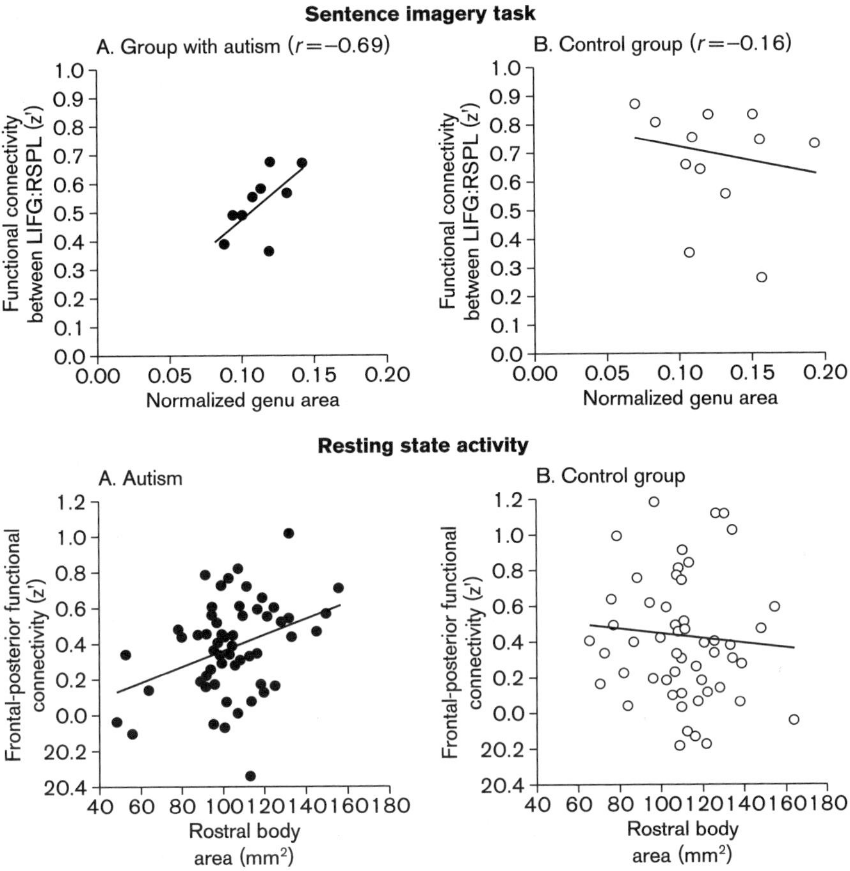

(B)

Figure 3.1 Continued

Fourth, several recent diffusion tensor imaging (DTI) studies of white matter in autism have found abnormalities in the connective tracts, particularly in fractional anisotropy, a measure of coherence of directionality of white matter fibers. At very young ages (two to three years), there is evidence of *increased* fractional anisotropy in autism, particularly in the frontal lobe and corpus callosum (Ben Bashat et al., 2007), consistent with early overgrowth of white matter, discussed above. By five years of age, however, fractional anisotropy is reduced for tracts that connect regions within the frontal lobes (Sundaram et al., 2008). In older children and adolescents (10- to 18-year-olds), there is reduced fractional anisotropy in specific frontal-posterior tracts in autism (Sahyoun, Belliveau, Soulières, Schwartz, & Mody, 2010), as well as autism-related differences in hemispheric lateralization of fractional anisotropy in the arcuate fasciculus connecting frontal, parietal, and temporal cortices (Fletcher et al., 2010; Knaus et al., 2010). One study of children and adolescents with autism found reduced fractional anisotropy in white matter adjacent to the ventromedial prefrontal cortices, anterior cingulate gyri, temporoparietal junction, and in the corpus callosum (Barnea-Goraly et al., 2004). Reduced fractional anisotropy persists into adulthood in the corpus callosum and in tracts in the frontal and temporal lobes (Alexander et al., 2007; Keller, Kana, & Just, 2007; Lee et al., 2007). Cumulatively, these studies provide clear evidence of a relationship between autism and disruption of the white matter that provides the anatomical connectivity among frontal and posterior brain regions, a disruption that is exacerbated with development. The DTI finding most relevant to the theory proposed in this chapter is reduced fractional anisotropy in an area of the left anterior corona radiata, consistent with either the left uncinate fasciculus (connecting the frontal and temporal lobes) or the left inferior frontal-occipital fasciculus, observed in a sample of 52 adults and adolescents with autism compared to age- and IQ-matched controls (Keller and Just, 2009a).

These converging findings suggest that reductions in communication and connectivity among cortical regions may be part of the pervasive core processing deficits in autism (Belmonte et al., 2004; Courchesne & Pierce, 2005a, 2005b; Herbert et al., 2004; Just et al., 2004; Keller et al., 2007; Rippon, Brock, Brown, & Boucher, 2007). Below, we describe a theory of autism based on disruption of cortical connectivity.

UNDERCONNECTIVITY THEORY

The cortical underconnectivity theory (Just et al., 2004, 2007) posits that interregional (systems-level) connective circuitry in the brain is disrupted in autism. In particular, the communication bandwidth between frontal areas and posterior cortical areas is proposed to be lower in autism than in control participants. The theory proposes a causal relationship between the anatomical, physiological (brain activity), and psychological phenomena. Thus, any psychological process which requires extensive coordination between frontal and posterior brain regions is susceptible to disruption, particularly when the task is complex and requires integration of different types of cortical computations. Underconnectivity is proposed as a unifying theory for explaining a range of deficits at the levels of psychological function, cortical function, and cortical anatomy, and the heterogeneity of possible connective disturbances could underlie the considerable heterogeneity of behavioral symptoms of autism. This is an initial attempt at an exhaustive theory, in the sense that no other independent factors that do not stem from or underlie connectivity aberrations are presumed to underlie autism.

Bandwidth Limitations in Autism

The bandwidth of a communication channel is the amount of information that can be transmitted per unit time, and this property is crucial for the functioning of a network of interconnected nodes whose mainstay is collaborative interaction. Human thought relies on co-activation of a network of cortical areas linked by white matter tracts providing anatomical connectivity. As discussed above, fMRI studies have demonstrated that synchronization between frontal and posterior areas is lower in autism (Just et al., 2004, 2007; Kana et al., 2006, 2007; Koshino et al., 2005; Villalobos et al., 2005). Figure 3.2A (see plate section) illustrates this deficit in connectivity when participants complete a Tower of London (TOL) problem-solving task, which entails activation of both frontal and parietal areas. We attribute the lower synchronization demonstrated in this and other tasks to a lower communication bandwidth between frontal and posterior areas in autism relative to controls, depicted schematically in Figures 3.2B and 3.2C. The model presented below demonstrates that a bandwidth constraint, coupled with increased autonomy of the parietal lobe, results in a reduction of frontal-parietal synchronization. The model also explains the behavioral differences in task performance seen between groups as a function of a frontal-parietal bandwidth constraint in autism.

The functional connectivities plotted in Figure 3.2A are means of correlations of activation times-series data, averaged over 18 participants in each group and over multiple pairs of activated frontal-parietal pairs of regions of interest. The correlations measure the degree to which the activation levels in two regions rise and fall together. Figure 3.3 illustrates the coordination of two regions for one participant with autism (top panel) and one control participant (bottom panel): a frontal region (left DLPFC) and a parietal region (left parietal). Visual inspection and the correlation coefficients indicate that the two curves are less correlated for the participant with autism compared to the control participant (and Figure 3.2A shows the mean frontal-parietal correlation for each group across all frontal-parietal pairs of regions). These figures illustrate functional underconnectivity in autism compared to controls in TOL problem-solving, and this pattern is replicated in many other tasks requiring synchronization of frontal and posterior areas.

Such functional underconnectivity of a very similar form has also been observed in autism in a number of diverse domains. One of these was a social task involving face perception and working memory, exhibiting reduced synchronization between the fusiform face area and a frontal area (Koshino et al., 2008). Another was a Theory of Mind task in which the intentions of animated geometric objects were being inferred from their motions, exhibiting reduced functional connectivity between the medial frontal area and the right posterior superior temporal area (both associated with Theory of Mind processing) (Kana et al., 2009). Another study was a sentence comprehension task in which participants had to construct a visual image in order to evaluate whether the sentence was true or false, requiring coordination between a frontal language area and a parietal spatial processing area (Kana et al., 2006). Yet another was a task requiring complex inhibition, displaying reduced frontal-parietal connectivity (Kana et al., 2007). Finally, even in a resting state when participants were not performing any assigned task, the functional underconnectivity in autism between frontal and posterior regions continued to be manifested (Cherkassky et al., 2006). The diversity of these tasks speaks to the generality of the functional underconnectivity phenomenon.

Figures 3.2A and 3.3 depict the main phenomenon for which the computational modeling, described below, attempts to provide a postulated mechanism—that is, a lowered communication bandwidth. A key assumption is that

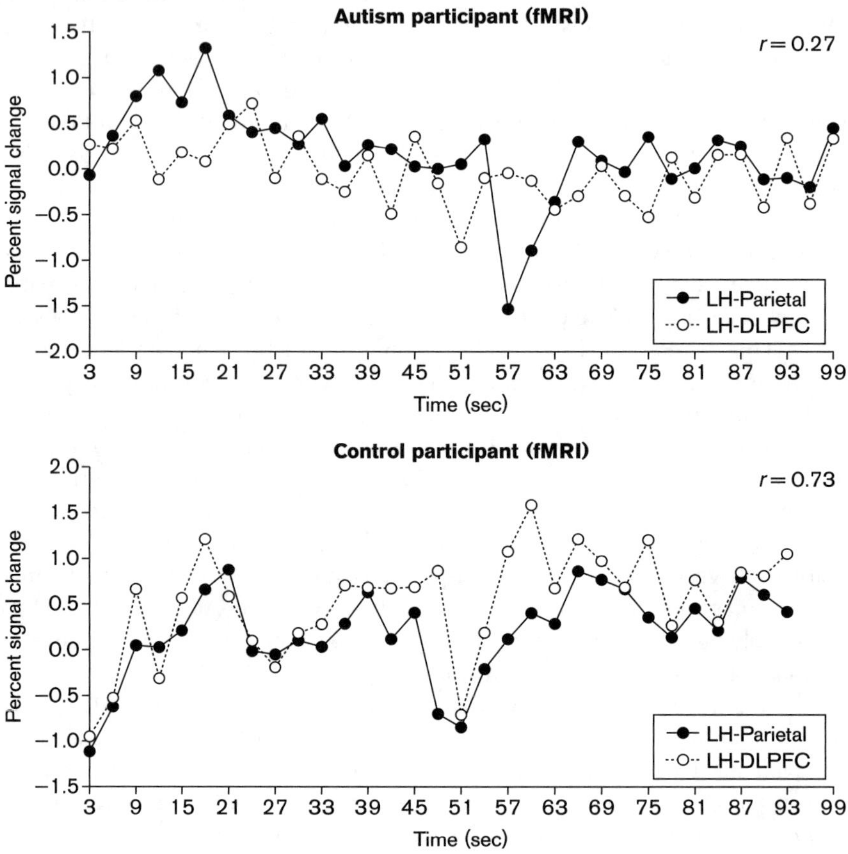

Figure 3.3 Higher frontal-parietal functional connectivity between the two activation time series in a control participant (correlation r = .73) (bottom panel) in the Tower of London task than in an autism participant (r = .27) (top panel) (data from Just et al., 2007).

lowering the bandwidth will produce an adaptation in the system. Adaptation in a computer network illustrates that agents in a collaborative environment can become more autonomous when inter-agent communication is impaired (Stone & Veloso, 1999), and communication networks can switch to an asynchronous mode when bandwidth decreases (Fall, 2003). Analogously, the underconnectivity theory of autism predicts that decreased cortical bandwidth could result in concomitant adaptations in cortical functioning, most probably increased posterior (in this case, parietal) autonomy from frontal influences. Moreover, it is also plausible that decreased bandwidth could give rise to increased functional connectivity among posterior regions.

COMPUTATIONAL MODELING OF BRAIN FUNCTION AND COGNITION

Here we briefly describe a recent computational account (Just et al., 2012) of the lower frontal-posterior functional connectivity and longer response times in autism in a high-level visual problem-solving task, the Tower of London. The model is expressed within the 4CAPS cognitive neuroarchitecture, which accounts for cortical function in terms of a set of collaborating computational centers intended to correspond to cortical centers (Just & Varma, 2007). The autism model of the Tower of London task is an adaptation of a previous TOL model developed to account for the brain activation and performance of typically developing individuals (Newman, Carpenter, Varma, & Just, 2003). (The task required re-arranging the positions of three distinctive balls in three suspended pool pockets until they matched a specified goal [or ending] configuration, as shown in Figure 3.4.) The model contained two frontal centers and two parietal centers. The autism model contained two adaptations. One was a lowering of the communication bandwidth between the frontal and parietal centers, which slowed performance when a center had to wait longer for critical input from another center. The second adaptation was an increased autonomy accorded to the parietal centers, such that they were enabled to proceed

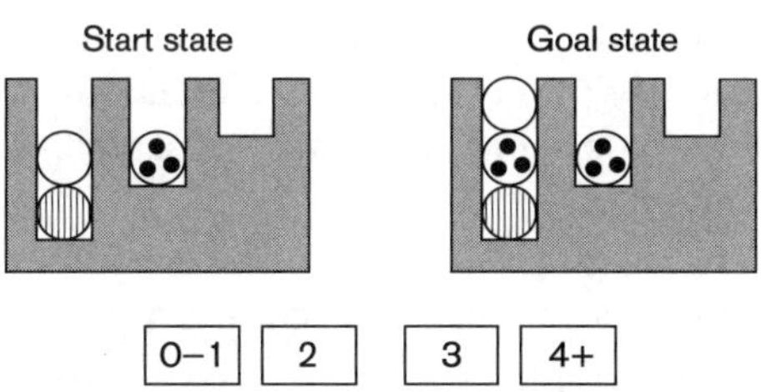

Figure 3.4 A sample Tower of London problem. This display shows a three-move problem and a schematic diagram showing the response buttons to indicate the number of moves required.

without frontal input in certain circumstances. (An example of one such circumstance occurs during the last move of a problem: If a parietal center is proposing a move in the puzzle that would be the last move of a successful solution, then in the autism model that parietal center is enabled to make the move without requiring the input from the frontal executive centers that would normally collaborate in selecting this move.)

The autism model shows lower functional connectivity between frontal and parietal centers, compared to the original model. When the correlations of the time series for all possible pairs of frontal and parietal centers are averaged for the control model and the full autism model, the resulting difference in functional connectivity strongly resembles the corresponding group difference found in the fMRI data (shown in Figure 3.2A). The autism model also shows increased response times, and the participants with autism did. In addition, the autism model can predict the frontal-parietal functional connectivity of individual participants with autism by making the frontal-posterior bandwidth proportional to an index of that individual's white matter properties. The model thus provides an integrated explanation of how the postulated mechanisms account for some of the central brain imaging and behavioral findings in autism.

Cause, Effect, and Adaptation

The observed brain functioning in autism likely results from both the brain changes introduced by autism and the brain's natural adaptations to the changes during many years of brain development. In this view, greater parietal autonomy and reliance on posterior brain areas is interpreted not as part of the primary physiological basis of autism, but as a functional consequence. The modeling described above reinforces the notion that an adapted system does not always function as well as an intact system might. When completing the more complex TOL problems that required the frontal areas of the brain to manage deeply embedded goals, the adapted system was less effective than an intact system. Lower performance might also occur in other tasks during which certain frontal processes cannot be performed or compensated for by a posterior center (such as Theory of Mind processing). On the other hand, as described below, the adapted system may be more effective in situations in which the frontal contributions may impede performance (such as searching for embedded figures in a distracting context).

SUMMARY OF PREVIOUS CONNECTIVITY-RELATED FINDINGS: COMMONALITIES ACROSS DOMAINS OF THOUGHT

The model can be extended to account for brain characteristics seen in autism while participants engage in a variety of tasks and types of thinking. A summary of the findings from studies of 10 types of tasks indicates a number of commonalities as well as specificities. One robust finding across studies is the frontal-posterior undersynchronization, which to date has been observed in every high-level thinking task that has been examined, including tasks of executive functioning, language, memory, social processing, and high-level perception, as well as in a resting state "task," as shown in the third column of Table 3.1. In many of these tasks, the corpus callosum of the participants with autism was reliably smaller than that seen in control participants (fourth column), and the corpus callosum size was correlated with the degree of frontal-posterior synchronization (fifth column). In addition, areas around the corpus callosum showed lower structural integrity in autism, as measured by fractional anisotropy in diffusion tensor imaging studies. Many of these studies also showed decreased activation in a frontal area and increased activation in a posterior association area, consistent with the model's tenets. Thus there are commonalities across domains of thought in the frontal-posterior undersynchronization, in the relation between undersynchronization and properties of the relevant white matter, and in the distribution of activation in the brain (less frontal and more posterior).

Domain-Specific Behavioral Findings in Autism

The brain characteristics of autism also have behavioral manifestations that are task-specific. For example, in pilot studies of the TOL puzzle, participants with autism had more difficulty with more complex problems than did IQ-matched control participants, necessitating an fMRI study design that excluded the most difficult problems. The right-hand column of Table 3.1 describes several behavioral manifestations of autism that are drawn from large behavioral studies (not necessarily from the corresponding brain-imaging studies). For instance, poorer comprehension of complex syntax in autism was observed in the Detroit Test of Oral Directions (Minshew, Goldstein, & Siegel, 1997), and good performance at word recognition was observed by Newman et al. (2007). In general, the tendency is for the autism group to process tasks in a way that relies less on functions that have a vital frontal component (e.g., executive functioning, complex language, Theory of Mind, or face, and social processing) and more on posterior functions (visual or other perceptual processing). This greater reliance on posterior areas may lead to processing that is more independent of frontal areas, more visual or featural in content, and, in some circumstances, more effective for persons with autism compared to neurotypical individuals.

Because this theory accounts for the neuroimaging and behavioral patterns of results in a wide variety of thinking tasks, it is likely that it can be extended to anticipate characteristics of thinking in autism in new situations. If the brain activity and thought processes in people without autism are understood well enough, then the theory-based model can provide a first-order prediction of what will occur in autism.

TABLE 3.1 Summary of Domain-General and Domain-Specific Autism Findings

		Domain-General Brain Phenomena in Autism					Domain-Specific Behavioral Phenomena in Autism
DOMAIN	**TASK**	**Lower frontal–posterior synchronization**	**Smaller corpus callosum**	**Correlation between corpus callosum and synchronization**	**Less frontal activation**	**More posterior activation**	
Executive	Tower of London puzzle (Just et al., 2007)	Yes	Yes	Yes	MFG	LG	Difficulty with more complex problems
Executive	Inhibition of high-level response (Kana et al., 2007)	Yes	—	—	R IFG	—	Impaired high-level inhibition
Executive	Inhibition of high-level response (Solomon et al., 2009)	Yes	—	—	MFG, R SFG	—	Impaired high-level inhibition
Language	Visual imagery in sentence comprehension (Kana et al., 2006)	Yes	Yes	Yes	L IFG, L MFG	L IPS, R SPL	Imagery activation even for more abstract sentences ("thinking in pictures")
Language	Sentence comprehension (Just et al., 2004)	Yes	—	—	L IFG, MFG	L STG	Difficulty with complex syntax; good word-reading
Memory	Working memory for alphabetic letters (Koshino et al., 2005)	Yes			L IFG, L MFG	L IT	Letters are coded relatively more visually than verbally
Social	Theory of Mind: animation (Kana et al., 2009)	Yes	Yes	—	MFG	R TPJ	Theory of Mind difficulties

TABLE 3.1 Continued

Social	Face memory (Koshino et al., 2008)	Yes	—	—	L IFG, MFG	—	Faces are treated as relatively more visual than social objects
Perception	Embedded Figures Test (Damarla et al., 2010)	Yes	Yes	Yes	MFG	R IPS, R SPL	Less interference from higher-order information
Resting State	Fixation (Cherkassky et al., 2006)	Yes	Yes	Yes	—	—	—
Resting State	Fixation (Kennedy & Courchesne, 2008)	Yes	Yes	Yes	—	—	—
Resting State	Fixation (Monk et al., 2009)	Yes	Yes	Yes	—	—	—
Diffusion Tensor Imaging	No task (Alexander et al., 2007; Barnea-Goraly et al., 2004; Keller et al., 2007)	—	Lower integrity	—	—	—	—

RELATION TO OTHER THEORIES OF AUTISM

This section compares underconnectivity theory with previous theoretical approaches to autism, such as the theories of weak central coherence (Frith, 1989), impaired complex information processing (Minshew et al., 1997), enhanced perceptual functioning (Mottron, Dawson, Soulieres, Hubert, & Burack, 2006), mindblindness (Baron-Cohen, 1995), impaired social processing and motivation (Dawson et al., 2002), and longer-distance cortical communication. Each of these theories captures some fundamental aspect of autism, and all of them are at least partially correct. However, many of these predecessor theories were developed before extensive brain-imaging studies of autism had been performed, focusing instead on behavioral data, so they tend not to be grounded in a biological substrate. We propose that it is this biological substrate that accounts for the diversity of symptoms supporting the diverse theories of autism. The underconnectivity theory provides a basis for comparison with some of the preceding theories described below.

Weak Central Coherence (WCC) Theory

Frith's (1989) theory of weak central coherence (WCC) attempts to explain the tendency in autism to focus on details at the expense of broader integrative information processing. Frith suggested that the flow of normal thought is similar to the flow of a river that imposes coherence among contributing streams or inputs; the theory hypothesizes that, in autism, there is weaker central coherence among the contributing streams of thought. The excellence of this analogy distracts from WCC theory's absence of a plausible underlying biological mechanism, although recently Frith and colleagues have attempted to relate neuroimaging results to WCC. By contrast, underconnectivity theory links together abnormalities in underlying biological structures (i.e., white matter tracts) and cortical communication processes with psychological processes (i.e., interregional communication and the sharing of representational elements). As with WCC theory, underconnectivity theory predicts weak coherence among ongoing processes, but specifically when the processes include communication between frontal and posterior areas. Underconnectivity theory interprets weak central coherence as an emergent system property arising from this reduced frontal-posterior communication bandwidth, which does not require the existence of a mechanism that arranges coherence, as WCC implicitly posits. Moreover, the 4CAPS computational model suggests that reduced long-distance bandwidth may result in more autonomous processing centers, resulting in impairments in functions involving a frontal contribution, particularly when a large processing load is being imposed on the system. In sum, WCC theory provides a useful organizing analogy that is applicable to a broad range of phenomena in autism, whereas underconnectivity theory additionally proposes an underlying mechanism that relates the biological and psychological levels.

Autism as a Complex Information Processing Disorder

Minshew and her colleagues (Minshew & Goldstein, 1998; Minshew et al., 1997; Williams, Goldstein, & Minshew, 2006) have observed impairment in autism across many domains when the complexity level of information processing is high. Lower-level processes are spared or even enhanced, but as tasks become more complex, impairment gets more pronounced. In this theory, complexity is not rigorously defined, but it may refer to a higher level of abstraction that the task requires. Underconnectivity theory attributes the complex information processing deficits to a specific biological substrate, frontal-posterior brain connectivity. The difficulties in complex information processing may occur when frontal involvement is mandatory for normal performance (presumably to support the high levels of abstraction), but in autism, the poor frontal-posterior connectivity (abnormally limited bandwidth) undermines the frontal contributions and hence performance is impaired.

Related to the description of autism as a complex information processing disorder is the *executive dysfunction theory of autism* (Hughes, Russell, & Robbins, 1994; Pennington & Ozonoff, 1996), which notes that executive dysfunction in autism tends to be observed in complex tasks. According to underconnectivity theory, executive dysfunction could arise from poor connectivity between the posterior regions and the frontal areas that perform executive functions. For instance, a problem-solving task like TOL requires the coordination between executive (frontal) and spatial (parietal) brain areas. Any limitation of such coordination in autism may manifest itself as a deficit in problem-solving or in executive functioning.

Enhanced Perceptual Functioning (EPF)

Mottron and his colleagues (2006) have hypothesized that autism involves enhancement of certain types of perceptual processing. They argue that, compared to control participants, perceptual processing in autism is locally oriented; includes enhanced low-level discrimination and perception of simple static stimuli; and entails greater use of posterior brain regions in complex visual tasks. Individuals with autism have diminished perception of complex movement, and low-level information processing is autonomous from higher-order operations. This extensive list of the perceptual characteristics in autism bears a good correspondence to the underconnectivity theory position, particularly the theory's postulation of increased autonomy of posterior centers.

Specifically, the bias in autism towards local rather than global processing is attributed by underconnectivity theory to the lower frontal-posterior communication bandwidth, resulting in the degradation of top-down or global influences. Underconnectivity theory also suggests that functional connectivity among posterior areas may actually be *higher* in autism than controls because the decrease in frontal-posterior traffic could lead to increased posterior autonomy and posterior-posterior bandwidth. In sum, any enhancements in autism in some lower-level perceptual functions may arise secondarily from poorer connectivity between frontal and more posterior (perceptual) areas. Moreover, underconnectivity theory provides a biologically based explanation for some of the perceptual phenomena on which the EPF approach focuses.

Mindblindness

The mindblindness theory (Baron-Cohen, 1995) suggests that the deficits seen in individuals with autism during Theory of Mind (ToM) processing are centrally causal to the disorder. Many behavioral and neuroimaging studies have demonstrated this deficit (e.g., Baron-Cohen, 1989; Happé, 1995; Tager-Flusberg, 1992; Castelli, Frith, Happé, & Frith, 2002; Kana et al., 2009) and its biological substrates in the right posterior superior temporal sulcus and the nearby temporo-parietal junction, and the medial frontal area. Underconnectivity theory posits that, in autism, bandwidth limitations impede the normal communication between these areas, resulting in the observable deficits in ToM.

A recent fMRI study explicitly measured the functional connectivity between the frontal and posterior regions of the ToM cortical network (Kana et al., 2009). The participants viewed an animated interaction between two geometric figures, including trials in which the intentionality of the figures could be inferred (the ToM condition). In the original PET study of ToM using these figures, Castelli et al. (2002) found that the correlation across subjects between the average level of activity in the superior temporal sulcus (an area associated with ToM and the perception of biological motion) and extrastriate cortex was lower across autistic participants than across control participants. Using fMRI, Kana and colleagues (2009) found a reliable reduction in the *synchronization* of the activation (across points in time) between frontal and posterior ToM areas in the group with autism relative to the control group during the ToM task, as the underconnectivity theory predicted.

Underconnectivity theory is a more general approach than ToM or mindblindness theory, which can be viewed as an instance of reduced frontal-posterior connectivity. The specific roles of the frontal and posterior components of the ToM network are still debated; however, our studies suggest that these cortical areas work together during ToM processing and that this collaboration is disrupted in autism.

Impaired Social Processing and Motivation

Some researchers have attributed a central or causal role to the prominent social interaction deficits seen in individuals with autism (Dawson et al., 2002; Schultz et al., 2003). Contemporary brain-imaging studies of autism have discovered aberrations in cortical processing of social tasks. For example, one of the key brain areas involved in processing faces (the fusiform face area, or FFA) demonstrates hypoactivation with some displacement of location for people with autism compared to controls (Schultz, 2005; Schultz et al., 2000). However, by expanding the focus to the cortical *network* involved in such tasks, the abnormality can be seen as a result of underconnectivity. In a study using the n-back working memory task with faces as stimuli, Koshino and colleagues (2008) found abnormal FFA activation, but also reported several other network disturbances. First, the autism group had lower functional connectivity between the FFA and frontal areas than did the control group. Second, individuals with autism had less activation in the right posterior ToM areas (posterior middle and superior temporal area), suggesting that social processing was evoked to a lower degree in autism. Because FFA dysfunction is not the only abnormality in neural functioning of social processes, it appears that autism is not just a social processing deficit, but a neural systems disorder, involving abnormal interaction among areas responsible for processing social stimuli, such as faces.

Another proposed explanation for impaired social processing in autism centers around atypical development of the ability to *initiate* joint attention (IJA) (Mundy, Sigman, & Kasari, 1994; Mundy, Sullivan, & Mastergeorge, 2009). This theory suggests that social referencing and learning depends on the initiation of joint attention, which requires close collaboration between temporo-parietal and frontal areas. This proposal is consistent with the underconnectivity theory in that the frontal-posterior communication system is compromised in autism, which would lead to an impairment of IJA as well as a relative preservation of joint attention capabilities that do not involve frontal areas.

Other social processing tasks that are impaired in autism can also be interpreted as connectivity problems. One study investigated the processing of the gaze of an avatar, who looked either towards a visual stimulus in its field of view (an appropriate behavior) or inappropriately away from the stimulus (Pelphrey, Morris, & McCarthy, 2005). For control participants, the posterior superior temporal sulcus (STS) activated differentially to the avatar's appropriate versus inappropriate gaze shifts; however, there was no differential response in STS in participants with autism. The authors suggested that "[i]n individuals with autism, the connection between higher level [frontal] systems and the STS region may be broken, and thus the higher level systems do not engage and maintain activation in the STS region." Again, this pattern is consistent with the theory of frontal-posterior underconnectivity.

Overall, complex social processing involves many brain regions, usually including frontal areas. For proper functioning, these regions require intact connectivity that enables effective communication of information among them. The high informational demands of these tasks are often overlooked, yet the complexity of social thought necessitates a communication infrastructure that is no less sophisticated than any other type of thought. Perhaps social processing requires an even more finely integrated system, which could explain why social deficits are particularly apparent in autism.

Long-Distance Connectivity

Some researchers have suggested that long-range, but not short-range, brain connectivity may be disrupted in autism (Belmonte et al., 2004; Lewis & Elman, 2008). These theorists suggest that the enlargement of brain size in autism during the early stages of development, described above (Aylward, Minshew, Field, Sparks, & Singh, 2002; Courchesne et al., 2001; Courchesne, Carper, & Akshoomoff , 2003; Piven et al., 1995; Sparks et al., 2002), increases the cortical distance between key processing centers, resulting in disruption of distant inter-regional communication. Specifically, this hypothesis predicts that individuals with autism will have lower fMRI-measured functional connectivity than the control group only for long-distance pairs of areas of activation.

In order to test this hypothesis, we reanalyzed the functional connectivity data in the Just et al. (2007) Tower of London study described above. From 15 functional regions of interest (ROIs), there were 105 pair-wise measures of z′-transformed functional connectivity. The pairs were categorized as either long- or short-distance using a median split of the Euclidean distances between the centroids of the two ROIs. Contrary to the long-distance hypothesis, there was no interaction between the group difference in functional connectivity with the distance between two ROIs ($F(1, 34) = 0.27$, $p = .61$). Although the functional connectivity decreased with Euclidean distance between ROI centroids ($F(1, 34) = 324.85$, $p < .0001$), it did so similarly for both autism and control groups. By contrast, underconnectivity theory posits that the connection distance is not as critical as whether the connection is between a frontal area and a posterior cortical area. Indeed, the underconnectivity theory correctly predicts an interaction between group and the frontal-parietal vs. other-pairs variable ($F(1,34) = 6.30$, $p < .02$), with the autism group showing reliably lower functional connectivity only for frontal-parietal pairs (Just et al., 2007).

While it may seem improbable that a neurobiological factor could selectively affect frontal-posterior tracts, but not other long-distance connections, it is actually biologically plausible. The frontal lobes are implicated in many of the developmental mechanisms that may be relevant to autism, including glial activation and neuroinflammation (Vargas et al., 2005); minicolumnopathy (Casanova et al., 2006); increase in neuron number (Courchesne et al., 2011); and early brain overgrowth (Carper et al., 2002, Carper & Courchesne, 2005; Herbert et al., 2004). Given the protracted maturation of frontal lobe circuitry, these abnormalities could affect only frontal-posterior tracts, resulting in underconnectivity specifically along white matter connecting cortical centers in those areas (Courchesne & Pierce, 2005a, 2005b). Based on the fMRI studies of functional connectivity and the DTI studies of structural connectivity reviewed here, it is clear that connections involving the frontal lobes are affected more than others.

QUESTIONS RAISED BY THE THEORY

The underconnectivity theory provides a useful theoretical framework, but it has not yet been applied to investigations of several outstanding questions about autism. In its current form, we view the theory as preliminary, anticipating that future research will result in considerable refinement, expansion, and modification. Below we raise some key, but unanswered, questions generated by the theory.

Other Connectivity Disturbances

Several types of other connectivity abnormalities besides functional underconnectivity could emerge, through the use of fMRI or other techniques. Further study could find alterations in connectivity among neural systems or intraregional communication, including the possibility of *increased* connectivity between some areas. Other techniques that could be brought to bear on studies of neural connectivity in autism include histology, electrophysiology, morphometry, and diffusion imaging. Specifically, it will be most interesting to use some combination of these approaches to investigate white matter and gray matter abnormalities, as well as the relation between functional and anatomical abnormalities in autism.

Task Effects in Connectivity

Although we have reported functional underconnectivity in a number of different types of thinking relevant to autism (executive function, perception, language, social processing, inhibition), this phenomenon has not been studied in many other types of relevant tasks, including tasks without frontal involvement, tasks with non-visual input (auditory, haptic, gustatory, or olfactory), and simple motor tasks. We assume that the disruption in connectivity only applies between frontal and posterior regions because the studies supporting this theory focused on tasks with frontal involvement, but ensuing studies could falsify this assumption.

Investigation with Lower-Functioning and Younger Participants

Most of the functional connectivity studies to date have been conducted with high-functioning individuals with autism, but this research should be extended to include lower-functioning participants. Although it is more difficult to acquire imaging data from low-functioning individuals, it should be possible to study this population's resting state functional connectivity, which has been shown to be impaired in high-functioning autism (Cherkassky et al., 2006; Kennedy & Courchesne, 2008; Monk et al., 2009). Another extension might examine younger participants with autism in order to understand the ontology of functional underconnectivity and the development of white matter that supports cortical connectivity.

Relation of Underconnectivity Theory to Other Clinical Populations

Comparison of possible cortical communication disturbances across neurological conditions could be informative about the nature of connectivity. For example, Herbert et al. (2004) found several areas of white matter that were larger in autism and also in participants with developmental language delay, compared to controls, although there were some areas affected only in one disorder and not the other. Understanding the patterns of commonalities and specificities in disordered anatomical and functional connectivity may reveal possible branching points in development of different syndromes.

Another disorder that involves disruption of white matter, like autism and developmental language delay, is dyslexia (e.g., Deutsch et al., 2005). Recently, we demonstrated that the white matter abnormalities associated with poor reading skills in children can be improved with training (Keller & Just, 2009b). If white matter is modifiable with behavioral therapies, as this study showed, there is hope that behavioral therapies for autism might also be able to modify a connectivity deficit.

Etiology of Underconnectivity

Underconnectivity theory does not attempt to account for the pathophysiological origins of autism, although it provides guidance for such a search. Underconnectivity theory could be easily linked to genomics, since it already integrates some of the known pathophysiological and neuropsychological aspects of autism. For instance, one tentative hypothesis proposes that autism is caused by developmental dysregulation of inter-regional brain connectivity (Geschwind & Levitt, 2007).

SUMMARY

Underconnectivity theory proposes that autism can be characterized as a neural systems disorder marked by frontal-posterior communication impairments caused by lowered bandwidth. The abnormal flow of information between frontal and posterior areas results in deficits in tasks that require substantial frontal contributions, as well as increased reliance on posterior cortical regions. This increased dependence on processing in more posterior regions could hamper performance during tasks that necessitate inputs from the frontal cortex, including for higher-level strategies and concepts. The diversity of behavioral symptoms in autism may be due to the wide range of activities that involve substantial frontal participation.

The 4CAPS computational model of autism (Just et al., 2012) provides a sufficiency proof of underconnectivity theory. By recreating the conditions proposed by underconnectivity theory—that is, lower frontal-posterior bandwidth and more autonomy of posterior cortical centers—the model reproduces several key phenomena observed in fMRI studies of autism using the TOL task, including observed reaction times, fMRI activation, and group and individual differences in functional connectivity. In addition, the model accounts for group differences in a wide variety of tasks across different domains (as shown in Table 3.1).

Although white matter differences form at least part of the biological basis of autism, future studies should search for concomitant or even causal gray matter abnormalities. New imaging technologies can trace white matter tracts in great detail, thereby transforming some of these theoretical considerations into empirical issues. A theory of frontal-posterior underconnectivity in autism provides an initial framework to guide such future research.

ACKNOWLEDGMENTS

This research was supported by the Autism Centers of Excellence Grant HD055748 from the National Institute of Child Health and Human Development, the National Institute of Mental Health Grant MH029617, and the Office of Naval Research Grant N00014–07–1–0041.

NOTE

1. Corresponding author. Address correspondence to: Marcel Adam Just, Carnegie Mellon University, Department of Psychology, 5000 Forbes Avenue, Pittsburgh, PA 15213, Phone: 412-268-2791, Fax: 412-268-2804, Email: just@cmu.edu.

REFERENCES

Alexander, A. L., Lee, J. E., Lazar, M., Boudos, R., DuBray, M. B., Oakes, T. R.,… Lainhart, J. E. (2007). Diffusion tensor imaging of the corpus callosum in autism. *NeuroImage, 34*, 61–73.

Asperger, H. (1944). Autistic psychopathy in childhood. Translated in U. Frith (Ed.) (1991), *Autism and Asperger's syndrome* (pp. 37–92). Cambridge: Cambridge University Press.

Assaf, M., Jagannathan, K., Calhoun, V. D., Miller, L., Stevens, M. C., Sahl, R.,… Pearlson, G. D. (2010). Abnormal functional connectivity of default mode subnetworks in autism spectrum disorder patients. *NeuroImage, 53*, 247–256.

Aylward, E. H., Minshew, N. J., Field, K., Sparks, B. F., & Singh, N. (2002). Effects of age on brain volume and head circumference in autism. *Neurology, 59*, 175–183.

Bailey, A., Luthert, P., Dean, A., Harding, B., Janota, I., Montgomery M.,… Lantos, P. (1998). A clinicopathological study of autism. *Brain, 121*, 101–117.

Barnea-Goraly, N., Kwon, H., Menon, V., Eliez, S., Lotspeich, L., & Reiss, A. L. (2004). White matter structure in autism: Preliminary evidence from diffusion tensor imaging. *Biological Psychiatry, 55*, 323–326.

Baron-Cohen, S. (1989). Are autistic children "behaviourists"? *Journal of Autism and Developmental Disorders, 19*, 579–600.

Baron-Cohen, S. (1995). *Mindblindness: An essay on autism and theory of mind.* Cambridge, MA: MIT Press.

Baslow, M. H. (2003). N-acetylaspartate in the vertebrate brain: Metabolism and function. *Neurochemical Research, 28*, 941–953.

Belmonte, M. K., Allen, G., Beckel-Mitchener, A., Boulanger, L. M., Carper, R. A., & Webb, S. J. (2004). Autism and abnormal development of brain connectivity. *Journal of Neuroscience, 24*, 9228–9231.

Ben Bashat, D., Kronfeld-Duenias, V., Zachor, D. A., Ekstein, P. M., Hendler, T., Tarrasch, R.,… Ben Sira, L. (2007). Accelerated maturation of white matter in young children with autism: A high B value DWI study. *NeuroImage, 37*, 40–47.

Carlsson M. L. (1998). Hypothesis: Is infantile autism a hypoglutamatergic disorder? Relevance of glutamate – serotonin interactions for pharmacotherapy. *Journal of Neural Transmission, 105*, 525–535.

Carper, R. A., & Courchesne, E. (2005). Localized enlargement of the frontal cortex in early autism. *Biological Psychiatry, 57*, 126–133.

Carper, R. A., Moses, P., Tigue, Z. D., & Courchesne, E. (2002). Cerebral lobes in autism: Early hyperplasia and abnormal age effects. *NeuroImage, 16*, 1038–1051.

Casanova, M. F., van Kooten, I. A., Switala, A. E., van Engeland, H., Heinsen, H., Steinbusch, H. W.,… Schmitz, C. (2006). Minicolumnar abnormalities in autism. *Acta Neuropathologica, 112*, 287–303.

Castelli, F., Frith, C., Happé, F., & Frith, U. (2002). Autism, Asperger syndrome and brain mechanisms for the attribution of mental states to animated shapes. *Brain, 125*, 1839–1849.

Cherkassky, V. L., Kana, R. K., Keller, T. A., & Just, M. A. (2006). Functional connectivity in a baseline resting-state network in autism. *NeuroReport, 17*, 1687–1690.

Chung, M. K., Dalton, K. M., Alexander, A. L., & Davidson, R. J. (2004). Less white matter concentration in autism: 2D voxel-based morphometry. *NeuroImage, 23*, 242–251.

Coben, R., Clarke, A. R., Hudspeth, W., & Barry, R. J. (2008). EEG power and coherence in autistic spectrum disorder. *Clininical Neurophysiology, 119*, 1002–1009.

Courchesne, E., Campbell, K., & Solso, S. (2011). Brain growth across the life span in autism: Age-specific changes in anatomical pathology. *Brain Research, 1380*, 138–145.

Courchesne, E., Carper, R., & Akshoomoff, N. (2003). Evidence of brain overgrowth in the first year of life in autism. *Journal of the American Medical Association, 290*, 337–344.

Courchesne, E., Karns, C. M., Davis, H. R., Ziccardi, R., Carper, R. A., Tigue, Z. D.,… Courchesne, R. Y. (2001). Unusual brain growth patterns in early life in patients with autistic disorder: An MRI study. *Neurology, 57*, 245–254.

Courchesne, E., & Pierce, K. (2005a). Why the frontal cortex in autism might be talking only to itself: Local over-connectivity but long-distance disconnection. *Current Opinion in Neurobiology, 15*, 225–230.

Courchesne, E., & Pierce, K. (2005b). Brain overgrowth in autism during a critical time in development: Implications for frontal pyramidal neuron and interneuron development and connectivity. *International Journal of Developmental Neuroscience, 23*, 153–170.
Courchesne, E., Redcay, E., & Kennedy, D. P. (2004). The autistic brain: Birth through adulthood. *Current Opinion in Neurology, 17*, 489–496.
Courchesne, E., Redcay, E., Morgan, J. T., & Kennedy, D. P. (2005). Autism at the beginning: Microstructural and growth abnormalities underlying the cognitive and behavioral phenotype of autism. *Developmental Psychopathology, 17*, 577–597.
Coyle, J. T., Leski, M. L., & Morrison, J. H. (2002). The diverse roles of L-glutamic acid in brain signal transduction. In K. L. Davis, D. Charney, J. T. Coyle., C. Nemeroff (Eds.), *Neuropsychopharmacology: The fifth generation of progress* (pp. 71–79). Philadelphia: Lippincott, Williams, and Wilkins.
Damarla, S. R., Keller, T. A., Kana, R. K. Cherkassky, V. L. Williams, D. L., Minshew, N. J., & Just, M. A. (2010). Cortical underconnectivity coupled with preserved visuospatial cognition in autism: Evidence from an fMRI study of an embedded figures task. *Autism Research, 5*, 273–279.
Dawson, G., Webb, S., Schellenberg, G. D., Dager, S., Friedman, S., Aylward, E., & Richards, T. (2002). Defining the broader phonotype of autism: Genetic, brain, and behavioral perspectives. *Developmental Psychopathology, 14*, 581–611.
Deutsch, G. K., Dougherty, R. F., Bammer, R., Siok, W. T., Gabrieli, J. D. E., & Wandell, B. (2005). Children's reading performance is correlated with white matter structure measured by diffusion tensor imaging. *Cortex, 41*, 354–363.
Fall, K. (2003). A delay-tolerant network architecture for challenged internets. *Intel Research Technical Report* (IRB-TR-03–003), Intel Corporation.
Fletcher, P. T., Whitaker, R. T., Tao, R., DuBray, M. B., Froehlich, A., Ravichandran, C.,… Lainhart, J. E. (2010). Microstructural connectivity of the arcuate fasciculus in adolescents with high-functioning autism. *NeuroImage, 51*, 1117–1125.
Friedman, S. D., Shaw, D. W., Artru, A. A., Richards, T. L., Gardner, J., Dawson, G.,… Dager, S. R. (2003). Regional brain chemical alterations in young children with autism spectrum disorder. *Neurology, 60*, 100–107.
Frith, U. (1989). *Autism: Explaining the enigma*. Oxford, UK: Blackwell.
Geschwind, D. H., & Levitt, P. (2007). Autism spectrum disorders: Developmental disconnection syndromes. *Current Opinion in Neurobiology, 17*, 103–111.
Giedd, J. N., Blumenthal, J., Jeffries, N. O., Castellanos, F. X., Liu, H., Zijdenbos, A.,… Rapoport, J. L. (1999). Brain development during childhood and adolescence: A longitudinal MRI study. *Nature Neuroscience, 2*, 861–863.
Happé, F. G. E. (1995). The role of age and verbal ability in the Theory of Mind task performance of subjects with autism. *Child Development, 66*, 843–855.
Hardan, A. Y., Minshew, N. J., & Keshavan, M. S. (2000). Corpus callosum size in autism. *Neurology, 55*, 1033–1036.
Hartline, D. K., & Colman, D. R. (2007). Rapid conduction and the evolution of giant axons and myelinated fibers. *Current Biology, 17*, R29–R35.
Herbert, M. R., Ziegler, D. A., Makris, N., Bakardjiev, A., Hodgson, J., Adrien, K. T.,… Caviness, V. S., Jr. (2003). Larger brain and white matter volumes in children with developmental language disorder. *Developmental Science, 6*, F11–F22.
Herbert, M. R., Ziegler, D. A., Makris, N., Filipek, P. A., Kemper, T. L., Normandin, J. J.,… Caviness, V. S., Jr. (2004). Localization of white matter volume increase in autism and developmental language disorder. *Annals of Neurology, 55*, 530–540.

Hisaoka, S., Harada, M., Nishitani, H., & Mori, K. (2001). Regional magnetic resonance spectroscopy of the brain in autistic individuals. *Neuroradiology, 43*, 496–498.

Hughes, C., Russell, J., & Robbins, T. W. (1994). Evidence for executive dysfunction in autism. *Neuropsychologia, 32*, 477–492.

Jäncke, L., Preis, S., & Steinmetz, H. (1999). The relation between forebrain volume and midsagittal size of the corpus callosum in children. *NeuroReport, 10*, 2981–2985.

Jäncke, L., Staiger, J. F., Schlaug, G., Huang, Y., & Steinmetz, H. (1997). The relationship between corpus callosum size and forebrain volume. *Cerebral Cortex, 7*, 48–56.

Jones, T. B., Bandettini, P. A., Kenworthy, L., Case, L. K., Milleville, S. C., Martin, A., & Birn, R. M. (2010). Sources of group differences in functional connectivity: An investigation applied to autism spectrum disorder. *NeuroImage, 49*, 401–414.

Just, M. A., Cherkassky, V. L., Keller, T. A., Kana, R. K., & Minshew, N. J. (2007). Functional and anatomical cortical underconnectivity in autism: Evidence from an FMRI study of an executive function task and corpus callosum morphometry. *Cerebral Cortex, 17*, 951–961.

Just, M. A., Cherkassky, V. L., Keller, T. A., & Minshew, N. J. (2004). Cortical activation and synchronization during sentence comprehension in high-functioning autism: Evidence of underconnectivity. *Brain, 127*, 1811–1821.

Just, M. A., Keller, T. A., Malave, V. L., Kana, R. K., & Varma, S. (2012). Autism as a neural systems disorder: A theory of frontal-posterior underconnectivity. *Neuroscience and Biobehavioral Reviews, 36*, 1292–1313.

Just, M. A., & Varma, S. (2007). The organization of thinking: What functional brain imaging reveals about the neuroarchitecture of complex cognition. *Cognitive, Affective, and Behavioral Neuroscience, 7*, 153–191.

Kana, R. K., Keller, T. A., Cherkassky, V. L., Minshew, N. J., & Just, M. A. (2006). Sentence comprehension in autism: Thinking in pictures with decreased functional connectivity. *Brain, 129*, 2484–2493.

Kana, R. K., Keller, T. A., Cherkassky, V. L., Minshew, N. J., & Just, M. A. (2009). Atypical frontal-posterior synchronization of Theory of Mind regions in autism during mental state attribution. *Social Neuroscience, 4*, 135–152.

Kana, R. K., Keller, T. A., Minshew, N. J., & Just, M. A. (2007). Inhibitory control in high-functioning autism: Decreased activation and underconnectivity in inhibition networks. *Biological Psychiatry, 62*, 198–206.

Kanner, L. (1943). Autistic disturbances of affective contact. *Nervous Child, 2*, 217–250.

Keller, T. A., & Just, M. A. (2009a). Reduced fractional anisotropy and increased radial diffusivity in high-functioning autism: A large-sample whole-brain diffusion tensor imaging study. Poster presented at 15th Annual Meeting of the Organization for Human Brain Mapping, San Francisco, CA, June 2009.

Keller, T. A., & Just, M. A. (2009b). Altering cortical connectivity: Remediation-induced changes in the white matter of poor readers. *Neuron, 64*, 624–631.

Keller, T. A., Kana, R. K., & Just, M. A. (2007). A developmental study of the structural integrity of white matter in autism. *NeuroReport, 18*, 23–27.

Kennedy, D. P., & Courchesne, E. (2008). The intrinsic functional organization of the brain is altered in autism. *NeuroImage, 39*, 1877–1885.

Knaus, T. A., Silver, A. M., Kennedy, M., Lindgren, K. A., Dominick, K. C., Siegel, J., & Tager-Flusberg, H. (2010). Language laterality in autism spectrum disorder and typical controls: A functional, volumetric, and diffusion tensor MRI study. *Brain and Language, 112*, 113–120.

Koshino, H., Carpenter, P. A., Minshew, N. J., Cherkassky, V. L., Keller, T. A., & Just, M. A. (2005). Functional connectivity in an fMRI working memory task in high-functioning autism. *NeuroImage, 24*, 810–821.

Koshino, H., Kana, R. K., Keller, T. A., Cherkassky, V. L., Minshew, N. J., & Just, M. A. (2008). fMRI investigation of working memory for faces in autism: Visual coding and underconnectivity with frontal areas. *Cerebral Cortex, 18*, 289–300.

Lee, J. E., Bigler, E. D., Alexander, A. L., Lazar, M., DuBray, M. B., Chung, M. K.,… Lainhart, J. E. (2007). Diffusion tensor imaging of white matter in the superior temporal gyrus and temporal stem in autism. *Neuroscience Letters, 424*, 127–132.

Levitt, J. G., O'Neill, J., McCracken, J. T., Guthrie, D., Toga, A. W., & Alger, J. R. (2003). Proton magnetic resonance spectroscopic imaging in childhood autism. *Biological Psychiatry, 54*, 1355–1366.

Lewis, J. D., & Elman, J. L. (2008). Growth-related neural reorganization and the autism phenotype: A test of the hypothesis that altered brain growth leads to altered connectivity. *Developmental Science, 11*, 135–155.

Manes, F., Piven, J., Vrancic, D., Nanclares, V., Plebst, C., & Starkstein, S. E. (1999). An MRI study of the corpus callosum and cerebellum in mentally retarded autistic individuals. *Journal of Neuropsychiatry and Clinical Neuroscience, 11*, 470–474.

Mason, R. A., Williams, D. L., Kana, R. K., Minshew, N. J., & Just, M. A. (2008). Theory of Mind disruption and recruitment of the right hemisphere during narrative comprehension in autism. *Neuropsychologia, 46*, 269–280.

Minshew, N. J., & Goldstein, G. (1998). Autism as a disorder of complex information processing. *Mental Retardation and Developmental Disabilities Research Reviews, 4*, 129–136.

Minshew, N. J., Goldstein, G., & Siegel, D. J. (1997). Neuropsychologic functioning in autism: Profile of a complex information processing disorder. *Journal of the International Neuropsychological Society, 3*, 303–316.

Mizuno, A., Liu, Y., Williams, D. L., Keller, T. A., Minshew, N. J., & Just, M. A. (2011). The neural basis of deictic shifting in linguistic perspective-taking in high-functioning autism. *Brain, 134*, 2422–2435.

Mizuno, A., Villalobos, M. E., Davies, M. M., Dahl, B. C., & Muller, R. A. (2006). Partially enhanced thalamocortical functional connectivity in autism. *Brain Research, 1104*, 160–174.

Monk, C. S., Peltier, S. J., Wiggins, J. L., Weng, S. J., Carrasco, M., Risi, S., & Lord, C. (2009). Abnormalities of intrinsic functional connectivity in autism spectrum disorders. *NeuroImage, 47*, 764–772.

Mottron, L., Dawson, M., Soulieres, I., Hubert, B., & Burack, J. A. (2006). Enhanced perceptual functioning in autism: An update, and eight principles of autistic perception. *Journal of Autism and Developmental Disorders, 36*, 27–43.

Mundy, P., Sigman, M., & Kasari, C. (1994). Joint attention, developmental level, and symptom presentation in children with autism. *Development and Psychopathology, 6*, 389–401.

Mundy, P., Sullivan, L., & Mastergeorge, A. M. (2009). A parallel and distributed-processing model of joint attention, social cognition, and autism. *Autism Research, 2*, 2–21.

Murias, M., Webb, S. J., Greenson, J., & Dawson, G. (2007). Resting state cortical connectivity reflected in EEG coherence in individuals with autism. *Biological Psychiatry, 62*, 270–273.

Newman, S. D., Carpenter, P. A., Varma, S., & Just, M. A. (2003). Frontal and parietal participation in problem solving in the Tower of London: fMRI and computational modeling of planning and high-level perception. *Neuropsychologia, 41*, 1668–1682.

Newman, T. M., Macomber, D., Naples, A. J., Babitz, T., Volkmar, F., & Grigorenko, E. L. (2007). Hyperlexia in children with autism spectrum disorders. *Journal of Autism and Developmental Disorders, 37*, 760–774.

Noonan, S. K., Haist, F., & Müller, R. A. (2009). Aberrant functional connectivity in autism: Evidence from low-frequency BOLD signal fluctuations. *Brain Research, 1262*, 48–63.

Otsuka, H., Harada, M., Mori, K., Hisaoka, S., & Nishitani, H. (1999). Brain metabolites in the hippocampus-amygdala region and cerebellum in autism: An 1H-MR spectroscopy study. *Neuroradiology, 41*, 517–519.

Pelphrey, K. A., Morris, J. P., & McCarthy, G. (2005). Neural basis of eye gaze processing deficits in autism. *Brain, 128*, 1038–1048.

Pennington, B. F., & Ozonoff, S. (1996). Executive functions and developmental psychopathology. *Journal of Child Psychology and Psychiatry, 37*, 51–87.

Piven, J., Arndt, S., Bailey, J., Havercamp, S., Andreasen, N. C., & Palmer, P. (1995). An MRI study of brain size in autism. *American Journal of Psychiatry, 152*, 1145–1149.

Piven, J., Bailey, J., Ranson, B. J., & Arndt. S. (1997). An MRI study of the corpus callosum in autism. *American Journal of Psychiatry, 154*, 1051–1056.

Polleux, F., & Lauder, J. M. (2004). Toward a developmental neurobiology of autism. *Mental Retardation and Developmental Disabilities Research Review, 10*, 303–317.

Ringo, J. L. (1991). Neuronal interconnection as a function of brain size. *Brain, Behavior, and Evolution, 38*, 1–6.

Rippon, G., Brock, J., Brown, C., & Boucher, J. (2007). Disordered connectivity in the autistic brain: Challenges for the "new psychophysiology". *International Journal of Psychophysiology, 63*, 164–172.

Rubenstein, J. L., & Merzenich, M. M. (2003). Model of autism: Increased ratio of excitation/inhibition in key neural systems. *Genes, Brain, and Behavior, 2*, 255–267.

Sahyoun, C. P., Belliveau, J. W., Soulières, I., Schwartz, S., & Mody, M. (2010). Neuroimaging of the functional and structural networks underlying visuospatial vs. linguistic reasoning in high-functioning autism. *Neuropsychologia, 48*, 86–95.

Schipul, S. E., Keller, T. A., & Just, M. A. (2011). Inter-regional brain communication and its disturbance in autism. *Frontiers in Systems Neuroscience, 5*, 10.

Schipul, S. E., Williams, D. L., Keller, T. A., Minshew, N. J., & Just, M. A. (2012). Distinctive neural processes during learning in autism. *Cerebral Cortex, 22*, 937–950.

Schultz, R. T. (2005). Developmental deficits in social perception in autism: The role of the amygdala and fusiform face area. *International Journal of Developmental Neuroscience, 23*, 125–141.

Schultz, R. T., Gauthier, I., Klin, A., Fulbright, R. K., Anderson, A. W., Volkmar, F.,… Gore, J. C. (2000). Abnormal ventral temporal cortical activity during face discrimination among individuals with autism and Asperger syndrome. *Archives of General Psychiatry, 57*, 331–340.

Schultz, R. T., Grelotti, D. J., Klin, A., Kleinman, J., Van der Gaag, C., Marois, R., & Skudlarski, P. (2003). The role of the fusiform face area in social cognition: Implications for the pathobiology of autism. *Philosophical Transactions of the Royal Society of London B: Biological Sciences, 358*, 415–427.

Shannon, C. (1949). Communication in the presence of noise. *Proceedings of the IRE, 37*, 10–21.

Shih, P., Shen, M., Ottl, B., Keehn, B., Gaffrey, M. S., & Muller R. A. (2010). Atypical network connectivity for imitation in autism spectrum disorder. *Neuropsychologia, 48*, 2931–2939.

Solomon, M., Ozonoff, S. J., Ursu, S., Ravizza, S., Cummings, N., Ly, S., & Carter, C. S. (2009). The neural substrates of cognitive control deficits in autism spectrum disorders. *Neuropsychologia, 47*, 2515–2526.

Sparks, B. F., Friedman, S. D., Shaw, D. W., Aylward, E. H., Echelard, D., Artru, A. A.,… Dager, S. R. (2002). Brain structural abnormalities in young children with autism spectrum disorder. *Neurology, 59*, 184–192.

Stone, P., & Veloso, M. (1999). Task decomposition and dynamic role assignment for real-time strategic teamwork. In J. P. Muller, M. P. Singh, & A. S. Rao (Eds.), *Intelligent Agents V: Agents, Theories, Architectures, and Languages, ATAL '98, vol. 1555* (pp. 293–308). Berlin/Heidelberg: Springer.

Sundaram, S. K., Kumar, A., Makki, M. I., Behen, M. E., Chugani, H. T., & Chugani, D. C. (2008). Diffusion tensor imaging of frontal lobe in autism spectrum disorder. *Cerebral Cortex, 18*, 2659–2665.

Tager-Flusberg, H. (1992). Autistic children's talk about psychological states: Deficits in the early acquisition of a theory of mind. *Child Development, 63*, 161–172.

Turner, K. C., Frost, L., Linsenbardt, D., McIlroy, J. R., & Müller, R. A. (2006). Atypically diffuse functional connectivity between caudate nuclei and cerebral cortex in autism. *Behavioral and Brain Functions, 2*, 34–45.

Vargas, D. L., Nascimbene, C., Krishnan, C., Zimmerman, A. W., & Pardo, C. A. (2005). Neuroglial activation and neuroinflammation in the brain of patients with autism. *Annals of Neurology, 57*, 67–81.

Vidal, C. N., Nicolson, R., De Vito, T. J., Hayashi, K. M., Geaga, J. A., Drost, D. J.,… Thompson, P. M. (2006). Mapping corpus callosum deficits in autism: An index of aberrant cortical connectivity. *Biological Psychiatry, 60*, 218–225.

Villalobos, M. E., Mizuno, A., Dahl, B. C., Kemmotsu, N., & Muller, R. A. (2005). Reduced functional connectivity between V1 and inferior frontal cortex associated with visuomotor performance in autism. *NeuroImage, 25*, 916–925.

Waiter, G. D., Williams, J. H. G., Murray, A. D., Gilchrist, A., Perrett, D. I., & Whiten, A. (2005). Structural white matter deficits in high-functioning individuals with autistic spectrum disorder: A voxel-based investigation. *NeuroImage, 24*, 455–461.

Waxman, S. G. (1980). Determinants of conduction velocity in myelinated nerve fibers. *Muscle Nerve, 3*, 141–150.

Weng, S. J., Wiggins, J. L., Peltier, S. J., Carrasco, M., Risi, S., Lord, C., and Monk, C. S. (2010). Alterations of resting state functional connectivity in the default network in adolescents with autism spectrum disorders. *Brain Research, 1313*, 202–214.

Williams, D. L., Goldstein, G., & Minshew, N. J. (2006). Neuropsychologic functioning in children with autism: Further evidence for disordered complex information-processing. *Child Neuropsychology, 12*, 279–298.

4

Implicit Learning and Reward Systems Deficit in Autism

A Mechanism for Social Learning Deficit?

ASHLEY A. SCOTT-VAN ZEELAND
Scripps Transnational Science Institute, La Jolla, CA

SUSAN BOOKHEIMER
University of California, Los Angeles, CA

A perplexing issue in autism research concerns why the cluster of seemingly independent phenotypical deficits co-occurs in this neurodevelopmental disorder. At face value, it is difficult to conceptualize language delay, social skills impairment, and repetitive behaviors as related functions. While general models such as those positing abnormal cellular organization or altered connectivity predict more system-wide impairments, these models alone cannot simultaneously account for both the range and the specificity of deficits seen in autism. We propose that the striatally mediated reward circuitry underlying implicit habit learning may play an important role in the development of many of the symptoms of autism across all three diagnostic domains. Habit learning here refers to developing the ability to respond to regularities in the environment without awareness of the regularities or of the ability to respond to them, as described below.

Known sequelae of striatal abnormalities include impaired implicit learning (Knowlton, Mangels, & Squire, 1996); abnormal responses to reward (Czernecki et al., 2002); and motor abnormalities such as repetitive and stereotypic behaviors (Kurlan, 2004; Saka & Graybiel, 2003). Among implicitly learned behaviors are those relevant to language, including the use and understanding of syntax and nonverbal communication, which are impaired in autism. Additionally, while children with autism spectrum disorders (ASD) are able to form interpersonal attachments, they do not respond to social rewards as typically developing (TD) children do and show less motivation to seek socially rewarding stimuli, such as the smiling face of a caregiver. It has been suggested that this lack of bias to orient to a caregiver's face may be a result of the child's not finding that face particularly "rewarding" to view (Dawson, Meltzoff, Osterling, Rinaldi, & Brown, 1998; Dawson, Webb, & McPartland, 2005; Schultz, 2005). The model of striatal dysfunction proposed here integrates well with existing neuroscientific data, including functional magnetic resonance imaging (fMRI) findings and current models positing long-range connectivity impairment.

Accounts of implicit learning deficits in autism are not new; however, the term *implicit learning* has been used to describe several different processes, each with a unique underlying neuroanatomy (Heindel, Salmon, Shults, Walicke, & Butters, 1989). For instance, Bowler, Matthews, and Gardiner (1997) used a word-stem completion task to look at implicit memory (here defined as non-conscious influences on memory) in autism and Asperger's, finding no strong evidence for a primary deficit in this type of implicit memory. Using a perceptual priming task, Renner, Klinger, and Klinger (2000) similarly found no evidence for implicit learning differences in ASD. However, in these studies, implicit learning referred specifically to repetition priming. Single-unit recordings in monkeys show that repetition priming is characterized by a reduction in neural firing rate for repeated items in the cortex originally processing the stimuli; similar results are found in human neuroimaging studies (Henson, Shallice, & Dolan, 2000; James, Humphrey, Gati, Menon, & Goodale, 1999; Koustaal et al., 2001).

We also distinguish these processes from *incidental learning*. For instance, some children with autism learn very detailed information (e.g., baseball statistics) despite never having been intentionally taught this information. However, this type of learning is still explicit, as it involves the subject (consciously) attending to the information and memorizing the explicit and deterministic associations, processes reliant on the hippocampal-based episodic memory system.

This chapter discusses implicit learning processes associated with the skill or habit learning system, which relies on subcortical striatal systems. In their seminal study of habit learning, Knowlton, Squire, and Gluck (1994) developed a probabilistic classification task, the Weather Prediction Task, in which subjects saw pairs of cards that presented different patterns. Subjects were told a certain card pattern would be associated with a particular outcome, either *Rain* or *Sunshine*. After seeing a pair of cards, participants were asked to predict the outcome based on the pattern they saw. The relationship between any card pattern and the outcome was actually probabilistic (e.g., a pattern was associated with *Rain* 67% of the time and *Sunshine* 33%). From the subjects' point of view, the relationship between the cards and the outcome was seemingly random. However, their behavior showed a slow but significant learning curve, and over time subjects could correctly predict the outcome with the highest associated probability more often than chance. If, after they showed evidence of learning, subjects were explicitly asked to identify an outcome associated with a particular card pair, they performed at chance. In this instance, the subjects had learned the associations, but did not consciously know that they had learned. Unlike a traditional learning task with a deterministic outcome (i.e., each card is associated with the same outcome every time [100%]), in a probabilistic task a particular outcome is only correct a portion of the time (e.g., 67%). However, given many repetitions of these stimuli, subjects' behaviors show that they do in fact learn the associations. Thus learning occurs, but entirely without awareness, and it is apparently stable over time.

Habit learning may occur when outcomes are probabilistic or in a context in which memorization is discouraged or impossible; it can occur after repeated exposure, regardless of whether the information is verbally conveyed, intentionally taught, or simply observed. In a series of experiments, Schwartz and Hashtroudi (1991) found that habit learning and repetition priming produced different characteristic responses to factors such as word frequency, suggesting these learning processes are separable. Knowlton et al. (1996) demonstrated that habit learning depends on striatal and not hippocampal learning systems when they found that patients with amnesia (with damage to limbic-diencephalic regions) were able to demonstrate learning on the habit learning task, while patients with Parkinson's disease (with damage to the neostriatum) were not. The anatomical findings were later confirmed by an fMRI study (Poldrack, Prabhakaran, Seger, & Gabrieli, 1999) demonstrating that the caudate in particular is sensitive to implicit learning. A study by Rodriguez, Aron, and Poldrack (2006) showed that implicit learning is augmented by reward feedback, which is mediated by the ventral striatum. The dorsal and ventral striatum are intrinsically linked during reward-based learning in a loop that includes the medial prefrontal cortex, orbitofrontal cortex, and amygdala, as well as several other regions. (The striatum, a component of the basal ganglia, is a subcortical brain structure consisting of the caudate nucleus and the putamen.) Evidence from human and animal studies indicates that the striatal and hippocampal learning systems are competitive in nature (Poldrack & Packard, 2003), suggesting that impairment in one would result in over-reliance on the other. Moody, Bookheimer, Vanek, and Knowlton (2004) found support for this proposal in patients with Parkinson's, who showed enhanced hippocampal activity and reduced striatal activity compared to control subjects.

IMPLICIT LEARNING IN AUTISM

Procedural learning is one type of habit learning that has been found to be impaired in autism. The serial reaction time (SRT) task is a motor-sequence learning task in which subjects have to make a button-press response to a set of directional stimuli presented in a sequence; unbeknownst to the subject, for some blocks, the sequences are repeated, while for other blocks the sequences are novel. Although subjects are unaware of the structure of the task, response time (RT) performance indicates shorter response times for repeated compared to novel sequences. Using the SRT task, Mostofsky, Goldberg, Landa, and Denckla (2000) found that children with autism did not show the characteristic advantage in RT for repeated vs. novel sequences compared to TD children; they hypothesized that this may be due to cerebellar abnormalities. From these data, Kriete and Noelle (2009) developed a neurocomputational model positing disruption of the dopamine system in fronto-striatal circuits as underlying the implicit learning deficit. In the past few years, our laboratory has conducted several fMRI studies in children with autism that, despite presenting very different tasks, show similar group differences in the frontal cortex and the striatum, particularly under implicit learning conditions. Based on these and other fMRI studies, we argue that a breakdown in fronto-striatal circuits underlying implicit learning can account for the range of symptoms seen in autism. This perspective attributes a critical role to the habit learning system in acquiring language, in social learning, and in reward responsiveness that may affect social motivation.

Implicit Learning and Language

Studies on language acquisition in infants have demonstrated that statistical regularities in speech streams may guide one of the earliest steps in linguistic decoding: word segmentation (Aslin, Saffran, & Newport, 1998; Saffran, Aslin, & Newport, 1996; Thiessen & Saffran, 2003). In fact, the degree to which infants successfully segment speech has been linked to later language ability in preschool (Newman, Ratner, Jusczyk, Jusczyk, & Dow, 2006). In a study of speech segmentation in adults, McNealy, Mazziotta, and Dapretto (2006) adapted the speech segmentation task of Saffran et al. (1996) for use in fMRI to identify brain regions associated with the acquisition of novel "word" boundaries. These stimuli consisted of tri-syllabic phoneme strings with probabilistic word boundaries. The construction of the stimuli resulted in the transitional probability, or probability that one syllable would follow another, being higher within the tri-syllabic pseudowords than across the word boundaries. Aside from activity within canonical language regions, they found significant activation of the basal ganglia. Interestingly, as the cues to word boundaries decreased, activity in the basal ganglia increased. Consistent with the evidence for the role of the striatum in probabilistic learning, these findings implicate the basal ganglia in calculating the statistical features of speech that allow us to learn word boundaries. Acquisition of other language skills, such as grammar, may also rely on calculations of statistical dependencies across linguistic units (Gomez & Gerken, 1999) and thus might also depend on the fronto-striatal system. In fact, in an fMRI investigation of artificial grammar learning in normal adults, the striatum was found to be significantly more active when conditions were grammatical as opposed to when they were not (Lieberman, Chang, Chiao, Bookheimer, & Knowlton, 2004).

Marked impairments in linguistic and communication skills are hallmark features of autism, with many ASD individuals exhibiting quite limited linguistic repertoires or completely lacking spoken language (Bailey, Phillips, & Rutter, 1996; Rapin & Dunn, 1997). In a recent study, we examined the responsiveness of the striatum during word segmentation in a sample of children with and without autism (Scott-Van Zeeland, McNealy et al., 2010). We hypothesized that difficulty in implicit learning may account for the language delay and stereotyped speech deficits often seen in autism. Using the same fMRI paradigm as McNealy et al. (2006, 2010), we found that, unlike TD children, children with autism did not show a facilitatory effect of increasing cues to word boundaries in fronto-temporal-parietal networks. This finding suggests that, in autism, the brain is not as sensitive to the statistical structures of linguistic properties of the speech stream and automatically processes only the pre-linguistic properties of the stimuli. We then investigated how activity in the brain changed during increasing exposure to the speech streams in order to identify regions likely involved in learning as function of exposure. These analyses identified significant learning-related signal increases in the basal ganglia and left temporo-parietal cortex only in TD children. As a group, the children with autism showed no evidence of statistical learning-related activity in the basal ganglia. Moreover, the level of communicative impairment in children with autism was inversely correlated with signal increases in these same regions during exposure to the artificial languages. Thus, individuals with autism who showed the most severe communicative impairments also demonstrated the least amount of striatal activity, while those with stronger communicative abilities had more activity.

It thus appears that striatal processing of the statistical properties of speech streams, important for the earliest steps of language learning, is impaired in autism. In addition to people with autism, individuals with known basal ganglia dysfunction, such as patients with Parkinson's disease and Huntington's disease, are impaired on implicit learning tasks (Knowlton et al., 1996) and have demonstrated deficits in the acquisition of language rules (De Diego-Balaguer et al., 2008; Lieberman, Friedman, & Feldman, 1990; Lieberman et al., 1992). Together these findings implicate the striatum as an important structure for the statistically based implicit learning that gives rise to language acquisition. Dysfunction of this system early in development may form the basis of the language impairment seen in autism.

Implicit Learning and Social Motivation

The inability to engage with the social world in a typical manner is one of the defining characteristics of autism. Whereas TD infants show a preference for social over non-social stimuli (Legerstee, Anderson, & Schaffer, 1998), children who develop autism show decreased motivation to attend to social stimuli as early as the child's first birthday (Dawson et al., 1998; Osterling & Dawson, 1994). Developmentally, children with autism spectrum disorders also show impairments in other social skills, such as imitation (Williams, Whiten, & Singh, 2004) and joint attention (Bruinsma, Koegel, & Koegel, 2004). These early skills may help young children develop empathy by understanding the perspectives, intentions, and actions of others, as well as helping to foster language development (Kasari, Paparella, Freeman, & Jahromi, 2008; Kuhl, 2007; Mundy, Sigman, & Kasari, 1990). One hypothesis that accounts for this early difference in social attention posits that children with autism do not find social stimuli rewarding and therefore spend less time orienting to them, resulting in a cascade of negative consequences for the development of social cognition (Dawson et al., 1998, 2005; Schultz, 2005). Consistent with this hypothesis, a computational model by Triesch and colleagues (2006) suggests the development of social behaviors (e.g., gaze following, joint attention) may rely on reward-related learning. In this model, infants must not only be able to respond appropriately to a reward in the external environment, but must also be able to learn an association between that reward and the event that sometimes precedes it (e.g., a gaze shift by their caregiver). An inability either to learn the probabilistic association between the gaze shift and reward or to encode the reward value could lead to a failure to develop appropriate gaze following and joint attention skills, deficits characteristic of autism.

Anatomically, the reward system is supported by the ventral striatum, which receives inputs from the midbrain and has reciprocal connections to the frontal cortex, including anterior cingulate and orbitofrontal cortex. This reward system has been well defined in both animal models and human studies in response to primary rewards (e.g., food: O'Doherty, Deichmann, Critchley, & Dolan, 2002), as well as to secondary rewards (e.g., money: O'Doherty, Kringelbach, Rolls, Hornak, & Andrews, 2001; Thut et al., 1997; see also Knutson & Cooper, 2005, for a review). Importantly, this reward network has been shown to respond to social cues, including viewing pictures of happy faces (Phillips et al., 1998; Spreckelmeyer et al., 2009), of attractive faces (Aharon et al., 2001), and of loved ones (Bartels & Zeki, 2004). Interestingly, while it was not a direct study of social reward processing, Dapretto and colleagues (2006) identified decreased activity in the ventral striatum in children with autism relative to TD children while viewing and imitating emotional faces during an fMRI task.

Rewards modulate learning in probabilistic classification tasks. During probabilistic learning, subjects implicitly predict the likelihood of a positive or negative outcome. The ventral striatum plays a critical role in responding to prediction errors, defined as instances in which there is a disparity between the predicted outcome and the actual outcome (Rodriguez et al., 2006). In a study, we modified the Weather Prediction Task to use with children with autism (Scott-Van Zeeland, Dapretto, Ghahremani, Poldrack, & Bookheimer, 2010) by adding social and non-social (monetary) rewards to augment learning of the probabilistic associations. Subjects saw random designs that were associated with a button press of either *1* or 2. Although the designs did not in any way suggest a particular number, we asked the participants to learn which designs went with which number. They pressed a button to indicate 1 or 2; the computer gave them feedback, but we told them beforehand that it was malfunctioning and would occasionally give them the wrong feedback (thereby creating an atmosphere in which relationships between patterns and outcomes would not be the same all the time). There were three conditions, such that the feedback was conveyed by either (1) *Correct* or *Incorrect* displayed on the screen; (2) a monetary reward, with depictions of coins appearing on the screen or crossed out to indicate the response was incorrect; or (3) a social reward, with a photo of a young woman either smiling or pouting. We did this as an event-related design and were able to model and analyze the reward responses and the stimulus responses separately. The feedback from the computer was probabilistic: Half of the feedback was random, so that participants could not learn any association, and half was deterministic, such that the picture was associated with 1 or 2 all of the time. Trial types were interspersed such that, from the subjects' point of view, the associations were random. We tested the subjects' awareness of the associations after the experiment with an explicit learning task, at which participants performed at chance, indicating that, if any learning occurred, it was implicit.

We first examined the extent to which subjects with autism showed a reward-related response in the ventral striatum independent of learning effects. Typically developing children showed activation in the ventral striatum for both social and monetary rewards. However, the magnitude of the ventral striatum response for children with autism was much smaller than for TD children in both reward types. This indicates that there may be a general problem in the reward response in autism. We investigated the effect of reward type on implicit learning by examining the prediction accuracy over the course of the task. Even though subjects had no explicit knowledge of the relationship between stimuli and outcome, TD children showed a positive learning curve in both conditions, with the effect slightly enhanced in the social reward condition. In contrast, there was no evidence of learning in the children with autism. This finding suggests a primary deficit in implicit learning in children with autism regardless of reward type. When we investigated responses during trials with deterministic feedback (when, theoretically, the children could have learned the associations between patterns and responses), we found a significant increase in activation in the dorsal striatum for TD children compared to those with autism. This difference provides additional evidence of reduced activity in regions responsible for implicit learning in children with autism. We also investigated the relationship between the control participants' magnitudes of activity in the ventral striatum with their individual scores on the Social

Responsiveness Scale (Constantino et al., 2003). (There was not enough activity in the ventral striatum in participants with autism to extend this analysis to both groups.) We found a negative correlation between the scores and brain activity, such that the better their social skills, the more activity the children had in their ventral striatum in response to social rewards. Thus, it appears that, even among TD children, the magnitude of the neural reward response is related to the development of social skills.

To summarize, we find evidence of two striatal-based deficits in autism related to implicit learning. First, ventral striatum activity was reduced in children with autism compared to controls, indicating a weaker reward-based responsiveness, a phenomenon that typically drives or enhances learning. Second, subjects with autism showed reduced learning of implicit associations, which was associated with less activity in the dorsal striatum. Activity in the ventral striatum is associated with social reciprocity in TD kids, suggesting that the basal ganglia are important areas for normal social development, likely in combination with the frontal lobe via fronto-striatal connections whose impairments could contribute to symptoms of autism.

RECOVERY OF "NORMAL" FUNCTION IN EXPLICIT PROCESSING

Assuming that there is a striatal deficit in autism that contributes to impairments in social learning, motor learning, and language acquisition, we may also make predictions about the role of this deficit during explicit processing. Specifically, we have hypothesized that the activation differences between children with and without autism observed in tasks involving implicit processes may be attenuated under explicit processing conditions.

Several studies support this hypothesis. Wang, Dapretto, Hariri, Sigman, and Bookheimer (2004) used an emotional face processing paradigm to examine differences in emotional responsiveness regions, specifically the amygdala, in children with ASD and TD children. In one condition, subjects matched a target face to another face with a similar expression. Subjects were not told to examine the emotion portrayed. This task activates the amygdala in adult controls (Hariri, Bookheimer, & Mazziotta, 2000), and it elicited robust amygdala activation in the TD children, but not in the ASD children. In a second condition, subjects were told to explicitly identify the emotions portrayed by the faces and give them a verbal label, thus requiring explicit processing of the facial activation. In this condition, the TD children showed a down-regulation of the amygdala response, while the ASD children showed a relative increase in the amygdala activation; as a result, there were no longer between-group differences in activation patterns. Thus, explicit instructions to attend to specific social information appeared to increase brain activity in relevant regions in children with ASD. A similar finding was reported by Wang, Lee, Sigman, and Dapretto (2007), who used a task tapping into the comprehension of irony in communication. In that study, subjects were presented with cartoon depictions of an event accompanied by a verbal utterance in which the tone of voice, facial expressions, or both were inconsistent with the content of the speech (e.g., given a cartoon depicting two children building with blocks and showing one of the children accidentally knocking down the other's blocks, the utterance of the second child was "Way to go!"). The stimuli were presented in two different conditions, one in which no instructions were given (passive viewing and listening), and the other in which the subjects were instructed to focus on the emotional content of the cartoon or the tone of voice. In the passive viewing condition, the ASD children failed to activate several brain regions that the TD children activated, particularly the medial prefrontal cortex. However, in the condition with explicit instructions to focus on emotional content, the activation patterns in the ASD children "normalized" and between-groups differences vanished.

The finding that increased stimulus salience may also normalize fMRI responses in autism could reflect the role of implicit processing deficits in explaining observed brain activation differences. Several studies over the years have shown a failure to activate the fusiform face area in autism in response to face stimuli (e.g., Schultz et al., 2000; Pierce, Müller, Ambrose, Allen, & Courchesne, 2001). However, using more salient stimuli (i.e., pictures of the faces of family members), children with autism showed robust activation in the fusiform gyrus (Pierce, Haist, Sedaghat, & Courchesne, 2004; Pierce & Redcay, 2008). This finding is inconsistent with the notion that ASD individuals lack a face-specialized brain region. Rather, an alternative explanation is that, while children with autism do not *automatically* process faces as a unique category, they are able to consciously process them with normal fusiform activation when their attention is explicitly directed to the relevant aspects of the stimuli.

Making the implicit explicit is one of the primary methods of teaching social skills to higher functioning children with autism. While TD individuals appear to automatically register rules of behavior, children with autism do not. Many therapeutic approaches to social skills training essentially operationalize and verbalize these unstated rules of engagement. For instance, Schrandt, Townsend, and Poulson (2009) taught children with ASD how to respond empathically through explicit teaching and modeling of behavior. Laushey, Heflin, Shippen, Alberto, and Fredrick (2009) found that children simply placed within peer groups showed no improvement in social skills, but when given explicit, rule-based instruction, they showed significant improvement. Such treatment approaches may capitalize on intact learning systems in ASD by encouraging memorization of rules that TD children learn without instruction.

FRONTAL-STRIATAL CONNECTIONS

While we have focused here on striatal function in isolation, it is important to note that these functions form part of a series of networks primarily involving connections to various regions in the frontal lobes. Alexander, DeLong, and Strick (1986) described no fewer than five fronto-striatal pathways that are important for motor functions, response inhibition, attentional and emotional modulation, and reward-related processing. In the studies reported above showing reductions in striatal activation among individuals with ASD (i.e., investigations of language learning, emotion imitation, reward processing, and implicit learning), the activation was also reduced in several frontal regions, including posterior inferior frontal, ventrolateral prefrontal, and medial prefrontal cortices. It is possible that the differences in striatal activation in autism are related to impaired connections in these fronto-striatal circuits, consistent with recent accounts proposing primary connectivity deficits in autism. Frontostriatal deficits have been reported in several other disorders, including attention deficit/hyperactivity disorder (e.g., Cubillo et al., 2010; Robbins 2007) and obsessive-compulsive disorder (Kathmann, Rupertseder, Hauke, & Zaudig, 2005), for which there are high rates of co-morbidity with autism (Cath, Ran, Smit, van Balkom, & Comijs, 2008; Leyfer et al., 2006), as well as acquired movement disorders, particularly Parkinson's, which has a different behavioral profile but may share some similarities with autism (e.g., a restricted behavioral repertoire and implicit learning deficits).

In summary, across a diverse set of tasks, we find evidence for impairments in autism in implicit learning involving the role of the striatal system in habit learning, and the frontal connections to this system. In TD children and adults, striatal regions are associated with processes and functions that compose some of the core deficits of autism, particularly reward processing in the ventral striatum. This deficit in reward processing, we suggest, is associated with poor social skill development and possibly with impairment in the social motivation that supports the functioning of a broader range of skills in neurotypical individuals. Reduced activation related to implicit learning in the dorsal striatum could result in a variety of problems associated with autism: poor social learning; impaired language learning; and possibly motor stereotypies. It could also lead to deficits in the procedural learning of motor actions, although this has not yet been studied systematically with respect to striatal activity in autism. A fair amount is known about these networks with regard to their specific directional pathways and the neurotransmitters and neuropeptides involved, and ultimately it may be possible to pharmacologically manipulate activity in these networks to augment implicit learning. Thus this new understanding of the biological basis of impaired habit learning in autism provides a valuable perspective on the breadth of the impairments in autism and their possible remediation.

REFERENCES

Aharon, I., Etcoff, N., Ariely, D., Chabris, C. F., O'Connor, E., & Breiter, H. C. (2001). Beautiful faces have variable reward value: fMRI and behavioral evidence. *Neuron, 32*, 537–551.

Alexander, G. E., DeLong, M. R., & Strick, P. L. (1986). Parallel organization of functionally segregated circuits linking basal ganglia and cortex. *Annual Review of Neuroscience, 9*, 357–381.

Aslin, R. N., Saffran, J. R., & Newport, E. L. (1998). Computation of conditional probability statistics by 8-month-old infants. *Psychological Science, 9*, 321–324.

Bailey, A., Phillips, W., & Rutter, M. (1996). Autism: Towards an integration of clinical, genetic, neuropsychological, and neurobiological perspectives. *Journal of Child Psychology and Psychiatry, 37*, 89–126.

Bartels, A., & Zeki, S. (2004). The neural correlates of maternal and romantic love. *NeuroImage, 21*, 1155–1166.

Bowler, D. M., Matthews, N. J., & Gardiner, J. M. (1997). Asperger's syndrome and memory: Similarity to autism but not amnesia. *Neuropsychologia, 35*, 65–70.

Bruinsma, Y., Koegel, R. L., & Koegel, L. K. (2004). Joint attention and children with autism: A review of the literature. *Mental Retardation and Developmental Disabilities Research Reviews, 10*, 169–175.

Cath, D. C., Ran, N., Smit, J. H., van Balkom, A. J., & Comijs, H. C. (2008). Symptom overlap between autism spectrum disorder, generalized social anxiety disorder, and obsessive-compulsive disorder in adults: A preliminary case-controlled study. *Psychopathology, 41*, 101–110.

Constantino, J. N., Davis, S. A., Todd, R. D., Schindler, M. K., Gross, M. M., Brophy, S. L., . . . Reich, W. (2003). Validation of a brief quantitative measure of autistic traits: Comparison of the social responsiveness scale with the autism diagnostic interview-revised. *Journal of Autism and Developmental Disorders,* 33, 427–433.

Cubillo, A., Halari, R., Ecker, C., Giampietro, V., Taylor, E., & Rubia, K. (2010). Reduced activation and inter-regional functional connectivity of fronto-striatal networks in adults with childhood Attention-Deficit Hyperactivity Disorder (ADHD) and persisting symptoms during tasks of motor inhibition and cognitive switching. *Journal of Psychiatric Research, 44*, 629–639.

Czernecki, V., Pillon, B., Houeto, J. L., Pochon, J. B., Levy, R., & Dubois, B. (2002). Motivation, reward, and Parkinson's disease: Influence of dopatherapy. *Neuropsychologia, 40*, 2257–2267.

Dapretto, M., Davies, M. S., Pfeifer, J. H., Scott, A. A., Sigman, M., Bookheimer, S. Y., & Iacoboni, M. (2006). Understanding emotions in others: Mirror neuron dysfunction in children with autism spectrum disorders. *Nature Neuroscience, 9*, 28–30.

Dawson, G., Meltzoff, A. N., Osterling, J., Rinaldi, J., & Brown, E. (1998). Children with autism fail to orient to naturally occurring social stimuli. *Journal of Autism and Developmental Disorders, 28*, 479–485.

Dawson, G., Webb, S. J., & McPartland, J. (2005). Understanding the nature of face processing impairment in autism: Insights from behavioral and electrophysiological studies. *Developmental Neuropsychology, 27*, 403–424.

De Diego-Balaguer, R., Couette, M., Dolbeau, G., Dürr, A., Youssov, K., & Bachoud-Lévi, A. C. (2008). Striatal degeneration impairs language learning: Evidence from Huntington's disease. *Brain, 131*, 2870–2881.

Gomez, R. L., & Gerken, L. (1999). Artificial grammar learning by 1-year-olds leads to specific and abstract knowledge. *Cognition, 70*, 109–135.

Hariri, A. R., Bookheimer, S. Y., & Mazziotta, J. C. (2000). Modulating emotional responses: Effects of a neocortical network on the limbic system. *Neuroreport, 11*, 43–48.

Heindel, W. C., Salmon, D. P., Shults, C. W., Walicke, P. A., & Butters, N. (1989). Neuropsychological evidence for multiple implicit memory systems: A comparison of Alzheimer's, Huntington's, and Parkinson's disease patients. *Journal of Neuroscience, 9*, 582–587.

Henson, R., Shallice, T., & Dolan, R. (2000). Neuroimaging evidence for dissociable forms of repetition priming. *Science, 287*, 1269–1272.

James, T. W., Humphrey, G. K., Gati, J. S., Menon, R. S., & Goodale, M. A. (1999). Repetition priming and the time course of object recognition: An fMRI study. *Neuroreport, 10*, 1019–1023.

Kasari, C., Paparella, T., Freeman, S., & Jahromi, L. B. (2008). Language outcome in autism: Randomized comparison of joint attention and play interventions. *Journal of Consulting and Clinical Psychology, 76*, 125–137.

Kathmann, N., Rupertseder, C., Hauke, W., & Zaudig, M. (2005). Implicit sequence learning in obsessive-compulsive disorder: Further support for the fronto-striatal dysfunction model. *Biological Psychiatry, 58*, 239–244.

Knowlton, B. J., Mangels, J. A., & Squire, L. R. (1996). A neostriatal habit learning system in humans. *Science, 273*, 1399–1402.

Knowlton, B. J., Squire, L. R., & Gluck, M. A. (1994). Probabilistic classification learning in amnesia. *Learning and Memory, 1*, 106–120.

Knutson, B., & Cooper, J. C. (2005). Functional magnetic resonance imaging of reward prediction. *Current Opinion in Neurology, 18*, 411–417.

Koutstaal, W., Wagner, A. D., Rotte, M., Maril, A., Buckner, R. L., & Schacter, D. L. (2001). Perceptual specificity in visual object priming: Functional magnetic resonance imaging evidence for a laterality difference in fusiform cortex. *Neuropsychologia, 39*, 184–199.

Kriete, T., & Noelle, D. C. (2009). Implicit learning deficits in autism: A neurocomputational account. In N. A. Taatgen, & H. van Rijn (Eds.), *Proceedings of the thirty-first annual conference of the Cognitive Science Society* (pp. 899–904). Austin, TX: Cognitive Science Society.

Kuhl, P. K. (2007). Is speech learning "gated" by the social brain? *Developmental Science, 10*, 110–120.

Kurlan, R. (2004). Disabling repetitive behaviors in Parkinson's disease. *Movement Disorders, 19*, 433–437.

Laushey, K. M., Heflin, L. J., Shippen, M., Alberto, P. A., & Fredrick, L. (2009). Concept mastery routines to teach social skills to elementary children with high functioning autism. *Journal of Autism and Developmental Disorders, 39*, 1435–1448.

Legerstee, M., Anderson, D., & Schaffer, A. (1998). Five- and eight-month-old infants recognize their faces and voices as familiar and social stimuli. *Child Development, 69*, 37–50.

Leyfer, O. T., Folstein, S. E., Bacalman, S., Davis, N. O., Dinh, E., Morgan, J., … Lainhart, J. E. (2006). Comorbid psychiatric disorders in children with autism: Interview development and rates of disorders. *Journal of Autism and Developmental Disorders, 36*, 849–861.

Lieberman, M. D., Chang, G. Y., Chiao, J., Bookheimer, S. Y., & Knowlton, B. J. (2004). An event-related fMRI study of artificial grammar learning in a balanced chunk strength design. *Journal of Cognitive Neuroscience, 16*, 427–438.

Lieberman, P., Friedman, J., & Feldman, L. S. (1990). Syntax comprehension deficits in Parkinson's disease. *Journal of Nervous and Mental Disease, 178*, 360–365.

Lieberman, P., Kako, E., Friedman, J., Tajchman, G., Feldman, L. S., & Jiminez, E. B. (1992). Speech production, syntax comprehension, and cognitive deficits in Parkinson's disease. *Brain and Language, 43*, 169–189.

McNealy, K., Mazziotta, J. C., & Dapretto, M. (2006). Cracking the language code: Neural mechanisms underlying speech parsing. *Journal of Neuroscience, 26*, 7629–7639.

McNealy, K., Mazziotta, J. C., & Dapretto, M. (2010). The neural basis of speech parsing in children and adults. *Developmental Science, 13*, 385–406.

Moody, T. D., Bookheimer, S. Y., Vanek, Z., & Knowlton, B. J. (2004). An implicit learning task activates medial temporal lobe in patients with Parkinson's disease. *Behavioral Neuroscience, 118*, 438–442.

Mostofsky, S. H., Goldberg, M. C., Landa, R. J., & Denckla, M. B. (2000). Evidence for a deficit in procedural learning in children and adolescents with autism: Implications for cerebellar contribution. *Journal of the International Neuropsychological Society, 6*, 752–759.

Mundy, P., Sigman, M., & Kasari, C. (1990). A longitudinal study of joint attention and language development in autistic children. *Journal of Autism and Developmental Disorders, 20*, 115–128.

Newman, R., Ratner, N. B., Jusczyk, A. M., Jusczyk, P. W., & Dow, K. A. (2006). Infants' early ability to segment the conversational speech signal predicts later language development: A retrospective analysis. *Developmental Psychology, 42*, 643–655.

O'Doherty, J. P., Deichmann, R., Critchley, H. D., & Dolan, R. J. (2002). Neural responses during anticipation of a primary taste reward. *Neuron, 33*, 815–826.

O'Doherty, J., Kringelbach, M. L., Rolls, E. T., Hornak, J., & Andrews, C. (2001). Abstract reward and punishment representations in the human orbitofrontal cortex. *Nature Neuroscience, 4*, 95–102.

Osterling, J., & Dawson, G. (1994). Early recognition of children with autism: A study of first birthday home videotapes. *Journal of Autism and Developmental Disorders, 24*, 247–257.

Phillips, M. L., Bullmore, E. T., Howard, R., Woodruff, P. W., Wright, I. C., Williams, S. C.,... David, A. S. (1998). Investigation of facial recognition memory and happy and sad facial expression perception: An fMRI study. *Psychiatry Research, 83*, 127–138.

Pierce, K., Haist, F., Sedaghat, F., & Courchesne, E. (2004). The brain response to personally familiar faces in autism: Findings of fusiform activity and beyond. *Brain, 127*, 2703–2716.

Pierce, K., Müller, R. A., Ambrose, J., Allen, G., & Courchesne, E. (2001). Face processing occurs outside the fusiform "face area" in autism: Evidence from functional MRI. *Brain, 124*, 2059–2073.

Pierce, K., & Redcay, E. (2008). Fusiform function in children with an autism spectrum disorder is a matter of "who." *Biological Psychiatry, 64*, 552–560.

Poldrack, R. A., & Packard, M. G. (2003). Competition among multiple memory systems: Converging evidence from animal and human brain studies. *Neuropsychologia, 41*, 245–251.

Poldrack, R. A., Prabhakaran, V., Seger, C. A., & Gabrieli, J. D. (1999). Striatal activation during acquisition of a cognitive skill. *Neuropsychology, 13*, 564–574.

Rapin, I., & Dunn, M. (1997). Language disorders in children with autism. *Seminars in Pediatric Neurology, 4*, 86–92.

Renner, P., Klinger, L. G., & Klinger, M. R. (2000). Implicit and explicit memory in autism: Is autism an amnesic disorder? *Journal of Autism and Developmental Disorders, 30*, 3–14.

Robbins, T. W. (2007). Shifting and stopping: Fronto-striatal substrates, neurochemical modulation, and clinical implications. *Philosophical Transactions of the Royal Society of London, Biological Sciences, 362*, 917–932.

Rodriguez, P. F., Aron, A. R., & Poldrack, R. A. (2006). Ventral-striatal/nucleus-accumbens sensitivity to prediction errors during classification learning. *Human Brain Mapping, 27*, 306–313.

Saffran, J. R., Aslin, R. N., & Newport, E. L. (1996). Statistical learning by 8-month-old infants. *Science, 274*, 1926–1928.

Saka, E., & Graybiel, A. M. (2003). Pathophysiology of Tourette's syndrome: Striatal pathways revisited. *Brain and Development, 25*, S15–S19.

Schrandt, J. A., Townsend, D. B., & Poulson, C. L. (2009). Teaching empathy skills to children with autism. *Journal of Applied Behavior Analysis, 42*, 17–32.

Schultz, R. T. (2005). Developmental deficits in social perception in autism: The role of the amygdala and fusiform face area. *International Journal of Developmental Neuroscience, 23*, 125–141.

Schultz, R. T., Gauthier, I., Klin, A., Fulbright, R. K., Anderson, A. W., Volkmar, F.,... Gore, J. C. (2000). Abnormal ventral temporal cortical activity during face discrimination among individuals with autism and Asperger syndrome. *Archives of General Psychiatry, 57*, 331–340.

Schwartz, B. L., & Hashtroudi, S. (1991). Priming is independent of skill learning. *Journal of Experimental Psychology: Learning, Memory, and Cognition, 17*, 1177–1187.

Scott-Van Zeeland, A. A., Dapretto, M., Ghahremani, D. G., Poldrack, R. A., & Bookheimer, S. Y. (2010). Reward processing in autism. *Autism Research, 3*, 53–67.

Scott-Van Zeeland, A. A., McNealy, K., Wang, T., Sigman, M., Bookheimer, S. Y., & Dapretto, M. (2010). No neural evidence of statistical learning during exposure to artificial languages in children with autism. *Biological Psychiatry, 68*, 345–351.

Spreckelmeyer, K. N., Krach, S., Kohls, G., Rademacher, L., Irmak, A., Konrad, K.,... Gründer, G. (2009). Anticipation of monetary and social reward differently activates mesolimbic brain structures in men and women. *Social, Cognitive, and Affective Neuroscience, 4*, 158–165.

Thiessen, E. D., & Saffran, J. R. (2003). When cues collide: Use of stress and statistical cues to word boundaries by 7- to 9-month-old infants. *Developmental Psychology, 39*, 706–716.

Thut, G., Schultz, W., Roelcke, U., Nienhusmeier, M., Missimer, J., Maguire, R. P., & Leenders, K. L. (1997). Activation of the human brain by monetary reward. *Neuroreport, 8*, 1225–1228.

Triesch, J., Teuscher, C., Deak, G. O., & Carlson, E. (2006). Gaze following: Why (not) learn it? *Developmental Science, 9*, 125–147.

Wang, A. T., Dapretto, M., Hariri, A. R., Sigman, M., & Bookheimer, S. Y. (2004). Neural correlates of facial affect processing in children and adolescents with autism spectrum disorder. *Journal of the American Academy of Child and Adolescent Psychiatry, 43*, 481–490.

Wang, A. T., Lee, S. S., Sigman, M., & Dapretto, M. (2007). Reading affect in the face and voice: Neural correlates of interpreting communicative intent in children and adolescents with autism spectrum disorders. *Archives of General Psychiatry, 64*, 698–708.

Williams, J., Whiten, A., & Singh, T. (2004). A systematic review of action imitation in autistic spectrum disorder. *Journal of Autism and Developmental Disorders, 34*, 285–299.

5

Autism Susceptibility Genes and Normal Variation

Connecting Genes to Brain Structure and Function

DANIEL H. GESCHWIND
University of California, Los Angeles, CA

The organizing paradigm for our genetic research in autism is based on a neurodevelopmental model whereby cognition derives from the function of brain structures that are formed via the interactions of genes with the environment during development. In other words, our goal is to connect genes to brain to cognition. The brain structures that we refer to are not static; the brain is a dynamic structure whose gross anatomy and microscopic, chemical, and molecular structure develop in conjunction with the environment to produce cognitive function and, conversely, the environment (experience) modifies structure. From the standpoint of autism, and from the standpoint of my lab, we are trying to connect DNA, RNA, and other genetic structures to cognitive functions to determine what happens to cause the behavioral dysfunctions seen in this disorder (Figure 5.1). Using this model, we can harness the power of genetic methodologies to shed light on what happens during the development of the brain to lead to the syndrome that we later observe and call autism, in its many diverse varieties. This diversity and the emerging heterogeneity of autism have led us to conceive of autism spectrum disorders (Emilsson et al., 2008) as *the autisms* rather than a single unitary entity (Geschwind, 2009).

The overriding goal of the study of autism and genetics is to determine the autisms' etiologies. Currently, autism is defined based on observation of

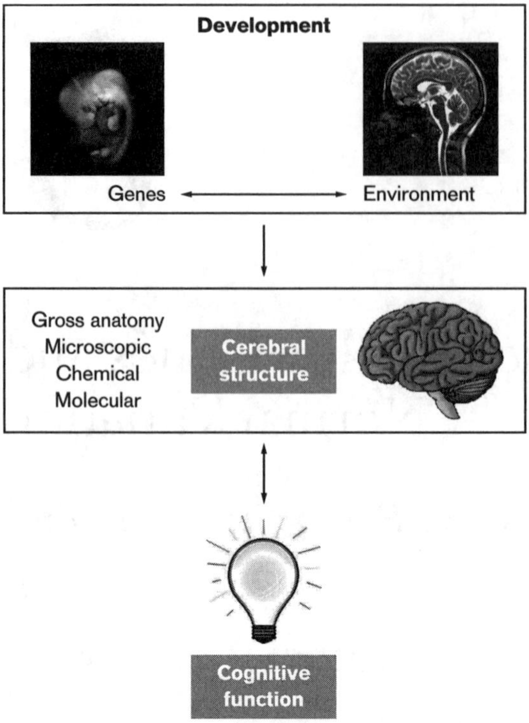

Figure 5.1 Connecting genes to brain to cognition in the autisms. Genes interact with environmental and stochastic factors during fetal and post-natal development, affecting the cerebral structure that underlies all human behavior and cognition. This structure is not static, but dynamic, and ranges in scale from the highly plastic chemical, molecular, and microscopic structures to neural circuits and the visible gross anatomy. The understanding of behavior and cognition is therefore rooted in an understanding of this dynamic structure, which itself is critically dependent on cognitive function (environment) for its normal development; hence the bi-directional arrow connecting cerebral structure to cognitive function. From a developmental perspective, what one may observe at a given epoch likely reflects an initial genetic insult modified by alterations in developmental trajectory caused by alterations in experience.

cognition and behavior, so diagnosis and treatment are often uncertain. If we can identify a more definitive etiology for any given case, we can improve treatment and hopefully in the future can tailor therapies to the individual. In this regard, the genetic findings over the past several years have been spectacular, identifying several dozen potential risk genes, none of which individually accounts for more than 1% of ASD cases, but when combined may account for 10% to 20% of cases (Abrahams & Geschwind, 2008; Cook & Scherer, 2008; O'Roak & State, 2008). At the same time, these data have shown that the clinical syndrome of autism, while highly heritable, is genetically very heterogeneous. Also, while common genetic variation contributes to autism, the effect of any given common polymorphism is very small relative to the phenotype of ASD. This suggests that perhaps the phenotype of ASD could be only weakly related to the intermediate phenotype (specific brain circuit or behavior) that the genetic polymorphism actually influences. These emerging data also support the role of more penetrant, rare mutations in the etiology of autism.

This chapter will first discuss the evidence supporting the notion that autism has a significant genetic origin, explain how we find genes that may be associated with autism, describe which genes have already been identified, and finally, explain what the genes are teaching us about autism and how we can begin to connect these genes to brain, and to cognition and behavior.

GENETIC FACTORS CONTRIBUTE SIGNIFICANTLY TO AUTISM RISK

There are three major sources of study indicating that autism has a strong genetic origin: twin studies, family studies, and investigation of the many known syndromes and chromosomal disorders strongly associated with autism. Twin studies have shown that the heritability (the extent of genetic contribution) of autism is about as high as is observed in common medical conditions; in fact, to my knowledge, the heritability of ASD is among the highest of all neuropsychiatric syndromes. Identical (monozygotic, MZ) twins have 100% of their genes in common, and they have a 60% to 70% concordance rate for strict DSM-IV autistic disorder. The MZ concordance rate is even higher for ASD, approaching 90% in some series (including autism, Asperger's, and pervasive developmental disorders [PDD]) (Bailey et al., 1995; Folstein & Rutter, 1977; Rutter, 2000). Fraternal (dizygotic, DZ) twins, who share 50% of their genes, have an average concordance of about 5% or 10% for strict autism, and slightly higher for ASD. Unfortunately, these numbers are based on studies that are fairly small; it is likely in the coming years that more accurate and up-to-date information will be published based on larger series. However, the MZ numbers are consistent across studies and universally demonstrate a very high heritability, at least 70% and up to 90%, depending on the method of calculation (Bailey et al., 1995; Rutter, 2000). But, even with this high heritability, there still is some room for the influence of the environment.

The second source of study, family studies, shows that if one sibling has autistic disorder, the risk for the next sibling is about 10%. The current rate of strict autistic disorder is a bit lower than one in 160, so, depending on how population risk/population prevalence is calculated, siblings of an autistic proband have a 20- to 50-fold increase in risk when compared to the general population (Abrahams & Geschwind, 2008; Gupta & State, 2007; Veenstra-Vanderweele, Christian, & Cook, 2004).

Both twin and family studies clearly show a person's risk for developing autism is greatly increased if a first-degree relative has autism. The issue is that, despite its high heritability, the mode of inheritance is not known. High heritability does not mean that a single major gene causes autism and does not inform our knowledge of the mode of inheritance. Most of the literature of ASD genetics predicts two, three, or more polymorphisms in genes interacting in any given patient to cause ASD. This "common variant–common disease" paradigm is consistent with other common diseases that have a significant genetic contribution (e.g., high blood pressure, obesity, diabetes, metabolic syndrome). In contrast to standard Mendelian genetics, where the genetic factors are thought of as causal, most common diseases are thought to be due to what is referred to as *complex genetics*. It should be emphasized that complex genetics is distinct from notions of clinical complexity or heterogeneity, which adds another layer of difficulty to the study of ASD. Conditions with complex genetic models are defined as having multiple genes acting together, usually with environmental factors, to contribute to the phenotype (Veenstra-Vanderweele et al., 2004). Each gene contributes a portion of the risk. Another factor is *variable penetrance*, meaning that not all carriers of a particular risk allele display the phenotype. Finally, *variable expressivity*, or differences in the way a phenotype is expressed, contributes to the complex genetics of autism. Although both reduced penetrance and reduced expressivity are also observed in Mendelian disorders, they are universal in complex genetic disorders. I will describe the methods used to discern some of the underlying complexities later in the chapter.

The investigation of syndromes and chromosomal disorders that co-occur with autism is the third major source of study of autism genetics. This approach has gained more and more traction as rare disorders with major gene mutations have been found to contribute to a significant proportion of autism risk. Hopefully in the future, we will be able to use advanced technology to understand prognosis in different kinds of autism that co-occur with different genetic disorders. Remarkably, based on current techniques, about 10% to 15% of individuals with autism have identifiable genetic disorders (Abrahams & Geschwind, 2008; O'Roak & State, 2008). Clinicians have known for years that Fragile X accounts for approximately 1% to 2% of cases of ASD, with about 25% of patients with Fragile X having an ASD (Bailey et al., 1993; Brown et al., 1986). A harbinger of recent advances that will be further discussed below, nearly a decade ago Ed Cook and colleagues discovered the maternal inherited duplication of chromosome 15q11–13 that accounts for 1% to 2% of ASD (Cook et al., 1997). There also are rarer genetic syndromes in which a high proportion of the patients have an autism spectrum disorder or autistic features (Abrahams & Geschwind, 2008); for example, at least 60% of patients with Timothy syndrome, a very rare cardiac conduction abnormality, have autism. These data emphasize a role for rare genetic disorders in autism, while highlighting its extraordinary etiological heterogeneity.

ESTABLISHMENT OF A SHARED PATIENT RESOURCE (AGRE)

How do researchers find autism genes, given all of this complexity? The first step is to recruit a very large sample size, no matter what method one is using. To that end, a group of parents and scientists created the Autism Genetic Resource Exchange (AGRE; www.AGRE.org) (Geschwind, 2001; Lajonchere & AGRE Consortium, 2010) under the financial support and in partnership with the Cure Autism Now Foundation (now Autism Speaks). The idea was to create a shared resource, where the families were collected so as to bring new investigators into the field and provide those already in the field with additional samples. This was in contrast to the usual paradigm in human genetics, where investigators hoard families that they collect; these precious resources become an individual investigator's competitive advantage in research. AGRE was formed based on the realization that one group could not do all of the research needed to advance ASD genetics and that it would take large sample sizes, collaboration, and many different approaches. This has clearly turned out to be true.

AGRE is an open resource consisting of biomaterials, phenotype data, and genetic data from families with one or more member with autism. When we started AGRE, most of the scientists involved were not engaged in autism genetics, including my own lab. After AGRE had developed for three years and had data from about 200 families, only two or three groups had really used it to any consequence. The most successful group was led by Conrad Gilliam, then at Columbia University, who genotyped the entire AGRE collection of samples and performed the first genome-wide linkage studies in AGRE (Liu et al., 2001; Yonan et al., 2003). Subsequently, a group of collaborative investigators from several institutions, including Columbia, University of Chicago, and UCLA, began to perform genetic studies in the AGRE cohort to provide a proof of principle that this kind of resource was actually valuable and could lead to advances in autism genetics. Now, about 1,000 families are in the database and over 150 groups have accessed AGRE. There are over 100 publications that employ the database or biomaterials; nearly every major autism genetics study, including the recently published genome-wide association studies (Wang & Wang, 2009; Weiss et al., 2008), is based on AGRE, making it the single major genetic resource in the field. It is unfortunate that most genetic studies of other neurologic or psychiatric diseases do not share their data widely, which would clearly accelerate research in the field. NIH is changing to mandate data and sample sharing, which will surely hasten progress in all fields of scientific endeavor involving human diseases by bringing new research ideas into the field and allowing access to critical patient samples for research. For this to be truly successful, the right data has to be shared in the appropriate format, along with biomaterials, and in a timely manner.

FINDING ASD SUSCEPTIBILITY GENES

With such a wealth of information, it becomes much easier to do genetic studies of autism. How does one use the three major approaches available to geneticists: (a) assessment of chromosome anomalies and structural variation, (b) linkage studies, and (c) association studies? What have we learned from these approaches?

Chromosomal Disorders

Investigating chromosome anomalies is essentially identification of chromosomal structural variation, which often causes genetic syndromes that are related to autism (Vorstman et al., 2006). As we know from Down syndrome, where the abnormality is genetic, but not inherited (an extra chromosome 21), cytogenetically visible structural chromosome abnormalities contribute significantly to neurodevelopmental conditions such as intellectual disability. Until about five years ago, light microscopes were used to study chromosomal karyotypes; only chromosomal anomalies greater than three million base pairs were able to be identified. As methods improve, we are finding smaller and smaller pieces of abnormal chromosomes, to the point where we can now scan the genome fairly efficiently for structural chromosomal variants below the single gene size (about 10,000–50,000 base pairs) using microarrays (Edelmann & Hirschhorn, 2009; Mefford et al., 2009; Vissers, de Vries, & Veltman, 2010). These variants can be gains or losses of genetic material, and when larger than 1,000, base pairs are referred to as copy number variations (CNV). Each of us actually has approximately a dozen CNV that are relatively small, not entire chromosomes, but pieces of chromosomes. A neurotypical person can have deletions (one chromosome on the autosomes or none on the X chromosome) or duplications (three or more copies of a chromosome), but the CNV that we are searching for are those that occur more frequently in ASD than in controls. To do these fine-grained analyses, researchers use microarray techniques. This and other technologies continue to improve the resolution of these studies, allowing more detailed analysis of the genome. As whole genome sequencing becomes affordable over the next few years, it will largely supplant the techniques that we currently use.

As discussed above, syndromes and recurrent CNV account for 10% to 15% of ASDs. For example, recently, several research groups identified a region on 16p that, when duplicated or deleted, increased the risk for autism almost 100-fold and was observed in nearly 1% of ASD cases (Kumar et al., 2008; Weiss et al., 2008). Subsequent studies indicate that duplications may not be nearly as pathogenic as deletions, and at the same time they indicate an association with broader phenotypes, including schizophrenia susceptibility (McCarthy et al., 2009).

In addition to syndromes, there is another class of rare genetic variants that are not recurrent, called *de novo CNV*. These structural chromosomal abnormalities occur such that the parents do not have the mutation, but rather they occur de novo in the gamete, as in Down syndrome. In this case, the child ends up with a genetic problem that was not inherited from the parents. These rare de novo CNV were first described in autism by Jonathan Sebat and Michael Wigler and account for 2% or 10% of autism cases depending on the population studied (Bucan et al., 2009; Glessner et al., 2009; Marshall et al., 2008; Sebat et al., 2007). When combined with the genetic syndromes and recurrent CNV (which are also syndromes) described above, this means that at least 10% to 20% of ASD cases have a de novo CNV, recurrent CNV, or genetic syndrome that is likely to be a major contributor to their ASD.

Genetic Linkage and Association

Studying genetic linkage is a very simple concept. A researcher looks within families to determine if there are any regions on a chromosome that are co-inherited with the condition. A given region is of interest if it is found only in people within the family who have the condition and not in people without the condition. In autism, often sibling pair designs are used. Here one asks if the sharing of genetic markers deviates significantly from the 50% that we expect in siblings. I will not focus on the results of genetic linkage studies of ASD in this chapter, and instead refer the reader to several recent reviews that address this topic (Abrahams & Geschwind, 2008; Folstein & Rosen-Sheidley, 2001; Lamb, Moore, Bailey, & Monaco, 2000).

Genetic association is population-based rather than family-based. In genetic association studies, we try to find genetic variants that are significantly more frequent in cases than in controls. The genetic code is made up of four letters, so if there is an alteration in one of those letters, it is called a *single nucleotide polymorphism* (SNP). An important thing to remember about these variants is that we all vary with each other perhaps one variant every 1,000 base pairs, depending on the region of the genome. However, genetic association studies look for SNPs or other forms of genetic variation that are seen more frequently in those with autism than those who are controls. The study of SNPs, alterations in one base pair, contrasts with the study of copy number variations, abnormalities in more than 1,000 base pairs, which can also be detected by microarray. SNPs and large CNV form two contrasting examples of the size spectrum of the classes of genetic variation that may be associated with a neurodevelopmental syndrome such as ASD. Here, I will discuss our association results in the context of the discussion of endophenotypes in the next section.

It is important to consider that, even among major CNV that are likely to be the major cause of a child's condition, few if any that we currently know of only cause autism; most can lead to intellectual disability, and some increase the risk for global developmental delay, or even schizophrenia (Abrahams & Geschwind, 2008; Cantor & Geschwind, 2008; Cook & Scherer, 2008). Therefore, it seems likely that most of these rare major or Mendelian mutations are modified by environmental, genetic, or epigenetic factors to lead to autism. Regardless of variability in the neurodevelopmental syndrome caused by any given mutation, these major effect mutations currently account for between 10% and 20% of cases of autism (Abrahams & Geschwind, 2008). What about the other 80% of people with autism? It is possible that they have rare (Mendelian) mutations that we still have not discovered or that their autism comes from the interaction of common variance with various environmental factors (complex genetics). There are many questions still to be answered to understand the genetic basis for autism in the other 80% of cases, and I will use the rest of the chapter to explain our work trying to identify these factors.

GENETIC HETEROGENEITY IN AUTISM

During the initial genome scans performed by Conrad Gilliam and his group at Columbia, a few loci that looked interesting were identified (Liu et al., 2001; Yonan et al., 2003). However, as Dr. Gilliam noted at the time (personal communication), even as AGRE tripled in size, it did not proportionately increase our power to detect linkage. In fact, in the most recent genetic linkage study, a collaboration between almost every major group in autism genetics in the world that included 1,200 families, there were no statistically significant linkage results (Autism Genome Project Consortium, 2007); no linkage peak in this study reached genome-wide significance, despite a tenfold increase in sample size from the original AGRE linkage scan (Liu et al., 2001) and the earlier International Molecular Genetics Study of Autism Consortium scan (1998). This is evidence of remarkable genetic heterogeneity.

Figure 5.2 (adapted from Abrahams & Geschwind, 2008, see plate section) illustrates the regions that have been identified and replicated in multiple studies. In Figure 5.2, red and yellow bars correspond to de novo losses and gains, respectively, that are observed in cases but not in controls. Green bars correspond to genes that are observed to modulate ASD risk (either through a rare syndrome or genetic association); light green and dark green bars represent promising or probable candidate genes, respectively. Regions shaded in purple correspond to linkage peaks. The red areas are the copy number variations that are deletions, the yellow are the duplications, and the purple are linkage peaks. Note that virtually every group has had a nominal linkage peak on chromosome 7q. In other words, a very broad region of 7q, especially 7q35, has been a consistent finding in linkage studies, as supported by meta-analysis (Badner & Gershon, 2002).

One region that has been implicated more than once with genome-wide significance is chromosome 17q, which is related primarily to male risk for autism in AGRE (Cantor et al., 2005; Stone et al., 2004). There are other regions for which, as we add families and add markers, the evidence appears to increase: for example, chromosome 11 and chromosome 5. These may be important hot spots; however, 1,200 families are not enough to truly understand the intricacies of the genetics affecting autism. For other complex diseases, such as diabetes, studies are able to identify and reproduce a number of loci when they are in the realm of 5,000 to 10,000 cases and controls, which is likely to be the minimum sample size needed for autism studies to establish very solid findings, and not just hit the low-hanging fruit. We have identified chromosomes 7 and 17, and maybe 11 and 5, but there are a lot more to be found.

Another point worth mentioning is that, even if a gene is found to be associated with autism, researchers still have to determine what that particular gene does. If one can connect a gene to a specific aspect of cognition and behavior, rather than the entire syndrome, we can hope to begin to understand the mechanism underlying disease susceptibility and move to better mechanistically driven treatments.

ENDOPHENOTYPES IN ASD

In the meantime, how should researchers address the issue of heterogeneity? If the core domains of autism are conceived of as distinguishable entities, a perspective that makes sense from a cognitive neuroscience standpoint, researchers can separately investigate language systems, social behavior systems, and repetitive/restrictive behavior systems (Figure 5.3, adapted from Geschwind, 2008, see plate section). Figure 5.3A illustrates the concept that ASD susceptibility may in some cases reflect the contribution of normal variation in heritable, potentially distinct core components of autism (endophenotypes). Figure 5.3B shows a simplified model of how a variety of risk variants, large and small, may contribute to ASDs in aggregate. In Figure 5.3A, normal variation in language, social, and repetitive/restrictive behaviors is illustrated as overlapping, but distinct functions, with the green and red sections demarcating the highest level of functioning and progressive abnormality, respectively. Under such a scheme, moderate abnormality in all three areas is necessary to have autism, but significant, isolated abnormality in one area leads to a more circumscribed condition, such as specific language impairment for deficits in language. Patients with Asperger's syndrome have normal language, but lie in the red zone for the other two components. Each of these heritable cognitive-behavioral components, or endophenotypes, although genetically complex, is likely to be less heterogeneous than the syndrome of autism. These endophenotypes can be studied separately to increase power to detect common genetic risk variants.

In Figure 5.3B, the contribution of genetic or environmental factors is emphasized by size or position of each representative weight. Mendelian mutations, such as de novo CNV, are depicted as a large ball, because they are considered causal in many cases and would tip the balance, placing an individual essentially into the red in all categories shown in Figure 5.3A (pleiotropy), resulting in autism. This category of autism risk in an individual is represented by the green circle to the right. The reality, however, is that there are few mutations known to be acting alone (i.e., are fully causal). Many mutations, including those that are recurrent, are not fully penetrant, and some patients have more than one de novo CNV. Similarly, most mutations, even rare mutations such as neuroligin 4, or recurrent mutations such as deletion 16p, show variable expressivity; for example, they could result in developmental delay or mental retardation (MR) in some individuals or lead to autism in others. The environment, epigenetic factors, or other common variants that might modulate the endophenotypes could be tipping the balance towards autism in a child who would have otherwise had mild or moderate MR. This model is shown in the purple circle to the right, in which another piece of the puzzle in addition to the major effect gene is needed to cause autism in the individual. In other cases, multiple common variants, each with small to intermediate effect and related to different components, would push an individual towards the right of the distribution and, along with environmental or epigenetic factors, could result in an ASD. This is depicted in the bottom, multicolored circle to the right of the figure. Each of these scenarios, or a combination, as shown at the right in the three contrasting models of autism genetic risk in the individual, may be acting in a given individual with autism. Defining the extent to which each contributes on a population level to ASD is a goal of current genetic research.

These systems may task on some of the same brain regions in some cases, but the overall distributed brain circuits underlying each of these domains can initially be thought of as distinct (it has been established in neurological research for almost a hundred years that it is possible for patients with brain injuries to be affected in only one of these systems very specifically). However, the notion is to study these domains separately because these endophenotypes (more elemental, biologically based aspects of a disorder that may be governed by fewer susceptibility genes) may be more closely related to individual genetic risk factors than is the entire broad syndrome of ASD. To optimize the gene search, endophenotypes must be associated with the disease, continuously distributed, and heritable, and therefore often observed in affected relatives at a higher rate than in the general population (Gottesman & Gould, 2003).

In autism, such endophenotypes include deficits in language, social behavior, and nonverbal communication; repetitive behaviors; increased head circumference; and even biochemical factors, such as differential gene expression (Chen, Kono, Geschwind, & Cantor, 2005; Duvall et al., 2007; Geschwind, 2008; Nishimura et al., 2007). These domains are certainly not simple, but separately relating them to genetic risk is simpler than investigating the entire syndrome at once. Family studies by Anthony Bailey, Joseph Piven, and

Patrick Bolton, among others (Bailey, Palferman, Heavey, & Le Couteur, 1998; Bolton et al., 1994; Bolton, Pickles, Murphy, & Rutter, 1998; Constantino et al., 2006; Folstein et al., 1999; Fombonne, Bolton, Prior, Jordan, & Rutter, 1997; Pickles et al., 2000; Piven, Palmer, Jacobi, Childress, & Arndt, 1997), show that there is a broad phenotype and that aspects of language delays, social cognition, or repetitive/restrictive behavior are more often seen in first-degree relatives than in the general population. Distinct aspects of autistic-like impairment segregate unaffected family members, similar to what is observed in the general population (Constantino & Todd, 2003, 2005; Ronald et al., 2006; Ronald, Happé, Price, Baron-Cohen, & Plomin, 2006). Therefore, using quantitative measures of specific endophenotypes permits the use of all family members; the quantitative trait loci (QTL) approach does not require what some may consider an arbitrary separation of affected from unaffected subjects.

An example of this endophenotype approach is a line of study initiated in 2001 by Alarcón and coworkers (Alarcón, Yonan, Gilliam, Cantor, & Geschwind, 2005). Here, investigators studied the AGRE cohort to identify whether there were chromosomal regions linked to the endophenotype of language delay. The initial study was relatively crude, taking advantage of data collected as part of the diagnostic evaluations rather than using specifically designed quantitative measures of language function. The researchers analyzed the Autism Diagnostic Interview-Revised (ADI-R) measures of "age at first word" and "age at first phrase" for all the children in the cohort and showed that the measures were highly heritable. Quantitative linkage analysis revealed a likely locus linked to "age at first word" (a surrogate for spoken language delay) on chromosome 7q35 that overlapped with the broader autism locus in that region (Alarcón, Cantor, Liu, Gilliam, & Geschwind, 2002). Rather than using a discrete measure and classifying people as affected or unaffected, the extent of phenotype-sharing (similarity in language delay) was regressed against genotype-sharing (alleles of markers on 7q35). Evidence for linkage to this region was subsequently identified in an independent cohort, but only about 40% of families showed linkage to this region, consistent with genetic heterogeneity (Alarcón et al., 2005). Interestingly, the locus was not important for those who had severe dysphasia or were mute; only milder impairment (language delay by 12 to 36 months) was relevant to this region, suggesting that this locus might be related to normal variation in language (Alarcón et al., 2005), which was later supported by Vernes et al. (2008).

Another way to address phenotype heterogeneity in autism using endophenotypes is to stratify the sample so that subjects are divided into discrete groups based on the presence or absence of the phenotype, in this case, language delay. This method has one major disadvantage: Because it divides the sample into smaller cohorts, it can reduce power. As larger samples are developed, stratification will become more feasible. Such stratification has provided some evidence for linkage to language endophenotypes (Bradford et al., 2001;

Buxbaum et al., 2004), but the significance of these results is uncertain because none of these loci have been replicated (Liu, Paterson, & Szatmari, 2008; Spence et al., 2006). In contrast, relying on the phenotype of sex has produced some interesting results. Given the four-to-one ratio of males to females in autistic disorder, Stone and colleagues (2004) contrasted the genetics of male-only families (those with two or more affected male children, and no affected females) to families that had one or more affected females. The researchers found clear genome-wide evidence for multiple sex-specific risk alleles. In fact, in a later study, Cantor et al. (2005) independently replicated a linkage peak on chromosome 17q at genome-wide significance in male-only families. This stands as the only formally replicated peak in autism genetics using identical methods in an independent sample (Abrahams & Geschwind, 2008).

QTL ANALYSIS IDENTIFIES CNTNAP2

Alarcón and colleagues (2005) expanded on their earlier (2002) study that found a chromosome 7q locus related to language delay. In the later study, this locus was not genome-wide significant, but ordered subset analysis provided additional evidence for the importance of this region in a subset of families (Alarcón et al., 2005). To identify the causal gene, we tested the entire 15Mb linkage region for genetic association by genotyping SNPs at high density across the genes in the region. We performed the analysis in two stages to have enough power, treating the first stage as a hypothesis-generating experiment so as to limit multiple testing issues in the second stage. The results of the hypothesis testing identified one gene, contactin associated protein-like 2, or CNTNAP2 (Alarcón et al., 2008), showing association with language delay. This was not a genome-wide study or a candidate gene study, but a regional, linkage-directed association study assessing all of the genes in the linkage region, and CNTNAP2 was the only gene that showed reasonable evidence for association. Work by others (Arking et al., 2008) has shown that common variation in a different region of this gene was related to the broad spectrum of ASD. Further, Bakkaloglu and colleagues (2008) found several unique rare variants in CNTNAP2 in multiple cases of ASD that were not observed in several thousand controls, implicating rare mutations as well.

However, the most irrefutable data implicating CNTNAP2 in ASD came from Strauss et al. (2006), who found a large Amish family with a recessive mutation in CNTNAP2 causing a condition referred to as Symptomatic Focal Epilepsy. These patients have seizures associated with intellectual disability and, remarkably, an ASD is observed in almost 70% of cases. In addition, almost half the patients have a neuronal migration disorder visible on MRI. My interpretation of these data is that functional alteration of this gene triggered a neuronal migration abnormality that led to seizures and language regression/delay (when the seizures are treated, the language improves, although the deficits are not cured) and frequently leads to an ASD.

Perhaps even more remarkable to us was that major foci of the seizures experienced in affected members of this family were in the anterior temporal lobe and the frontal lobe. This finding was exciting, as we had previously identified CNTNAP2 as one of a few genes focally enriched in human perisylvian language regions, in this case, specifically in the frontal and temporal cortices (Abrahams et al., 2007). No such enrichment in anterior frontotemporal cortex was observed in mice, consistent with the emergence and expansion of these regions in primates (Abrahams et al., 2007). This pattern of gene expression is very unusual; in the hundreds of genes we investigated, only a handful followed this pattern, including the MET gene (Mukamel et al., 2011), another gene found to be important in autism risk (Campbell et al., 2006). Thus, genetic evidence converges with developmental anatomical data to implicate cortical striatal-thalamolimbic circuitry known to be involved in certain aspects of social cognition, language learning, and attention in ASD.

CNTNAP2 COMPRISES PART OF A BROADER LANGUAGE-RELATED CIRCUITRY

Knowing that CNTNAP2 is expressed in highly evolved, language-related brain regions, and knowing that common variation in this gene is associated with quantitative variation in language delay while rare mutations cause epilepsy, language delay, and ASD, we wondered whether CNTNAP2 could be related to general language variation among all individuals, rather than being limited to ASD. Subsequent collaborative work led by Simon Fisher and Tony Monaco demonstrated that this was the case in a well-defined cohort of patients with specific language impairment (SLI) (Vernes et al., 2008; Monaco, 2007). SLI is highly heritable. Autistic children do poorly in one of the most heritable markers of SLI, non-word repetition (NWR). Remarkably, after testing more than 30 SNPs across the 2.5 million base pairs of sequence that spans the CNTNAP2 gene in about 180 sibling pairs with SLI, the same region implicated previously in language delay in ASD was found to be significantly associated with NWR (Vernes et al., 2008). This demonstrates that essentially the same region of the genome, in fact a small region of the same gene, is modulating language delay across two different clinical conditions, possibly through the same mechanism affecting function and development of the relevant brain regions.

To further investigate the relation of CNTNAP2 to other molecular components of human language circuitry, the group studied FOXP2, the only gene that has been definitively connected to language circuitry in humans (Fisher, Vargha-Khadem, Watkins, Monaco, & Pembrey, 1998; Lai, Fisher, Hurst, Vargha-Khadem, & Monaco, 2001). FOXP2 is a transcription factor, meaning that it functions by binding to DNA to regulate the levels of other genes. Vernes et al. (2008) found that FOXP2 bound to CNTNAP2 and showed, using an in vitro assay, that FOXP2 binding could potentially regulate the levels of CNTNAP2.

It is worthwhile to speculate that these findings are the potential rudimentary beginnings of identification of a molecular circuit related to language (Figure 5.4). We can start with the knowledge that there is a transcription factor important for human speech and language, FOXP2, that turns on and off several genes, including CNTNAP2, that are involved critically in the development of brain regions important for higher human cognition, including language. Genetic variation in some of these genes, including CNTNAP2, modulates language function. Furthermore, genes such as CNTNAP2 (and perhaps MET) that have very specific patterns of expression in the developing

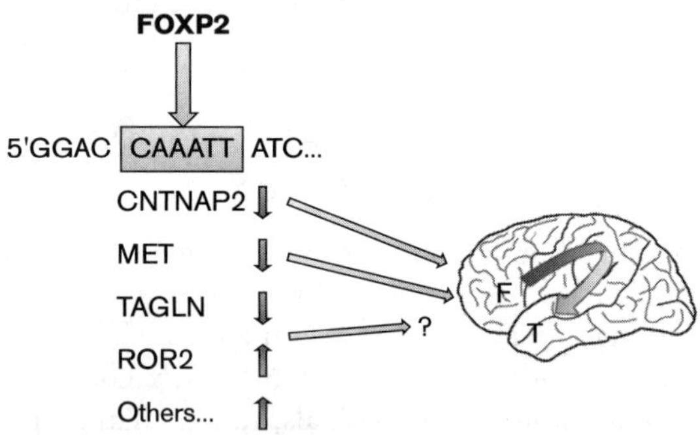

Figure 5.4 Connecting genes to brain: An "entry-level" molecular circuitry for language. The perisylvian language-related circuit is roughly outlined in the thick arrow on the right side of the figure. The molecular circuit starts with the transcription factor FOXP2, which functions to regulate the expression of other genes by binding to regulatory regions coded by their DNA sequence, indicated in the shaded box. Many downstream targets have been identified, including CNTNAP2 and MET, both of which are implicated in autism. There are numerous other known FOXP2 targets, which also would be potentially part of this molecular pathway, most prominently several that differ between human and chimpanzee, such as TAGLN and ROR (Konopka et al., 2009). Rather than being specifically related to language per se, this rudimentary molecular pathway involves genes, such as CNTNAP2 and MET, that regulate the patterning and development of brain circuitry in the frontal lobe, temporal lobe, and striatum, as well as more posterior regions to which this circuit is connected (arrows). These regions are involved in many cognitive functions, including motor sequencing, planning, semantics, etc., that contribute to language, among other behavioral and cognitive functions. These circuits are built on top of more primitive circuits and have evolved and adapted to underlie language. It is hypothesized, but not yet known, that the other FOXP2 targets such as ROR and TAGLN are expressed in such a focal pattern in frontal or temporal as observed for CNTNAP2 and MET, respectively.

nervous system clearly are important to the proper development and function of these anterior brain regions.

This concept fits with many of the ideas that have characterized autism research in the past decade, such as local (minicolumn) abnormalities and the theory of long-distance underconnectivity (Casanova et al., 2006; Cherkassky, Kana, Keller, & Just, 2006; Just, Cherkassky, Keller, Kana, & Minshew, 2007). This concept of underconnectivity across long-range neural pathways in autism, especially in language areas, was first described by Marcel Adam Just and Nancy Minshew (Just, Cherkassky, Keller, & Minshew, 2004). Other cognitive neuroscientists studying autism have come to similar conclusions (Courchesne & Pierce, 2005), highlighting a convergence of nearly a decade of imaging work in ASD and new findings in genetics. The crucial next step to test this hypothesis firmly is to combine genetics and imaging to evaluate whether ASD-related variation in CNTNAP2 modulates the functional connectivity of the regions in which it is expressed.

A BROADER SYNTHESIS: DEVELOPMENTAL DISCONNECTION

CNTNAP2 is one of perhaps several dozen ASD risk genes identified to date (Abrahams & Geschwind, 2008; Gupta & State, 2007). How do these findings in CNTNAP2 relate to the other genes that have been identified? With respect to CNTNAP2, I have described an example of the last few years' progress. Similar work can be done for other risk variants, a crucial step in moving from identification of genes to understanding how this genetic variation contributes to human brain dysfunction that underlies ASD. However, it is clear that the study of genetics in autism is not going to produce an easy answer; ASD is not due to one simple, single, obvious molecular pathway (Bill & Geschwind, 2009), or disruption of a single anatomical region. Additionally, ASD is not defined by etiology, but by observation of behavior and cognition. Essentially, what is observed in ASD is dysfunction of the circuits in the anterior part of the brain: frontal lobes, temporal lobes, and areas in other regions that are connected with them. The deficits in autism are related to functioning and connectivity of these higher-order association areas—that is, those responsible for rapid integration of multimodal information, as is necessary for language and social cognition in humans. Many different molecular pathways are likely to lead to such developmental disconnection, ranging from dendritic maturation and synaptic function to neuronal migration, axon outgrowth, and pathfinding (Geschwind & Levitt, 2007; Bill & Geschwind, 2009). Given the centrality of social cognition and language deficits in ASD and the known neural substrates that underlie these functions, our current model is that the key commonality connecting the various etiological forms of ASD is likely to be involvement of the frontal lobe and its connections.

SUMMARY

In summary, autism has a large genetic risk, but its etiology is multifactorial. Rare genetic variation contributes to at least 10% of ASD cases and is likely to explain more. However, understanding the contribution of common variation and its interaction with rare variances is still an important next step, as very few of the major gene mutations specifically cause only ASD. For research purposes, we should study traits that are related to underlying pathophysiology or biology (e.g., head circumference) instead of relying on clinical diagnostic-related measurements. To begin to connect genetics to the function of specific, highly evolved human brain circuits, research should focus on how genes affect function in subjects with a variety of abilities or clinical diagnoses, taking evolutionary data into account. Here, CNTNAP2 and its relation to a language function in ASD and SLI is a salient example. It is also important to understand the concept of developmental disconnection—that is, whether the genetic mutation affects the synapse, neuronal migration, neuronal differentiation, or lipid metabolism. The idea is that the pathophysiological commonality in the autisms is a subtle disconnection during brain development that impedes the normal patterns of frontal systems connectivity and subsequent functioning. Future work combining imaging and genetic information with different treatment modalities in humans will be critical to enhancing our understanding of ASD pathophysiology and development of more effective therapies.

AUTHOR NOTE

Daniel H. Geschwind, Professor, Departments of Neurology and Psychiatry, Director, UCLA Center for Autism Research Treatment (CART), and the Neurogenetics Program, Gordon and Virginia MacDonald Distinguished Chair in Human Genetics, University of California, Los Angeles.

ACKNOWLEDGMENTS

I would like to acknowledge present and former members of the lab, including Brett Abrahams, Maricela Alarcón, Giovanni Coppola, and Gena Konopka, who have made major contributions to the work reviewed here or helped with figures. In addition, I am grateful to my colleagues Susan Bookheimer, Rita Cantor, and Stanley F. Nelson for their continued collaboration. This research was supported by National Institute of Mental Health Grants MH081754 awarded to Daniel H. Geschwind and HD055784 awarded to Susan Bookheimer (Geschwind, project II PI).

Correspondence concerning this article should be addressed to Daniel H. Geschwind, Department of Neurology, UCLA, Gonda 2506, 695 Charles E Young Drive South, Los Angeles, CA 90095. E-mail: dhg@ucla.edu

REFERENCES

Abrahams, B. S., & Geschwind, D. H. (2008). Advances in autism genetics: On the threshold of a new neurobiology. *Nature Reviews Genetics, 9*, 341–355. doi:10.1038/nrg2346.

Abrahams, B. S., Tentler, D., Perederiy, J. V., Oldham, M. C., Coppola, G., & Geschwind, D. H. (2007). Genome-wide analyses of human perisylvian cerebral cortical patterning. *Proceedings of the National Academy of Sciences of the United States of America, 104*, 17849–17854. doi:10.107/pnas.0706128104.

Alarcón, M., Abrahams, B. S., Stone, J. L., Duvall, J. A., Perederiy, J. V., Bomar, J. M.,… Geschwind D. H. (2008). Linkage, association, and gene-expression analyses identify CNTNAP2 as an autism-susceptibility gene. *American Journal of Human Genetics, 82*, 150–159. doi:10.1016/j.ajhg.2007.09.005.

Alarcón, M., Cantor, R. M., Liu, J., Gilliam, T. C., & Geschwind, D. H. (2002). Evidence for a language quantitative trait locus on chromosome 7q in multiplex autism families. *American Journal of Human Genetics, 70*, 60–71.

Alarcón, M., Yonan, A. L., Gilliam, T. C., Cantor, R. M., & Geschwind, D. H. (2005). Quantitative genome scan and Ordered-Subsets Analysis of autism endophenotypes support language QTLs. *Molecular Psychiatry, 10*, 747–757. doi:10.1038/sj.mp.4001666.

Arking, D. E., Cutler, D. J., Brune, C. W., Teslovich, T. M., West K., Ikeda M.,… Chakravarti, A. (2008). A common genetic variant in the neurexin-superfamily member CNTNAP2 increases familial risk of autism. *American Journal of Human Genetics, 82*, 160–164. doi:10.1016/j.ajhg.2007.09.015.

Autism Genome Project Consortium. (2007). Mapping autism risk loci using genetic linkage and chromosomal rearrangements. *Nature Genetics, 39*, 319–328. doi:10.1038/ng1985.

Badner, J. A., & Gershon, E. S. (2002). Regional meta-analysis of published data supports linkage of autism with markers on chromosome 7. *Molecular Psychiatry, 7*, 56–66. doi:10.1038/sj/mp/4000922.

Bailey, A., Bolton, P., Butler, L., Le Couteur, A., Murphy, M., Scott, S.,… Rutter, M. (1993). Prevalence of the Fragile X anomaly amongst autistic twins and singletons. *Journal of Child Psychology and Psychiatry, 34*, 673–688.

Bailey, A., Le Couteur, A., Gottesman, I., Bolton, P., Simonoff, E., Yuzda, E., & Rutter, M. (1995). Autism as a strongly genetic disorder: Evidence from a British twin study. *Psychological Medicine, 25*, 63–77.

Bailey, A., Palferman, S., Heavey, L., & Le Couteur, A. (1998). Autism: The phenotype in relatives. *Journal of Autism and Developmental Disorders, 28*, 369–392.

Bakkaloglu, B., O'Roak, B. J., Louvi, A., Gupta, A. R., Abelson, J. F., Morgan, T. M.,… State M. W. (2008). Molecular cytogenetic analysis and resequencing of contactin associated protein-like 2 in autism spectrum disorders. *American Journal of Human Genetics, 82*, 165–173. doi:10.1016/j.ajhg.2007.09.017.

Bill, B. R., & Geschwind, D. H. (2009). Genetic advances in autism: Heterogeneity and convergence on shared pathways. *Current Opinion in Genetics and Development, 19*, 271–278. doi:10.1016/j.gde.2009.04.004.

Bolton, P., Macdonald, H., Pickles, A., Rios, P., Goode, S., Crowson, M.,… Rutter, M. (1994). A case-control family history study of autism. *Journal of Child Psychology and Psychiatry, 35*, 877–900.

Bolton, P. F., Pickles, A., Murphy, M., & Rutter, M. (1998). Autism, affective, and other psychiatric disorders: Patterns of familial aggregation. *Psychological Medicine, 28*, 385–395.

Bradford, Y., Haines, J., Hutcheson, H., Gardiner, M., Braun, T., Sheffield, V., & Piven, J. (2001). Incorporating language phenotypes strengthens evidence of linkage to autism. *American Journal of Medical Genetics, 105*, 539–547. doi:10.1002/ajmg.1497.

Brown, W. T., Jenkins, E. C., Cohen, I. L., Fisch, G. S., Wolf-Schein, E. G., Gross, A.,… Ritvo, E. (1986). Fragile X and autism: A multicenter survey. *American Journal of Medical Genetics, 23*, 341–352.

Bucan, M., Abrahams, B. S., Wang, K., Glessner, J. T., Herman, E. I., Sonnenblick, L. I.,… Hakonarson, H. (2009). Genome-wide analyses of exonic copy number variants in a family-based study point to novel autism susceptibility genes. *PLoS Genetics, 5*, e1000536. doi:10.1371/journal.pgen.1000536.

Buxbaum, J. D., Silverman, J., Keddache, M., Smith, C. J., Hollander, E., Ramoz, N., & Reichert, J. G. (2004). Linkage analysis for autism in a subset of families with obsessive-compulsive behaviors: Evidence for an autism susceptibility gene on chromosome 1 and further support for susceptibility genes on chromosome 6 and 19. *Molecular Psychiatry, 9*, 144–150. doi:10.1038/sj.mp. 4001465.

Campbell, D. B., Sutcliffe, J. S., Ebert, P. J., Militerni, R., Bravaccio, C., Trillo, S.,… Levitt, P. (2006). A genetic variant that disrupts MET transcription is associated with autism. *Proceedings of the National Academy of Sciences of the United States of America, 103*, 16834–16839. doi:10.1073/pnas.0605296103.

Cantor, R. M., & Geschwind, D. H. (2008). Schizophrenia: Genome, interrupted. *Neuron, 58*, 165–167. doi:10.1016/j.neuron.2008.04.007.

Cantor, R. M., Kono, N., Duvall, J. A., Alvarez-Retuerto, A., Stone, J. L., Alarcón, M.,… Geschwind, D. H. (2005). Replication of autism linkage: Fine-mapping peak at 17q21. *American Journal of Human Genetics, 76*, 1050–1056.

Casanova, M. F., van Kooten, I. A., Switala, A. E., van Engeland, H., Heinsen, H., Steinbusch, H. W.,… Schmitz, C. (2006). Minicolumnar abnormalities in autism. *Acta Neuropathologica, 112*, 287–303. doi:10.1007/s00401–006–0085–5.

Chen, G., Kono, N., Geschwind, D., & Cantor, R. (2005). Linkage of autism spectrum disorder: Evidence of a non-verbal communication locus on 8q24. Presented at the Annual Meeting, International Meeting for Autism Research, Boston, MA. May 5–7, 2005. IMFAR Abstracts No P1B217.

Cherkassky, V. L., Kana, R. K., Keller, T. A., & Just, M. A. (2006). Functional connectivity in a baseline resting-state network in autism. *Neuroreport, 17*, 1687–1690. doi:10.1097/01.wnr.0000239956.45448.4c.

Constantino, J. N., Lajonchere, C., Lutz, M., Gray, T., Abbacchi, A., McKenna, K.,… Todd, R. D. (2006). Autistic social impairment in the siblings of children with pervasive developmental disorders. *American Journal of Psychiatry, 163*, 294–296. doi:10.1176/aapi.ajp. 163.2.294.

Constantino, J. N., & Todd, R. D. (2003). Autistic traits in the general population: A twin study. *Archives of General Psychiatry, 60*, 524–530.

Constantino, J. N., & Todd, R. D. (2005). Intergenerational transmission of subthreshold autistic traits in the general population. *Biological Psychiatry, 57*, 655–660. doi:10.1016/j.biopsych.2004.12.014.

Cook, Jr., E. H., Lindgren, V., Leventhal, B. L., Courchesne, R., Lincoln, A., Shulman,

C.,… Courchesne, E. (1997). Autism or atypical autism in maternally but not paternally derived proximal 15q duplication. *American Journal of Human Genetics, 60*, 928–934.

Cook, Jr., E. H., & Scherer, S. W. (2008). Copy-number variations associated with neuropsychiatric conditions. *Nature, 455*, 919–923. doi:10.1038/nature07458.

Courchesne, E., & Pierce, K. (2005). Why the frontal cortex in autism might be talking only to itself: Local over-connectivity but long-distance disconnection. *Current Opinion in Neurobiology, 15*, 225–230. doi:10.1016/j.conb.2005.03.001.

Duvall, J. A., Lu, A., Cantor, R. M., Todd, R. D., Constantino, J. N., & Geschwind, D. H. (2007). A quantitative trait locus analysis of social responsiveness in multiplex autism families. *American Journal of Psychiatry, 164*, 656–662. doi:10.1176/appi.ajp.164.4.656.

Edelmann, L., & Hirschhorn, K. (2009). Clinical utility of array CGH for the detection of chromosomal imbalances associated with mental retardation and multiple congenital anomalies. *Annals of the New York Academy of Sciences, 1151*, 157–166. doi:10.1111/j.1749-6632.2008.03610.

Emilsson, V., Thorleifsson, G., Zhang, B., Leonardson, A. S., Zink, F., Zhu, J.,… Stefansson, K. (2008). Genetics of gene expression and its effect on disease. *Nature, 452*, 423–428. doi:10.1038/nature06758.

Fisher, S. E., Vargha-Khadem, F., Watkins, K. E., Monaco, A. P., & Pembrey, M. E. (1998). Localisation of a gene implicated in a severe speech and language disorder. *Nature Genetics, 18*, 168–170. doi:10.1038/ng0298-168.

Folstein, S., & Rutter, M. (1977). Infantile autism: A genetic study of 21 twin pairs. *Journal of Child Psychology and Psychiatry, 18*, 297–321.

Folstein, S. E., & Rosen-Sheidley, B. (2001). Genetics of autism: Complex aetiology for a heterogeneous disorder. *Nature Reviews Genetics, 2*, 943–955. doi:10.1038/35103559.

Folstein, S. E., Santangelo, S. L., Gilman, S. E., Piven, J., Landa, R., Lainhart, J.,… Wzorek, M. (1999). Predictors of cognitive test patterns in autism families. *Journal of Child Psychology and Psychiatry, 40*, 1117–1128.

Fombonne, E., Bolton, P., Prior, J., Jordan, H., & Rutter, M. (1997). A family study of autism: Cognitive patterns and levels in parents and siblings. *Journal of Child Psychology and Psychiatry, 38*, 667–683.

Geschwind, D. H. (2001). Sharing gene expression: An array of options. *Nature Reviews Neuroscience, 2*, 435–438. doi:10.1038/35077576.

Geschwind, D. H. (2008). Autism: Many genes, common pathways? *Cell, 135*, 391–395. doi:10.1016/j.cell.2008.10.016.

Geschwind, D. H. (2009). Advances in autism. *Annual Review of Medicine, 60*, 367–380. doi:10.1146/annurev.med.60.053107.121225.

Geschwind, D. H., & Levitt, P. (2007). Autism spectrum disorders: Developmental disconnection syndromes. *Current Opinion in Neurobiology, 17*, 103–111. doi:10.1016/j.conb.2007.01.009.

Glessner, J. T., Wang, K., Cai, G., Korvatska, O., Kim, C. E., Wood, S.,… Hakonarson, H. (2009). Autism genome-wide copy number variation reveals ubiquitin and neuronal genes. *Nature, 459*, 569–573. doi:10.1038/nature07953

Gottesman, I. I., & Gould, T. D. (2003). The endophenotype concept in psychiatry: Etymology and strategic intentions. *American Journal of Psychiatry, 160*, 636–645.

Gupta, A. R., & State, M. W. (2007). Recent advances in the genetics of autism. *Biological Psychiatry, 61*, 429–437. doi:10.1016/j.biopsych.2006.06.020.

International Molecular Genetics Study of Autism Consortium (1998). A full genome screen for autism with evidence for linkage to a region on chromosome 7q. *Human Molecular Genetics, 7*, 571–578.

Just, M. A., Cherkassky, V. L., Keller, T. A., Kana, R. K., & Minshew, N. J. (2007). Functional and anatomical cortical underconnectivity in autism: Evidence from an fMRI study of an executive function task and corpus callosum morphometry. *Cerebral Cortex, 17*, 951–961. doi:10.1093/cercor/bhl006.

Just, M. A., Cherkassky, V. L., Keller, T. A., & Minshew, N. J. (2004). Cortical activation and synchronization during sentence comprehension in high-functioning autism: Evidence of underconnectivity. *Brain, 127*, 1811–1821. doi:10.1093/brain/awh199.

Konopka, G., Bomar, J. M., Winden, K., Coppola, G., Jonsson, Z. O., Gao, F.,… Geschwind, D. H. (2009). Human-specific transcriptional regulation of CNS development genes by FOXP2. *Nature, 462*, 213–217. doi:10.1038/nature08549.

Kumar, R. A., KaraMohamde, S., Sudi, J., Conrad, D. F., Brune, C., Badner, J. A.,… Christian, S. L. (2008). Recurrent 16p11.2 microdeletions in autism. *Human Molecular Genetics, 17*, 628–638. doi:10.1093/hmg/ddm376.

Lai, C. S., Fisher, S. E., Hurst, J. A., Vargha-Khadem, F., & Monaco, A. P. (2001). A forkhead-domain gene is mutated in a severe speech and language disorder. *Nature, 413*, 519–523. doi:10.1038/35097076.

Lajonchere, C. M. & AGRE Consortium (2010). Changing the landscape of autism research: The Autism Resource Exchange. *Neuron, 68*, 187–191. doi:10.1016/j.neuron.2010.10.009.

Lamb, J. A., Moore, J., Bailey, A., & Monaco, A. P. (2000). Autism: Recent molecular genetic advances [published erratum appears in (2000) *Human Molecular Genetics*, 9, 1461]. *Human Molecular Genetics, 9*, 861–868.

Liu, J., Nyholt, D. R., Magnussen, P., Parano, E., Pavone, P., Geschwind, D.,… Gilliam, T. C. (2001). A genomewide screen for autism susceptibility loci. *American Journal of Human Genetics, 69*, 327–340.

Liu, X. Q., Paterson, A. D., & Szatmari, P. (2008). Genome-wide linkage analyses of quantitative and categorical autism subphenotypes. *Biological Psychiatry, 64*, 561–570. doi:10.1016/j.biopsych.2008.05.023.

Marshall, C. R., Noor, A., Vincent, J. B., Lionel, A. C., Feuk, L., Skaug, J., & Scherer, S. W. (2008). Structural variation of chromosomes in autism spectrum disorder. *American Journal of Human Genetics, 82*, 477–488. doi:10/1016/j.ajhg.2007.12.009.

McCarthy, S. E., Makarov, V., Kirov, G., Addington, A. M., McClellan, J., Yoon, S.,… Sebat, J. (2009). Microduplications of 16p11.2 are associated with schizophrenia. *Nature Genetics, 41*, 1223–1227. doi:10.1038/ng.474.

Mefford, H. C., Cooper, G. M., Zerr, T., Smith, J. D., Baker, C., Shafer, N.,… Eichler, E. E. (2009). A method for rapid, targeted CNV genotyping identifies rare variants associated with neurocognitive disease. *Genome Research, 19*, 1579–1585. doi:10.1101/gr.094987.109.

Monaco, A. P. (2007). Multivariate linkage analysis of specific language impairment (SLI). *Annals of Human Genetics, 71*, 660–673. doi:10.1111/j.1469–1809. 2007.00361.x.

Mukamel, Z., Konopka, G., Wexler, E., Osborn, G. E., Dong, H., Bergman, M. Y., Levitt, P., & Geschwind, D. H. (2011). Regulation of MET by FOXPT, genes implicated in higher cognitive dysfunction and autism risk. *Journal of Neuroscience, 31*, 11437–11442. doi:10.1523/JNEUROSCI.0181-11.2011.

Nishimura,Y., Martin, C. L., Vazquez-Lopez, A., Spence, S. J., Alvarez-Retuerto, A. I., Sigman, M.,... Geschwind, D. H. (2007). Genome-wide expression profiling of lymphoblastoid cell lines distinguishes different forms of autism and reveals shared pathways. *Human Molecular Genetics, 16*, 1682–1698. doi:10.1093/hmg/ddm116.

O'Roak, B. J., & State, M. W. (2008). Autism genetics: Strategies, challenges, and opportunities. *Autism Research, 1*, 4–17. doi:10.1002/aur.3.

Pickles, A., Starr, E., Kazak, S., Bolton, P., Papanikolaou, K., Bailey, A.,... Rutter, M. (2000). Variable expression of the autism broader phenotype: Findings from extended pedigrees. *Journal of Child Psychology and Psychiatry, 41*, 491–502.

Piven, J., Palmer, P., Jacobi, D., Childress, D., & Arndt, S. (1997). Broader autism phenotype: Evidence from a family history study of multiple-incidence autism families. *American Journal of Psychiatry, 154*, 185–190.

Ronald, A., Happé, F., Bolton, P., Butcher, L. M., Price, T. S., Wheelwright, S.,... Plomin, R. (2006). Genetic heterogeneity between the three components of the autism spectrum: A twin study. *Journal of the American Academy of Child and Adolescent Psychiatry, 45*, 691–699. doi:10.1097/01.chi.0000215325.13058.9d.

Ronald, A., Happé, F., Price, T. S., Baron-Cohen, S., & Plomin, R. (2006). Phenotypic and genetic overlap between autistic traits at the extremes of the general population. *Journal of the American Academy of Child and Adolescent Psychiatry, 45*, 1206–1214. doi:10.1097/01.chi.0000230165.54117.41.

Rutter, M. (2000). Genetic studies of autism: From the 1970s into the millennium. *Journal of Abnormal Child Psychology, 28*, 3–14. doi:10.1023/a:1005113900068.

Sebat, J., Lakshmi, B., Malhotra, D., Troge, J., Lese-Martin, C., Walsh, T., & Wigler, M. (2007). Strong association of de novo copy number mutations with autism. *Science, 316*, 445–449. doi:10.1126/science.1138659.

Spence, S. J., Cantor, R. M., Chung, L., Kim, S., Geschwind, D. H., & Alarcón, M. (2006). Stratification based on language-related endophenotypes in autism: Attempt to replicate reported linkage. *American Journal of Medical Genetics Part B: Neuropsychiatric Genetics, 141B*, 591–598.

Stone, J. L., Merriman, B., Cantor, R. M., Yonan, A. L., Gilliam, T. C., Geschwind, D. H., & Nelson, S. F. (2004). Evidence for sex-specific risk alleles in autism spectrum disorder. *American Journal of Human Genetics, 75*, 1117–1123.

Strauss, K. A., Puffenberger, E. G., Huentelman, M. J., Gottlieb, S., Dobrin, S. E., Parod, J. M.,... Morton, D. H. (2006). Recessive symptomatic focal epilepsy and mutant contactin-associated protein-like 2. *New England Journal of Medicine, 354*, 1370–1377.

Veenstra-Vanderweele, J., Christian, S. L., & Cook, Jr., E. H. (2004). Autism as a paradigmatic complex genetic disorder. *Annual Review of Genomics and Human Genetics, 5*, 379–405. doi:10.1146/annurev.genom.5.061903.180050.

Vernes, S. C., Newbury, D. F., Abrahams, B. S., Winchester, L., Nicod, J., Groszer, M.,... Fisher, S. E. (2008). A functional genetic link between distinct developmental language disorders. *New England Journal of Medicine, 359*, 2337–2345. doi:10.1056/NEJMoa0802828.

Vissers, L. E., de Vries, B. B., & Veltman, J. A. (2010). Genomic microarrays in mental retardation: From CNV to gene, from research to diagnosis. *Journal of Medical Genetics, 47*, 289–297. doi:10.1136/jmg.2009.072942.

Vorstman, J. A., Staal, W. G., van Daalen, E., van Engeland, H., Hochstenbach, P. F., & Franke, L. (2006). Identification of novel autism candidate regions through analysis of reported cytogenetic abnormalities associated with autism. *Molecular Psychiatry, 11*, 18–28. doi:10.1038/sj.mp. 4001757.

Wang, T. H., & Wang, H. S. (2009). A genome-wide association study primer for clinicians. *Taiwanese Journal of Obstetrics and Gynecology, 48*, 89–95.

Weiss, L. A., Shen, Y., Korn, J. M., Arking, D. E., Miller, D. T., Fossdal, R.,… Daly, M. J. (2008). Association between microdeletion and microduplication at 16p11.2 and autism. *New England Journal of Medicine, 358*, 667–675. doi:10.1056/NEJMoa075974.

Yonan, A. L., Alarcón, M., Cheng, R., Magnusson, P. K., Spence, S. J., Palmer, A. A.,… Gilliam, T. C. (2003). A genomewide screen of 345 families for autism-susceptibility loci. *American Journal of Human Genetics, 73*, 886–897.

Section III

Developmental Processes in Autism

6

What Do Early Signs Tell Us about the Developmental Roots of Autism?

SUSAN E. BRYSON
Dalhousie University, Nova Scotia, Canada

Over the past several years, considerable progress has been made in identifying the earliest behavioral signs of autism. This has been made possible largely by prospective studies of infants at risk for autism or a related autism spectrum disorder (ASD) (for a review, see Zwaigenbaum et al., 2009). By virtue of their increased familial risk (Bailey, Phillips, & Rutter, 1996), infants with an older sibling with ASD have been particularly informative, as they can be assessed for signs of ASD from birth or shortly afterwards, and then evaluated with reference to their later diagnostic status. Cumulatively, this research has had a major impact on efforts aimed at the earlier detection and treatment of ASD (Bryson, Zwaigenbaum, & Roberts, 2004; Johnson & Myers, 2007). Frontline clinicians are becoming more aware of the early signs of autism, and autism-targeted, early-screening initiatives are being debated and implemented in some jurisdictions (e.g., CAIRN Conference, 2009; First Signs, 2009). Two-year-olds and even younger children are increasingly being referred for an ASD diagnostic assessment, and evidence for the efficacy of autism-specific behavioral interventions for toddlers is beginning to emerge (Brian et al., 2008; Dawson et al., 2010; Vismara & Rogers, 2008). While we await empirical validation of these various initiatives, this is all very encouraging.

Equally importantly, prospective studies of at-risk infants provide rich opportunities to advance understanding of core mechanisms in ASD. They allow us to ask questions about mechanisms at multiple levels (i.e., the psychological, neurological, and biological) that give rise to the particular, albeit variable, expression of ASD. Studies of developmental mechanisms in infants at risk for ASD have the distinct advantage of being relatively unconfounded by the secondary effects of the atypical experiences so characteristic of children diagnosed with the disorder. While such endeavors hold promise for more targeted interventions, both biological and psychosocial/behavioral, it bears emphasizing that early detection efforts raise ethical as well as scientific issues that bear careful consideration (e.g., possible costs associated with anticipated but as yet unknown rates of false positives and false negatives, and availability of even earlier, evidence-based autism-specific intervention; cf. Emanuel, Wendler, & Grady, 2000).

In this chapter, I describe a large, multi-site prospective study of at-risk infants with an older sibling with ASD being conducted in Canada (Zwaigenbaum et al., 2005). I begin by outlining our findings on early behavioral signs of autism, with special reference to the timing of symptom onset, symptom severity, and cognitive and language profiles, as well as the enigmatic sex difference in ASD. I then turn to data on temperament and to experimental work on the early development of visual attention and its relationship to temperament in ASD. Throughout, consideration will be given to the broader autism phenotype—that is, cases with some but not the full complement (i.e., number or severity) of symptoms required for a diagnosis of autism or the lesser ASD. Although preliminary, I will speculate about mechanisms that may underlie the emergence and early manifestation of ASD.

A CANADIAN STUDY OF INFANT SIBLINGS AT RISK FOR ASD

Our prospective study includes infants at increased risk for ASD (all with an older sibling with ASD; hereafter *infant siblings*) and low-risk control infants with no first- or second-degree relatives with ASD. For both groups, the only exclusionary criteria are gestation less than 37 months, birth weight less than 2,500 grams, known genetic/chromosomal or neurological disorders, and severe sensory or motor impairment. The infants are enrolled in the study between six and 12 months of age and assessed at 3- to 6-month intervals until 24 months. At 36 months, the age at which reliable and stable ASD diagnoses are currently possible (Lord & Luyster, 2006), an independent "gold-standard" ASD diagnostic assessment is conducted blind to previous data. This 36-month assessment includes the Autism Diagnostic Observation Schedule (ADOS) (Lord et al., 2000), the Autism Diagnostic Interview-Revised (ADI-R) (Lord, Rutter, & Le Couteur, 1994), and expert clinical judgment using the DSM-IV-TR (American Psychiatric Association [APA], 2000), as well as reference to the profile of findings from contemporaneous measures of cognition, language, and adaptive skills.

Upon initiating our Infant Sibling Study in 1999, the first challenge was the absence of any formal instrument for assessing signs of autism in infants (i.e., those aged 18 months or younger). To address this need, and drawing on what was known about the early emergence of autism at that time (i.e., from retrospective data sources and our joint clinical experience), we developed a direct observational measure, the Autism Observation Scale for Infants (AOSI; Bryson, Zwaigenbaum, McDermott, Rombough, & Brian, 2008), to document and monitor signs of autism systematically in infants aged six to 18 months. The AOSI is an 18-item interactive play schedule in which the relative absence or presence of particular behaviors, including aspects of visual attention and reactivity, as well as sensory-motor, social-communicative, and play development, is rated on a scale from *0* to *2* or *3*, on which *0* implies no atypicality and higher values indicate increasing deviation from the norm. Inter-rater agreement and test-retest reliability of total scores on the AOSI are good to excellent (Bryson, Zwaigenbaum, et al., 2008), and data on its predictive validity are very promising (Brian et al., 2008; Zwaigenbaum et al., 2009). Below I will provide a summary of findings on the early development of infant siblings derived from both the AOSI and standardized measures of cognition and language. However, first we turn to data on recurrence risk for ASD and related developmental problems.

RECURRENCE ESTIMATES

To date, we have followed 225 high-risk infant siblings and 92 low-risk controls until at least three years of age. At age three years, 32 of the 225 infant siblings (14.2%) met "strict" diagnostic criteria for ASD (i.e., based on the revised ADOS algorithm [Gotham, Risi, Pickles, & Lord, 2007], Risi et al's [2006] ADI-R criteria, and expert clinical judgment using DSM-IV-TR [APA, 2000]). An additional 20 cases received a "clinical" ASD diagnosis but did not meet the above ADOS and/or ADI-R criteria, yielding a total of 23.1% diagnosed cases. Our male-to-female ratio is 1.9:1 (1.7:1 for strict and 2.3:1 for the clinical-alone cases; for details, see Zwaigenbaum et al., 2012; also see Ozonoff et al., 2011).

While eligible families have rarely declined to enroll in our study, it should be noted that the socioeconomic status of our families is skewed towards the middle and upper strata. There is also some suggestion of an age-related enrollment bias in our study (i.e., a slightly higher recurrence rate for infants enrolled at age 12 vs. 6 months), raising the possibility of over-representation of symptomatic versus non-symptomatic cases enrolling at 12 months. Thus, we cannot preclude possible bias, influenced by factors such as increased parental anxiety in families who have chosen to participate.

Similarly, while our recurrence estimates of 14.2%–23.1% are comparable to those reported in other infant sibling studies (Autism Speaks BSRC Meeting, 2009), relatively small sample sizes have thus far precluded a meta-analysis of factors such as method of ascertainment, case definition, family demographics, and sex and birth order of the older ASD sibling. In the meantime, it is clear from all infant sibling cohorts that ASD recurs with a frequency much higher than the 5%–10% estimated from the limited earlier data based on a narrower definition of ASD (Bailey et al., 1996).

We are surprised to note that our male-to-female ratio of about 2:1 is smaller than the 3–4:1 typically reported in population-based epidemiological studies of autism/ASD (for reviews, see Bryson, 1996, 1997; Fombonne, 2009; Gillberg & Wing, 1999). Our infant sibling cohort with ASD differs in that we have identified a relatively large number of more able girls and see no evidence of the usual sex difference in measured intelligence, whether using strict or clinical diagnostic criteria (Zwaigenbaum et al., 2012). This stands in contrast to more than three decades of research in which females with autism, and the more inclusive ASD, have been disproportionately represented in the lower IQ ranges (Fombonne, 2009; Lord, Schopler, & Revicki, 1982; Wing, 1981). Interestingly, our data resemble the 2:1 male-to-female ratio reported for more cognitively compromised children with ASD (e.g., Bryson, Bradley, Thompson, & Wainwright, 2008; Bryson & Smith, 1998; Gillberg & Wing, 1999). One outstanding question is whether more able females are less "autistic" than their male counterparts (cf. McLennan, Lord, & Schopler, 1993) and thus less likely to be diagnosed with ASD, particularly after the age of three years (an issue to be addressed as we follow our infant sibling cohort). While this might reflect social or other advantages conferred on females, claims that females may be less severely affected by other childhood disorders (e.g., specific reading disorder; Olson, 2002) implicate a more general sex-related phenomenon rather than something specific to ASD. In other words, ASD may simply represent the normal variation in sex-linked traits that places males at a somewhat higher risk for a range of developmental disorders (cf. Geschwind & Behan, 1982). On this assumption, it might be important to consider the possibility of a lower sex ratio (e.g., 2 vs. 3–4 males to 1 female) in the search for sex-linked genetic mechanisms in ASD. Evidence to date suggests that this might be particularly so for cases at higher genetic risk (i.e., those from multiplex vs. simplex families; cf. Zwaigenbaum et al., 2012).

Finally, having assessed over 400 infants, our findings suggest that infant siblings represent a wide spectrum, from those with virtually no autistic traits/symptoms to those who are severely affected by autism. While progress has been made in specifying core features of ASD in older children and adults (Frith & Happé, 1994; Happé & Frith, 2006), we have only begun to study their early manifestations in at-risk infants. Particularly striking are language and communication problems, social inhibition/anxiety, behavioral or cognitive inflexibility, and poor regulation of emotion. However, given the lack of well-operationalized and/or validated criteria for these constructs, particularly in children aged three years or younger, and our relatively short-term follow-up, little is known about the severity or stability of these problems.

Findings from the Mullen Scales of Early Learning (Mullen, 1995), a standardized measure of intellectual development, suggest that a substantial proportion of non-ASD infant siblings are at increased risk for language or more global developmental delays. At 36 months, 6.9% of our non-ASD siblings had low receptive and/or expressive language scores or global delays, based on a criterion of one and a half standard deviations below the norm on relevant Mullen subscales/scales. As we follow our entire infant sibling cohort into the early school years, the long-term significance of these and other early atypicalities in development will become apparent.

THE EARLY EMERGENCE OF ASD

Evidence from the AOSI, our direct measure of behavior, indicates that signs of autism begin to emerge between six and 12 months of age (Bryson et al., 2007; Zwaigenbaum et al., 2005; also see Ozonoff et al., 2010, for a replication). That is, ASD is not detectable at six months, but becomes increasingly evident by the end of the first year of life. Based on total AOSI scores, and using 36-month diagnostic status as the criterion, discrimination among groups (infant siblings with ASD, their non-ASD counterparts, and low-risk controls) is poor at six months but increases dramatically by 12 months. It may be significant that 12 months is also the age at which head circumference has been reported to increase in ASD (e.g., Cody-Hazlett et al., 2005). Details on findings from the AOSI, including its predictive validity at 12 months, will be provided in a subsequent paper (Bryson & Zwaigenbaum, in press), but two points bear emphasizing.

First, there is wide variability in the timing of onset, nature, and course of early ASD signs. As detailed in Bryson et al. (2007), there are two main subgroups of infant siblings with ASD: one with an early, 6- to 12-month onset of symptoms; and another with a later, 12- to 18-month onset. Infants with earlier symptoms appear more severely autistic, particularly as reflected in their lack of social engagement/responsiveness. While this "earlier–later onset" characterization captures the vast majority, there are cases, the exact proportion of which remains unclear, who show clear early signs of ASD (i.e., at 12 to 24 months, they are indistinguishable from those later diagnosed with ASD) but whose trajectories became more typical. The mechanisms by which some genetically high-risk toddlers shift into a more typical developmental trajectory are unknown. In other cases, infants with average or above-average cognitive and language development did not develop signs of ASD until after two years of age.

Second, infant siblings later diagnosed with ASD can be distinguished, as a group, from non-ASD siblings and controls by lower cognitive, communicative, and language scores by as early as 12 months of age (Bryson et al., 2007; Mitchell et al., 2006). Again, however, there was considerable variability within the ASD group (12-month composite Mullen standard scores ranged from 64 to 120). Critically, despite largely average intellectual ability at 12 months, about 20% of the ASD siblings showed a striking plateau in cognitive development between 12 and 36 months of age (resulting in composite Mullen standard scores of 50 or less at 24 and/or 36 months) (Bryson et al., 2007). All of these infants had the earlier, 6- to 12-month symptom onset pattern, and the deterioration was independent of sex. These findings argue for a re-conceptualization of regression in ASD, defined largely in terms of speech loss (e.g., Lord, Shulman, & DiLavore, 2004; but also see Luyster et al., 2005). Many of the infants described above had not developed any speech, although clearly there was a major disruption in their development.

Our findings also raise the question of whether very early and severe symptoms of autism, notably withdrawal and lack of engagement with others and things, interfere critically with subsequent cognitive and language development (cf. Schore, 1994). In other words, intellectual and language disability might not simply co-exist with autism, but rather be a product of it. In an attempt to identify possible mechanisms in the early emergence of ASD, we have also considered the role of temperament, data to which we now turn.

EARLY TEMPERAMENT PROFILES IN INFANT SIBLINGS

Temperament is defined as constitutionally based individual differences in reactivity and regulation (Rothbart & Bates, 1998). The reactive aspects of temperament (i.e., behavioral approach or withdrawal) are closely tied to motivation, whereas the regulatory aspects are linked to effortful (and ultimately executive) attentional control. Temperament is of particular interest because its various dimensions are more directly linked to underlying psychobiological mechanisms, governed by specific genes, than surface behaviors or symptoms (Rothbart & Posner, 2006; Whittle, Allen, Lubman, & Yücel, 2006). While temperament has been studied in children and adults with ASD (e.g., Hepburn & Stone, 2006; Janes, 2001; Soderstrom, Rastam, & Gillberg, 2002) and in their non-ASD relatives (e.g., Bailey, Palferman, Heavey, & Le Couteur, 1998; Hughes, Plumet, & Leboyer, 1999), we have extended this research by prospectively examining infants at increased risk for ASD (Garon et al., 2009). Specifically, Garon and colleagues asked three main questions:

1. Does temperament at 24 months distinguish ASD siblings from non-ASD siblings and controls at 36 months?
2. Does temperament predict 36-month diagnostic status beyond gender, symptom severity, and IQ at 24 months?
3. Does temperament at 24 months distinguish ASD subgroups at 36 months?

These questions were addressed by asking parents of our at-risk sibling cohort and low-risk controls to complete a temperament questionnaire, the Toddler Behavior Assessment Questionnaire-Revised (TBAQ-R) (Goldsmith, 1996; Rothbart, Ellis, Rueda, & Posner, 2003), as part of our routine 24-month battery.

Our temperament findings for toddlers with ASD are remarkably similar to those reported in older children and adults with ASD (e.g., Janes, 2001; Soderstrom et al., 2002), with several caveats. A discriminant function analysis, computed on the 24-month temperament subscale scores, revealed two significant functions (Garon, Bryson, & Smith, 2008). The first function, labeled *Behavioral/Social Approach* (BA), includes data from the TBAQ-R items measuring Positive Anticipation (largely social), Attention Shifting, and Activity Level, and accounted for 26.4% of the variance in temperament scores. The second function, labeled *Effortful Emotion Regulation* (EER), consisted of scale items assessing Inhibitory Control, Attention Shifting, Attention Focus, High Pleasure, Social Fear, Anger, and Soothability, accounting for 13.2% of the variance. Importantly, the BA function, defined by low positive anticipation, poor attention shifting, and high activity, distinguished ASD siblings from both their non-ASD counterparts and low-risk controls. In contrast, the EER function, defined by poor attention control, low positive emotion, high negative emotion, and difficultly being soothed, distinguished the low-risk controls from the high-risk siblings, regardless of later diagnosis. Note further that, at 24 months, temperament not only adds significantly to the prediction of diagnostic status (ASD vs. non-ASD) beyond symptom severity and IQ, but also moderates ASD symptom severity (indexed by ADOS algorithm scores; Lord et al., 2000), as predicted by Mundy and colleagues (2007).

Finally, within the sibling group, a cluster analysis revealed two ASD subgroups distinguished by age of diagnosis (corresponding to age of symptom onset), symptom severity, IQ, and BA. Infant siblings with lower BA have earlier diagnoses (symptom onset), more severe symptoms, and lower IQs, and may represent an extreme version of Sutton and colleagues' (2005) ASD subgroup with right cortical asymmetry. Low BA implicates the ascending dopamine/motivational pathways (e.g., Panksepp, 1998); a major disruption in these pathways may result in the emotional apathy and extreme withdrawal at the core of severe autism. In contrast, the EER component of temperament did not distinguish ASD subgroups or, as noted above, even the ASD siblings from their non-ASD counterparts. The implication here is that the broader autism phenotype (including cases not diagnosed with ASD) is characterized by poor descending cortical control of attention and emotion regulation. Below I describe our related work on the early development of visual-spatial attention and its association with emotion regulation.

VISUAL-SPATIAL ATTENTION AND EMOTION REGULATION IN INFANT SIBLINGS

In experimental work with children and adults with ASD, my graduate students and I have examined visual-spatial attention and its component *disengage*, *shift*, and *engage operations*. This early-developing form of attention, instantiated in neural substrates of the posterior attention system (primarily in the non-dominant, usually right, hemisphere), is of particular interest because of its critical role in the regulation of emotion, as well as various forms of learning (Posner, 1988; Rothbart & Posner, 2006). In order to move attention in visual space and thereby optimize the quality of "new" visual input, the infant must first *disengage* from the current focus and then *shift* and *engage* attention at the new target location so as to align the processing resources of the visual system. Development of the disengage operation also allows the infant to withdraw attention from distressing events and thereby regulate his/her state (Rothbart, Ziaie, & O'Boyle, 1992).

The posterior attention system and its spatially selective component operations form part of a larger network of interrelated attention systems that are organized at distinct levels and mediated by different neural regions (Posner, 1988; Posner & Dehaene, 1994). These include both a subcortical vigilance system, which maintains alertness and sustained attention, and an anterior executive system, which exerts volitional control and recruits resources necessary for goal-directed behavior. Towards the latter part of the first year of life, development of the frontal cortex allows the infant to exert increasing volitional control over visual orienting (Colombo, 2004; Johnson, 1990; Rothbart & Posner, 2006). Prior to this, the infant's attention is driven largely by external input, to which responses of the posterior attention system are relatively quick and automatic.

Evidence of the early development of the shift and disengage operations of visual attention comes largely from a simple visual-orienting task known as the Gap task. In this task, the infant's attention is engaged on a centrally located, colorful, and dynamic attractor stimulus when a second, peripheral stimulus is presented. The time it takes the infant to initiate an eye movement (saccade) to the second, peripheral stimulus is measured. The critical distinction is whether the timing of the two stimuli overlaps (resulting in both stimuli present on the screen at the same time) or not. Conditions under which a gap in timing occurs provide a measure of the shift operation: Offset of the attractor stimulus prior to onset of the peripheral stimulus serves to automatically disengage attention such that only a shift is required. Conditions in which the two stimuli overlap (i.e., the two compete for attention) provide a measure of the disengage operation: Attention must be disengaged first from the attractor stimulus before it can be shifted to the peripheral stimulus.

Using variants of the Gap Task, findings indicate that the disengage mechanism becomes operative at three to four months of age in typically developing infants, reflecting the increasing influence of cortical input (Atkinson, 1984, 2000; Hood & Atkinson, 1993; Johnson, Posner, & Rothbart, 1991, 1994; McConnell & Bryson, 2005). Overall, saccadic latencies to disengage and shift attention decrease over the first six months of age. At all ages, responses are slower during the overlap (Disengage) condition than the gap (Shift) condition, although this effect is largest in the younger infants and negligible in four- to six-month-olds. Moreover, and consistent with the claims of Rothbart and colleagues (1992), ease of disengaging attention at four to six months is associated with more positive emotion, less distress, and enhanced capacity to be soothed, as measured by parent-completed temperament questionnaires (Harman, Rothbart, & Posner, 1997; Johnson et al., 1991; McConnell & Bryson, 2005). Prior to four months of age, infants are able to focus their attention selectively, but once engaged on a particular stimulus, they have difficulty disengaging and thus moving their attention elsewhere. Rather, they tend to remain fixated for prolonged periods, a phenomenon known as *obligatory looking* (Stechler & Latz, 1966) or *sticky fixation* (Hood, 1995).

In related work, we and others have provided evidence of particular difficulties disengaging attention in ASD (Kawakubo et al., 2007; Kawakubo & Maekawa, 2005; Landry & Bryson, 2004; Rombough, 1998; also see Bryson, Landry, et al., 2004). Relative to matched controls, children with ASD are distinguished by abnormally long disengage latencies and associated distress behaviors (e.g., excessive mouthing, rapid and shallow breathing, and gaze avoidance) (Landry & Bryson, 2004). Indeed, on 20% of trials, children with ASD aged three to 12 years failed to disengage at all (i.e., remained stuck on one of two competing stimuli for the 8 s trial duration), similar to reports of typical two-month-olds (e.g., McConnell & Bryson, 2005). Independent of both chronological and mental age, children with ASD also demonstrated an asymmetry in visual orienting—that is, particular difficulty disengaging and moving attention towards the left side of space (Rombough, 1998). Left-sided assymmetries in disengaging and orienting attention have also been reported in older children and adults with ASD, on Posner's (1988) visual cueing task (Casey, Gordon, Mannheim, & Rumsey, 1993; Wainwright-Sharp & Bryson, 1993, 1996). Using fMRI during a similar visual orienting task, there is also evidence in adults with ASD of more generalized cortical activation to targets in the left visual field (Belmonte & Yurgelun-Todd, 2003).

Building on our preliminary findings with infant siblings (McMullen, 2004; Zwiagenbaum et al., 2005), we asked whether impaired disengagement might serve as an early marker of ASD (Bryson et al., under review). High-risk and control infants were assessed on the Gap Task at six and 12 months, and each time, their parents completed the Infant Behavior Questionnaire (Rothbart, 1981), a measure of temperament. Whereas no group differences were found for shift trials at either age, the groups differed in mean latencies to disengage attention at 12 (but not six) months. A significant linear effect showed that high-risk infant siblings who were later diagnosed with ASD took longer to disengage than the low-risk controls, with the non-ASD siblings falling in between. The ASD infant siblings were further distinguished from both the non-ASD siblings and controls by a left-sided asymmetry in disengaging attention, replicating findings with older children and adults (Casey et al., 1993; Rombough, 1998; Wainwright-Sharp & Bryson, 1993, 1996). Moreover, at 12 months, long left-directed disengage latencies were associated not only with an

ASD diagnosis, but also with a temperament profile characterized by low activity, reactivity and duration of orientation, high irritability, and difficulty being soothed. Long right-directed disengage latencies, in contrast, were only marginally related to ASD diagnostic status and high irritability.

Critical here are four main findings: (1) the age at which the disengage problem emerges in infants at risk for ASD; (2) the linear relationship between disengagement and diagnostic status in at-risk and control infants; (3) the disengage asymmetry in infants later diagnosed with ASD; and (4) the association between prolonged left-directed disengage latencies and key dimensions of temperament. Assuming that the anterior (frontal) attention system begins to develop by the end of the first year of life (e.g., Colombo, 2004; Johnson, 1990), our finding that the disengage problem emerges at 12 months could be taken as evidence of early dysfunctional volitional or executive control of attention in ASD (Bryson et al., under review). Executive dysfunction is well documented in older children and adults with ASD and in their non-ASD relatives (for reviews, see Bryson, Landry, & Wainwright, 1997; Hill, 2004; Ozonoff, 1995), although virtually nothing is known about its precursors. At 12 months, evidence of a linear relationship between disengaging attention and ASD diagnostic category, with subtle impairments in some non-ASD siblings, suggests that impaired disengagement forms part of the broader autism phenotype (Elsabbagh et al., 2009) and may be a precursor of the executive problems documented later in life.

At the same time, and not necessarily inconsistent with early executive dysfunction, the striking and virtually universal difficulty disengaging attention towards the left side of space, evident only in the ASD siblings, implicates right hemisphere dysfunction (cf. Orekhova et al., 2009; Roberts et al., 2010). Disruption in the *attention-arousal-activation* system (Heilman, Bowers, Valenstein, & Watson, 1986; Posner, 1988) may produce over- and/or under-activation of the right hemisphere, resulting in the unilateral spatial neglect-like phenomenon we predicted in ASD (Bryson, Wainwright-Sharp, & Smith, 1990). This possibility might be explored further through brain-imaging studies examining asymmetries in cortical activation.

The right hemisphere has also been implicated in nonverbal aspects of communication involving emotion and its regulation, particularly the regulation of negative states (Davidson, 2000; Schore, 1994; Wismer Fries & Pollak, 2007). Our finding that long left-directed disengage latencies are associated with key dimensions of temperament (notably high irritability and difficulty being soothed) is consistent with the claim that attention plays a critical role in regulating state (Rothbart et al., 1992) and with evidence implicating the right hemisphere in the regulation of negative emotion (Davidson, 2000; Schore, 1994; Wismer Fries & Pollak, 2007).

SUMMARY AND CONCLUDING REMARKS

In summary, our prospective infant sibling study reveals that ASD recurs in families with a frequency much greater than previously thought and perhaps with a lower sex ratio than reported in earlier studies. The latter finding reflects the inclusion of more able girls, who may appear less severely affected as they age. As we have documented elsewhere (Bryson et al., 2007; Zwaigenbaum et al., 2005), signs of autism are not evident at six months of age, but become so by 12 months in some children with ASD. While exceptions exist, there are two broad subgroups of infant siblings with ASD: an earlier, 6- to 12-month onset subgroup that differs from a later, 12- to 18-month onset subgroup by showing more severe ASD symptoms and lower IQs. A striking decrement in cognitive development, documented between 12 months and 24 and/or 36 months in about 20% of ASD cases, is also restricted to those with earlier symptom onset. With increasing efforts aimed at very early intervention, a critical outstanding question is whether intervention beginning at 12 months could place these children on a more positive trajectory of development.

At 24 months, ASD siblings are distinguished by a temperament profile marked by low Behavioral/Social Approach, manifested as extreme withdrawal in the early onset subgroup (Garon et al., 2009), which may contribute to their compromised cognitive and language development. In addition, the entire infant sibling cohort is distinguished by poor Effortful Emotion Regulation, suggesting that the regulatory (vs. reactive) component of temperament characterizes the broader autism phenotype. Finally, at 12 months, evidence of impaired attentional disengagement in the ASD siblings, and to a lesser extent in their non-ASD counterparts, suggests that this is both an early marker for ASD and a core dimension of the broader autism phenotype (cf. Happé & Frith, 2006). Several factors, notably the left-directed asymmetry in disengagement, its age of emergence, and its association with high irritability and poor emotion regulation, argue for right hemisphere dysfunction in ASD, possibly involving compromised executive/frontal input to the posterior attention system, although we await more direct evidence. Future studies might also determine whether problems with disengagement contribute to, or even underlie, other key features of ASD. These might include the development of joint attention and related social-communicative skills, as well as the ability to flexibly shift set and to process information at both global and local levels (e.g., Bryson, Landry, et al., 2004; Garon et al., 2009; Happé & Frith, 2006).

Finally, the present findings contribute to a growing body of research that has important implications for the earlier detection and treatment of ASD. The potential benefits to the many children and families affected by ASD are far reaching and well worth our efforts. Critically, these benefits depend on a commitment to targeted interventions that reflect advances in research on basic mechanisms in ASD.

ACKNOWLEDGMENTS

Many thanks to my collaborators (L. Zwaigenbaum, N. Garon, J. Brian, I. Smith, W. Roberts, and P. Szatmari), and all the families who have contributed to our research. I also thank Marcel Adam Just, an anonymous reviewer, and Jeff MacLeod for their helpful comments on an earlier draft of this manuscript.

REFERENCES

American Psychiatric Association (2000). *Diagnostic and statistical manual* (4th ed., text revision). Washington, DC: American Psychiatric Association.

Atkinson, J. (1984). Human visual development over the first six months of life: A review and a hypothesis. *Human Neurobiology, 3*, 61–74.

Atkinson, J. (2000). *The developing visual brain*. Oxford: Oxford Medical Publication.

Autism Speaks BSRC Meeting (2009, January). Sessions of the Annual *Baby Sibs Research Consortium (BSRC)*, Miami, FL.

Bailey, A., Palferman, S., Heavey, L., & Le Couteur, A. (1998). Autism: The phenotype in relatives. *Journal of Autism and Developmental Disorders, 28*, 369–392.

Bailey, A., Phillips, W., & Rutter, M. (1996). Autism: Towards an integration of clinical, genetic, neuropsychological, and neurobiological perspectives. *Journal of Child Psychology and Psychiatry, 37*, 89–126.

Belmonte, M. K., & Yurgelun-Todd, D. A. (2003). Functional anatomy of impaired selective attention and compensatory processing in autism. *Brain Research: Cognitive Brain Research, 17*, 651–664.

Brian, J., Bryson, S. E., Garon, N., Roberts, W., Smith, I. M., Szatmari, P., & Zwaigenbaum, L. (2008). Clinical assessment of autism in high-risk 18-month-olds. *Autism, 12*, 433–456.

Bryson, S. E. (1996). Brief report: Epidemiology of autism. *Journal of Autism and Developmental Disorders, 26*, 165–167.

Bryson, S. E. (1997). Epidemiology of autism: Overview and issues outstanding. In D. J. Cohen & F. R. Volkmar (Eds.), *Handbook of autism and pervasive developmental disorders* (2nd ed.) (pp. 41–46). New York, NY: Wiley & Sons.

Bryson, S. E., Bradley, E. A., Thompson, A., & Wainwright, A. (2008). Prevalence of autism among adolescents with intellectual disabilities. *Canadian Journal of Psychiatry, 53*, 449–459.

Bryson, S. E., Garon, N., McMullen, T., Brian, J., Smith, I., Roberts, W., & Zwaigenbaum, L. (under review). Impaired disengagement of attention and its relationship to emotion regulation in infants at high risk for ASD.

Bryson, S. E., Landry, R., Czapinski, P., McConnell, B., Rombough, V., & Wainwright, A. (2004). Autistic spectrum disorders: Causal mechanisms and recent findings on attention and emotion. *International Journal of Special Education, 19*, 14–22.

Bryson, S. E., Landry, R., & Wainwright, A. (1997). A componential view of executive function in autism: Review of recent evidence. In J. A. Burack & J. T. Enns (Eds.), *Attention, development, and psychopathology* (pp. 232–262). New York, NY: Guilford Press.

Bryson, S. E., & Smith, I. M. (1998). Epidemiology of autism: Prevalence, associated characteristics, and implications for research and service delivery. *Mental Retardation and Developmental Disabilities Research Reviews, 4*, 97–103.

Bryson, S. E., Wainwright-Sharp, A., & Smith, I. M. (1990). Autism: A developmental spatial neglect syndrome? In J. Enns (Ed.), *The development of attention: Research and theory* (pp. 405–427). Amsterdam: Elsevier.

Bryson, S. E. & Zwaigenbaum, L. (in press). The Autism Observation Scale for Infants. In V. B. Patel, V. R. Preedy & C. R. Martin (Eds.), *A comprehensive guide to autism*. Springer.

Bryson, S. E., Zwaigenbaum, L., Brian, J., Roberts, W., Szatmari, P., Rombough, V., & McDermott, C. (2007). A prospective case series of high-risk infants who developed autism. *Journal of Autism and Developmental Disorders, 37*, 12–24.

Bryson, S. E., Zwaigenbaum, L., McDermott, C., Rombough, V., & Brian, J. (2008). The Autism Observation Scale for Infants: Scale development and reliability data. *Journal of Autism and Developmental Disorders, 38*, 731–738.

Bryson, S. E., Zwaigenbaum, L., & Roberts, W. (2004). The early detection of autism in clinical practice. *Paediatrics and Child Health, 9*, 219–221.

CAIRN Conference (2009, October). *Research priorities in autism spectrum disorders: A forum for sharing and learning*. Sessions of the Annual Meeting of the Canadian Autism Intervention Research Network (CAIRN), Toronto, ON.

Casey, B. J., Gordon, C. T., Mannheim, G. B., & Rumsey, J. M. (1993). Dysfunctional attention in autistic savants. *Journal of Clinical and Experimental Neuropsychology, 15*, 933–946.

Cody-Hazlett, H., Poe, M., Gerig, G., Smith, R. G., Provenzale, J., Ross, A., & Piven, J. (2005). Magnetic resonance imaging and head circumference study of brain size in autism: Birth through age two years. *Archives of General Psychiatry, 62*, 1366–1376.

Colombo, J. (2004). Visual attention in infancy: Process and product in early cognitive development. In M. I. Posner (Ed.), *Cognitive neuroscience of attention* (pp. 329–341). New York, NY: Guilford Press.

Davidson, R. J. (2000). Affective style, psychopathology, and resilience: Brain mechanisms and plasticity. *American Psychologist, 55*, 1196–1214.

Dawson, G., Rogers, S., Munson, J., Smith, M., Winter, J., Greenson, J., & Varley, J. (2010). Randomized, controlled trial of an intervention for toddlers with autism: The Early Start Denver Model. *Pediatrics, 125*, 17–23.

Elsabbagh, M., Volein, A., Holmboe, K., Tucker, L., Csibra, G., Baron-Cohen, S., & Johnson, M. H. (2009). Visual orienting in the early broader autism phenotype: Disengagement and facilitation. *Journal of Child Psychology and Psychiatry, 50*, 637–642.

Emanuel, E. J., Wendler, D., & Grady, C. (2000). What makes clinical research ethical? *Journal of the American Medical Association, 283*, 2701–2711.

First Signs (2009). Developmental disability, early intervention, developmental delays, autism screening and early intervention autism: First signs. Available at: www.firstsigns.org.

Fombonne, E. (2009). Epidemiology of pervasive developmental disorders. *Pediatric Research, 65*, 591–598.

Frith, U., & Happé, F. (1994). Autism: Beyond "theory of mind." *Cognition, 50*, 115–132.

Garon, N., Bryson, S. E., & Smith, I. M. (2008). Executive function in preschoolers: A review using an integrative framework. *Psychological Bulletin, 134*, 31–60.

Garon, N., Bryson, S. E., Zwaigenbaum, L., Smith, I., Brian, J., Roberts, W., & Szatmari, P. (2009). Temperament and its relationship to autistic symptoms in a high-risk infant sib cohort. *Journal of Abnormal Child Psychology, 37*, 59–78.

Geschwind, N., & Behan, P. (1982). Left-handedness: Association with immune disease, migraine, and developmental learning disorder. *Proceedings of the National Academy of Sciences of the United States of America, 79*, 5097–5100.

Gillberg, C., & Wing, L. (1999). Autism: Not an extremely rare disorder. *Acta Psychiatrica Scandinavica, 99*, 399–406.

Goldsmith, H. H. (1996). Studying temperament via construction of the Toddler Behavior Assessment Questionnaire. *Child Development, 67*, 218–235.

Gotham, K., Risi, S., Pickles, A., & Lord, C. (2007). The Autism Diagnostic Observation Schedule: Revised algorithms for improved diagnostic validity. *Journal of Autism and Developmental Disorders, 37*, 613–627.

Happé, F., & Frith, U. (2006). The weak coherence account: Detail-focused cognitive style in autism spectrum disorders. *Journal of Autism and Developmental Disorders, 36*, 5–25.

Harman, C., Rothbart, M. K., & Posner, M. I. (1997). Distress and attention interactions in early infancy. *Motivation and Emotion, 21*, 27–43.

Heilman, K. M., Bowers, D., Valenstein, E., & Watson, R. T. (1986). The right hemisphere: Neuropsychological functions. *Journal of Neurosurgery, 64*, 693–704.

Hepburn, S. L., & Stone, W. L. (2006). Using Carey Temperament Scales to assess behavioral style in children with autism spectrum disorders. *Journal of Autism and Developmental Disorders, 36*, 637–642.

Hill, E. L. (2004). Executive dysfunction in autism. *Trends in Cognitive Sciences*, 8, 26–32.

Hood, B. M. (1995). Shift of visual attention in the infant: A neuroscience approach. In C. Rovee-Collier, & L. P. Lipsitt (Eds.), *Advances in infancy research* (pp. 163–216). Norwood, NJ: Ablex.

Hood, B. M., & Atkinson, J. (1993). Disengaging visual attention in the infant and adult. *Infant Behavior and Development, 16*, 405–422.

Hughes, C., Plumet, M. H., & Leboyer, M. (1999). Towards a cognitive phenotype for autism: Increased prevalence of executive dysfunction and superior spatial span amongst siblings of children with autism. *Journal of Child Psychology and Psychiatry, 40*, 705–718.

Janes, J. (2001). Executive function, emotion regulation, and maternal report of child temperament in children with PDD. Unpublished Master of Arts Thesis, University of Guelph, Guelph, ON.

Johnson, C. P., & Myers, S. M. (2007). Identification and evaluation of children with autism spectrum disorders. *Pediatrics, 120*, 1183–1215.

Johnson, M. H. (1990). Cortical maturation and the development of visual attention in early infancy. *Journal of Cognitive Neuroscience, 2*, 81–95.

Johnson, M. H., Posner, M. I., & Rothbart, M. K. (1991). Components of visual orienting in early infancy: Contingency learning, anticipatory looking, and disengaging. *Journal of Cognitive Neuroscience, 3*, 335–344.

Johnson, M. H., Posner, M. I., & Rothbart, M. K. (1994). Facilitation of saccades toward a covertly attended location in early infancy. *Psychological Science, 5*, 90–93.

Kawakubo, Y., Kasai, K., Okazaki, S., Hosokawa-Kakurai, M., Watanabe, K., Kuwabara, H., & Maekawa, H. (2007). Electrophysiological abnormalities of spatial attention in adults with autism during the gap overlap task. *Clinical Neurophysiology, 118*, 1464–1471.

Kawakubo, Y., & Maekawa, H. (2005). Spatial attention in individuals with autism: Gap overlap task with discrimination. *Japanese Journal of Special Education, 42*, 321–328.

Landry, R., & Bryson, S. E. (2004). Impaired disengagement of attention in young children with autism. *Journal of Child Psychology and Psychiatry, 45*, 1115–1122.

Lord, C., & Luyster, R. (2006). Early diagnosis of children with autism spectrum disorders. *Clinical Neuroscience Research, 6*, 189–194.

Lord, C., Risi, S., Lambrecht, L., Cook, E. H., Leventhal, B. L., DiLavore, P. C., & Rutter, M. (2000). The Autism Diagnostic Observation Schedule-Generic: A standard measure of social and communication deficits associated with the spectrum of autism. *Journal of Autism and Developmental Disorders, 30*, 205–223.

Lord, C., Rutter, M., & Le Couteur, A. (1994). Autism Diagnostic Interview-Revised: A revised version of a diagnostic interview for caregivers of individuals with possible pervasive developmental disorders. *Journal of Autism and Developmental Disorders, 24*, 659–685.

Lord, C., Schopler, E., & Revicki, D. (1982). Sex differences in autism. *Journal of Autism and Development Disorders, 12*, 317–330.

Lord, C., Shulman, C., & DiLavore, P. (2004). Regression and word loss in autistic spectrum disorders. *Journal of Child Psychology and Psychiatry, 45*, 936–955.

Luyster, R., Richler, J., Risi, S., Hsu, W. L., Dawson, G., Bernier, R., & Lord, C. (2005). Early regression in social communication in autism spectrum disorders: A CPEA study. *Developmental Neuropsychology, 27*, 311–336.

McConnell, B. A., & Bryson, S. E. (2005). Visual attention and temperament: Developmental data from the first six months of life. *Infant Behavior & Development, 28*, 537–544.

McLennan, J. D., Lord, C., & Schopler, E. (1993). Sex differences in higher functioning people with autism. *Journal of Autism and Developmental Disorders, 23*, 217–227.

McMullen, T. (2004). Disengagement of visual attention in infant siblings of children with autism. Unpublished master's thesis, York University, Toronto, ON.

Mitchell, S., Brian, J., Zwaigenbaum, L., Roberts, W., Szatmari, P., Smith, I., & Bryson, S. (2006). Early language and communication development of infants later diagnosed with autism spectrum disorders. *Journal of Developmental and Behavioral Pediatrics, 27*, S69–S78.

Mullen, E. M. (1995). *Mullen Scales of Early Learning* (AGS Edition). Circle Pines, MN: American Guidance Service Publishing.

Mundy, P. C., Henderson, H. A., Inge, A. P., & Coman, D. C. (2007). The modifier model of autism and social development in higher functioning children. *Research and Service for Persons with Severe Disabilities, 32*, 1–16.

Olson R. K. (2002). Dyslexia: Nature and nurture. *Dyslexia, 8*(3), 143–159.

Orekhova, E. V., Stroganova, T. A., Prokofiev, A. O., Nygren, G., Gillberg, C., & Elam, M. (2009). The right hemisphere fails to respond to temporal novelty in autism: Evidence from an ERP study. *Clinical Neurophysiology*. *120*(3), 520–529.

Ozonoff, S. (1995). Executive functions in autism. In E. Schopler, & G. B. Mesibov (Eds.), *Learning and cognition in autism* (pp. 199–219). New York, NY: Plenum Press.

Ozonoff, S., Iosif, A. M., Baguio, F., Cook, I. C., Hill, M. M., Hutman, T., & Young, G. S. (2010). A prospective study of the emergence of early behavioral signs of autism. *Journal of the American Academy of Child and Adolescent Psychiatry, 49*, 256–266.

Ozonoff, S., Young, G. S., Carter, A., Messinger, D., Yirmiya, N., Zwaigenbaum, L., . . .

Stone, W. L. (2011). Recurrence risk for autism spectrum disorders: A Baby Siblings Research Consortium study. *Pediatrics, 128*, e488–e495.

Panksepp, J. (1998). *Affective neuroscience: The foundations of human and animal emotions*. New York, NY: Oxford University Press.

Posner, M. I. (1988). Structures and function of selective attention. In T. Boll, & B. K. Bryant (Eds.), *Clinical neuropsychology and brain function: Research, measurement, and practice* (pp. 173–202). Washington, DC: American Psychological Association.

Posner, M. I., & Dehaene, S. (1994). Attentional networks. *Trends in Neurosciences, 17*, 75–79.

Risi, S., Lord, C., Gotham, K., Corsello, C., Chrysler, C., Szatmari, P., & Pickle, A. (2006). Combining information from multiple sources in the diagnosis of autism spectrum disorders. *Journal of the American Academy of Child and Adolescent Psychiatry, 45*, 1094–1103.

Roberts, T. P. L., Khan, S. Y., Rey, M., Monroe, J. F., Cannon, K., Blaskey, L.,… Edgar, J. C. (2010). MEG detection of delayed auditory evoked responses in autism spectrum disorders: Towards an imaging biomarker for autism. *Autism Research. 3*(1), 8–18.

Rombough, V. J. (1998). Visual-spatial attention in children with autism: Lateral versus vertical eye movements. Unpublished master's thesis, York University, Toronto, ON.

Rothbart, M. K. (1981). Measurement of temperament in infancy. *Child Development, 52*, 569–578.

Rothbart, M. K., & Bates, J. E. (1998). Temperament. In W. Damon, R. M. Lerner (Series Eds.), & N. Eisenberg (Vol. Ed.), *Handbook of child psychology: Volume 3, social, emotional, and personality development* (5th ed.) (pp. 105–176). New York: Wiley.

Rothbart, M. K., Ellis, L. K., Rueda, M. R., & Posner, M. I. (2003). Developing mechanisms of temperamental effortful control. *Journal of Personality, 71*, 1113–1144.

Rothbart, M. K., & Posner, M. I. (2006). Temperament, attention, and developmental psychopathology. In D. Cicchetti & D. J. Cohen (Eds.), *Developmental psychopathology: Developmental neuroscience* (2nd ed.) (pp. 465–501). Hoboken, NJ: Wiley.

Rothbart, M. K., Ziaie, H., & O'Boyle, C. G. (1992). Self-regulation and emotion in infancy. *New Directions for Child Development, 55*, 7–23.

Schore, A. N. (1994). *Affect regulation and the origin of the self: The neurobiology of emotional development*. Hillsdale, NJ: Erlbaum.

Soderstrom, H., Rastam, M., & Gillberg, C. (2002). Temperament and character in adults with Asperger syndrome. *Autism, 6*, 287–297.

Stechler, G., & Latz, E. (1966). Some observations on attention and arousal in the human infant. *Journal of the American Academy of Child Psychiatry, 5*, 517–525.

Sutton, S. K., Burnette, C. P., Mundy, P. C., Meyer, J., Vaughan, A., Sanders, C., & Yale, M. (2005). Resting cortical brain activity and social behavior in higher functioning children with autism. *Journal of Child Psychology and Psychiatry, 46*, 211–222.

Vismara, L. A., & Rogers, S. J. (2008). The Early Start Denver model: A case study of an innovative practice. *Journal of Early Intervention, 31*, 91–108.

Wainwright-Sharp, J. A., & Bryson, S. E. (1993). Visual orienting deficits in high functioning people with autism. *Journal of Autism and Developmental Disorders, 23*, 1–13.

Wainwright-Sharp, J. A., & Bryson, S. E. (1996). Visual-spatial orienting in autism. *Journal of Autism and Developmental Disorders, 26*, 423–438.

Whittle, S., Allen, N. B., Lubman, D. I., & Yücel, M. (2006). The neurobiological basis of temperament: Towards a better understanding of psychopathology. *Neuroscience and Biobehavioral Reviews, 30*, 511–525.

Wing, L. (1981). Sex ratios in early childhood autism and related conditions. *Psychiatry Research, 5*, 129–137.

Wismer Fries, A. B., & Pollak, S. D. (2007). Human emotions and the developing brain. In D. Coch, K. W. Fisher, & G. Dawson (Eds.), *Human behavior, learning, and the developing brain* (pp. 329–361). New York, NY: Guilford Press.

Zwaigenbaum, L., Bryson, S., Rogers, T., Roberts, W., Brian, J., & Szatmari, P. (2005). Behavioral manifestations of autism in the first year of life. *International Journal of Developmental Neuroscience, 23*, 143–152.

Zwaigenbaum, L., Bryson, S. E., Szatmari, P., Brian, J., Smith, I. M., Roberts, W.,… Roncadin, C. (2012). Sex differences in children with autism spectrum disorder identified within a high-risk infant cohort. *Journal of Autism and Developmental Disorders*. doi:10.1007/s10803-012-1515-y 22453928.

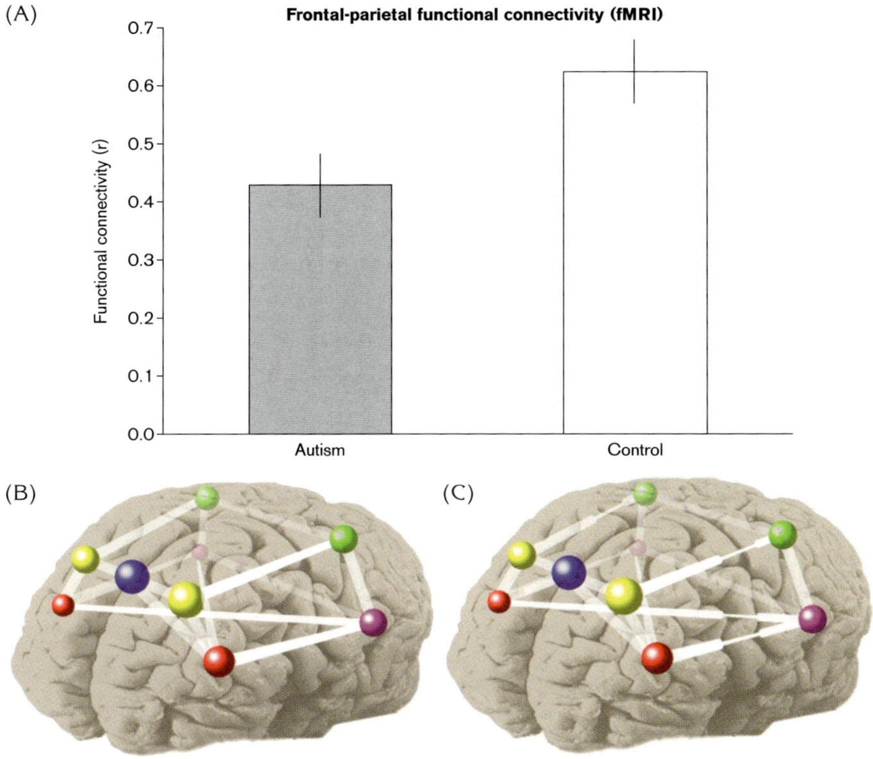

Figure 3.2 (A) Lower frontal-parietal functional connectivity in autism in the Tower of London task (data from Just et al., 2007); (B) Schematic depiction of typical systems connectivity; (C) Schematic depiction of lower bandwidth between frontal and posterior cortical centers in autism.

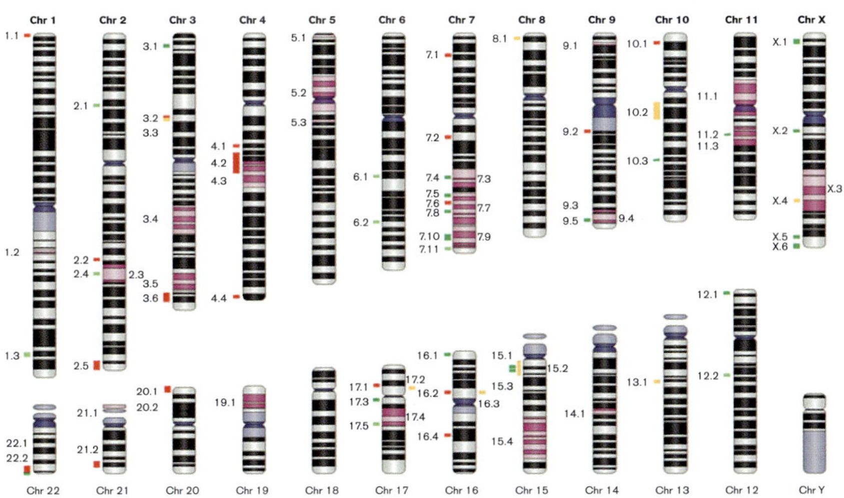

Figure 5.2 Loci implicated in ASD etiology.

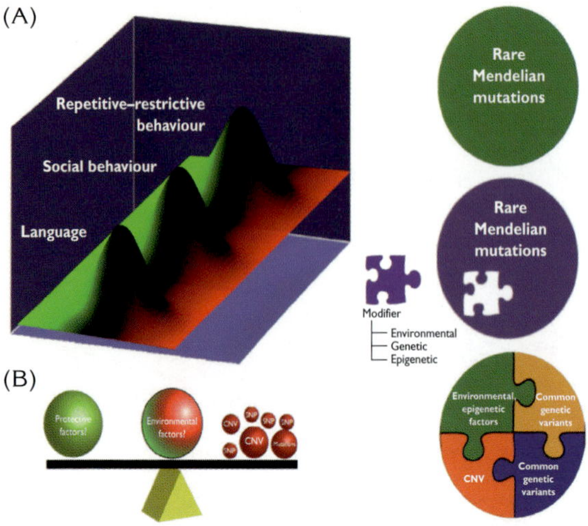

Figure 5.3 ASD and the normal continuum of cognition and behavior.

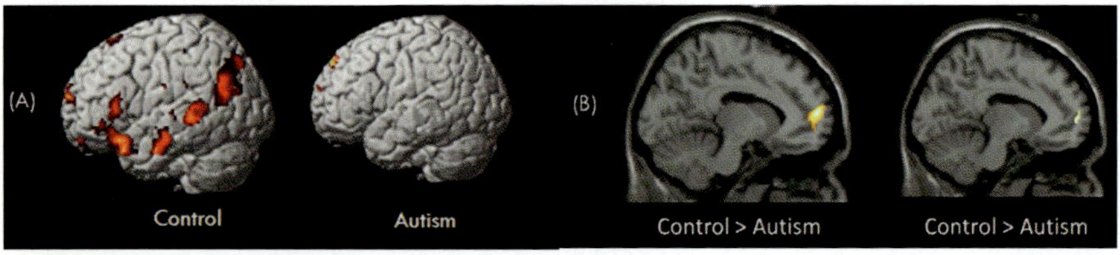

Figure 9.1 (A) Reduced activation in participants with autism in medial prefrontal cortex, left inferior frontal gyrus, and left posterior superior temporal sulcus when self- and other-judgment trials were compared to case-judgment trials ($p < .001$; $k = 25$); (B) Significant increase in activation in left MPFC in controls relative to autism during self vs. letter contrast (left) and other vs. letter contrast (right). In both contrasts, the autism group did not show greater activation in any region ($p < .001$; $k = 25$).

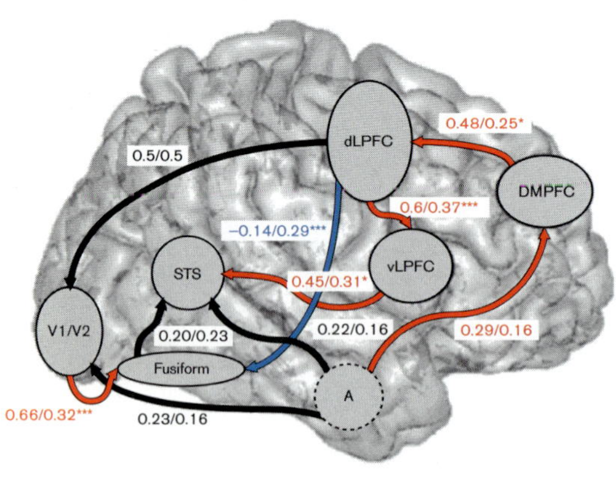

Figure 10.1 Effective connectivity illustrated using structural equation modeling during an explicit emotion processing task.

7

Social Engagement in the First Two Years of Life in Autism Spectrum Disorders

WARREN JONES
AMI KLIN
Marcus Autism Center, Emory University School of Medicine and Children's Healthcare in Atlanta, GA

OVERVIEW

Likely the greatest excitement in the past five years in research on autism spectrum disorders (ASD) has originated from molecular genetic studies (Varki, Geschwind, & Eichler, 2008), which have yielded an unprecedented number of important discoveries (e.g., Morrow et al., 2008; Sebat et al., 2007; Wang et al., 2009; Weiss et al., 2008). To leverage these discoveries in pursuit of causes of this vastly heterogeneous syndrome (Volkmar, Lord, Bailey, Schultz, & Klin, 2004), there is a need for successful systems biology approaches, leading the field from gene to cellular function to neuronal circuitries implicated in pathogenesis (Abrahams & Geshwind, 2008). With this ultimate goal in mind, our lab has researched, for the past eight years, developmentally early-emerging and evolutionarily highly conserved mechanisms of adaptive social action (e.g., Jones, Carr, & Klin, 2008; Klin, Jones, Schultz, Volkmar, & Cohen, 2002a, 2002b; Klin, Jones, Schultz, & Volkmar, 2003; Klin, Lin, Gorrindo, Ramsay, & Jones, 2009).

For human infants, a central task of social adaptation is engagement with caregivers. Given their fragility at birth, success on this task is of immediate survival value and of fundamental evolutionary significance. For example, a central skill facilitating adaptive success on this task is preferential attention to biological motion, which can be interpreted as a form of perceptual *life detector* (Johnson, 2006). Typically developing human infants exhibit this behavior within the first days of life (Simion, Regolin, & Bulf, 2008). It is highly conserved across species (Blake, 1993; Regolin, Tommasi, & Vallortigara, 2000) because it is critical for filial attachment and detection of predators (Johnson, 2006). In human infants, it facilitates perception of social signals and is a precursor to the capacity for attributing mental states to others (Frith & Frith, 1999). In a recent paper (Klin et al., 2009), we showed that this mechanism is fundamentally altered in two-year-olds with autism: They fail to preferentially orient to point-light displays of biological motion, attending instead to physical, not social, contingencies that are disregarded by controls—specifically, audiovisual synchronies between point lights and sounds. The relevance of this finding to elucidating core disabilities in autism was shown in a parallel study (Jones et al., 2008) in which we found that two-year-olds with autism show diminished preferential attention to the eyes of others, attending instead to the mouths of approaching adults. This presents a stark contrast to typical development: Newborns can distinguish a face looking towards them from a face looking away (Farroni, Csibra, Simion, & Johnson, 2002), and by three months, infants look more at a person's eyes than at other parts of the face (Haith, Bergman, & Moore, 1977). Taking these two studies together, we hypothesized that the toddlers with autism may have preferentially attended to mouths because, in the human face, this is the greatest source of audiovisual synchrony as lip motions occur synchronously with speech sounds (Jones & Klin, 2009; Klin et al., 2009). A wide range of foundational normative processes of socialization, including mutual gaze, gaze following, joint attention, and even language acquisition, are predicated on spontaneous searching for the eyes of others and increasing responsiveness to the gaze signals contained therein (Klin et al., 2002b). These are all core disabilities of the ASD phenotype (Volkmar et al., 2004).

In this chapter, we provide a description of some of our key studies to date involving infants and toddlers with ASD and summarize their potential utility in addressing two important grand challenges in autism research. First, given the vast etiologic heterogeneity (e.g., the multiplicity of implicated genetic processes), how can we account for the phenotypic *homogeneity*? Second, given the current unsatisfactory status of animal modeling in autism research, how can we utilize developmental psychopathology insights to hone in on more promising assays in developmental neurobiology research? This discussion is preceded by a brief summary of our developmental framework in approaching research of the pathogenesis of autism and related disorders.

DEVELOPMENTAL MODELS OF PATHOGENESIS IN ASD

At present, knowledge of the pathogenesis and expression of autism during the first years of life is still quite limited. Because children with autism are typically identified only at later stages of childhood (Chawarska et al., 2007), there is little experimental evidence measuring syndrome manifestation in infants and toddlers with ASD (Klin, Chawarska, & Volkmar, 2008). Nevertheless, mounting but largely indirect clinical evidence (Chawarska et al., 2007; Osterling, Dawson, & Munson, 2002; Volkmar, Stier, & Cohen, 1985; Werner, Dawson, Osterling, & Dinno, 2000; Zwaigenbaum et al., 2005) suggests that abnormalities are indeed present in the first year of life, prior to the later point in time when developmental concerns ultimately lead to clinical referrals. Direct observation and quantification of the early developmental progression of autism is still scant.

This gap in clinical and research knowledge is a critical one. The first two years of a baby's life encompass the most substantial and rapid period of neural and behavioral growth in postnatal human development (Johnson, 2001). For a condition as strongly heritable as autism (Rutter, 2005) and for one in which multifactorial genetic etiologies are likely to begin their impact on development from birth, if not before (Volkmar & Pauls, 2003), a thorough mapping of the first years of life in autism is a critical step for both understanding the pathogenesis of the condition as well as developing efforts for treatment and intervention (DiCicco-Bloom et al., 2006).

Knowledge of pathogenesis in autism is still largely theoretical. The timing of disruption(s), the particular aspects of development that are more or less affected, and the ensuing cascade of impact on processes of learning and socialization are all suggested by later evidence in children with autism but remain, at the time of first expression, functionally ill-defined (Klin et al., 2008; Zwaigenbaum et al., 2007). For example, a hallmark deficit in slightly older children with ASD, such as below-normal joint attention skills (Chawarska, Klin, & Volkmar, 2003; Mundy & Neal, 2000), may actually result from many different insults. It could be due to a disruption of a more basic ability, such as differential response to direct or averted gaze (which is present in typical development from the first days of life [Farroni et al., 2002]), or it could be due to reduced dyadic interactive skills (Dawson, Meltzoff, Osterling, Rinaldi, & Brown, 1998; Klin, 1991, 1992; Schultz, 2005); or from a mechanism affecting triadic interaction directly (Tomasello & Carpenter, 2007); or from an altered course of experience from which intact abilities become directed towards other ends. Viewed through this lens of developmental progression, skill deficits often noted in ASD, such as joint attention (Mundy & Neal, 2000) or Theory of Mind (Bates, 1979), may be culminations rather than starting points of pathogenesis.

A key aspect of the conceptual framework underlying our research is the notion that disruptions of socialization processes occurring at different times in development will result in different outcomes. This follows from the experience-expectant model of child development (Karmiloff-Smith, 2002; Oliver, Johnson, Karmiloff-Smith, & Pennington, 2000) in which the genetically determined schedule of neural maturation matches the timing of adaptive tasks. This process, for example, occurs in the timing of neural maturation of differentiated hand muscles involved in the critical act of grasping in primates (a critical milestone in particular for non-human primates that must, even in infancy, have the ability to cling to mother as she moves from branch to branch); mis-timing of the maturational process, too delayed or too precocious, may lead to the loss of that adaptive skill for the given organism (Anokhin, 1964). Thus illustrated, the importance of the timing of developmental skills generalizes to social-adaptive tasks. Following this model, success in these tasks prompts further development in an iterative process that builds on older structures to generate new ones. This process is ever-ongoing, resulting in successively more complex social-cognitive development (Bates, 1979). In this fashion, ontogeny realizes phylogenetic predispositions through the rapid movement of the child through universal social-adaptive tasks, jerrybuilding successful social and communicative babies (Johnson, 2001; Karmiloff-Smith, 2002; Klin et al., 2003; Oliver et al., 2000). Not unlike embryonic growth, we expect that the earlier the disruption of this process, the greater will be the developmental consequences. Given that earlier onset implies both a longer cascade of failures impacting later milestones and a possible arrest of development at the earlier stage of adaptation, earlier insults are likely to lead to more impaired outcomes.

This model also predicts that blockage of the normative social-adaptive trajectories will bias the child to forms of learning that are not grounded in social interaction. Preponderance of learning about the physical environment (e.g., physical over social contingencies) (Baron-Cohen, 1997; Baron-Cohen, Leslie, & Frith, 1986; Klin & Jones, 2006), rote speech over contextualized communication (Tager-Flusberg, Paul, & Lord, 2005), hyperlexia over conceptual reading (Grigorenko, Klin, & Volkmar, 2003), and memorization of facts and information over episodic and personal information (O'Shea, Fein, Cillessen, Klin, & Schultz, 2005) are features well-noted in later-life clinical expression that may arise from this social disinterest (Klin et al., 2003; Klin, Danovitch, Merz, Dohrmann, & Volkmar, 2007).

ATTENTION TO CONSPECIFICS IN TYPICAL DEVELOPMENT AND IN INFANTS AND TODDLERS WITH ASD: PREFERENTIAL ORIENTATION TO EYES

Within the first hours of life, typically developing babies attend preferentially to people. They distinguish and prefer their own mother's voice to that of an unknown woman, but prefer the sound of even an unknown woman's voice to silence (DeCasper & Fifer, 1980). As noted above, human newborns preferentially fixate on faces gazing at them rather than faces looking away (Farroni et al., 2002), and by three months they are drawn to the eye region when viewing speaking faces (Haith et al., 1977). Infants are also capable of imitating the facial gestures of a person while not mimicking similar movements made by a mechanical device (Meltzoff & Moore, 1992). This evidence suggests that typically developing babies have a predisposition to engage with the social aspects of their world. For them, the social dimension is what is most behaviorally salient and what consequently commands the greatest portion of the typically developing child's attention.

For children with autism, the available evidence suggests that this is not the case. The most robust markers for early diagnosis of children with autism center on disruptions to typical engagement with the social world: reduced interaction with and looking at others (Osterling et al., 2002; Werner et al., 2000); failure to respond to the calling of one's own name; diminished eye contact; and inability to join in imitative games and reciprocal vocalizations (Chawarska et al., 2007; Chawarska, Volkmar, & Klin, 2008; Dawson et al., 1998; Klin, 1991, 1992).

Work from our lab with a well-characterized 15-month-old toddler with autism (Klin et al., 2004) finds similar evidence (Klin & Jones, 2008). We presented this child with 10 video scenes, each lasting approximately 20 seconds

Figure 7.1 Caregiver stimuli.

and showing a female actor playing the role of caregiver (Figure 7.1) looking directly into the camera and entreating the child by engaging in childhood games (e.g., playing peek-a-boo). Visual fixation patterns were measured with eye-tracking technology. Non-fixation data (saccades, blinks, and off-screen fixations) were excluded from analyses. A typically developing 15-month-old toddler matched on nonverbal mental age and a typically developing nine-month-old baby matched on verbal age completed the same procedure for comparison. On-screen fixations were coded relative to four regions of interest: eyes, mouth, body (neck and contours around eyes and mouth, such as hair), and object (surrounding inanimate stimuli) (Figure 7.2B).

The toddler with autism showed an overriding preference for the mouth region rather than the eye region of the face relative to the nonverbal mental

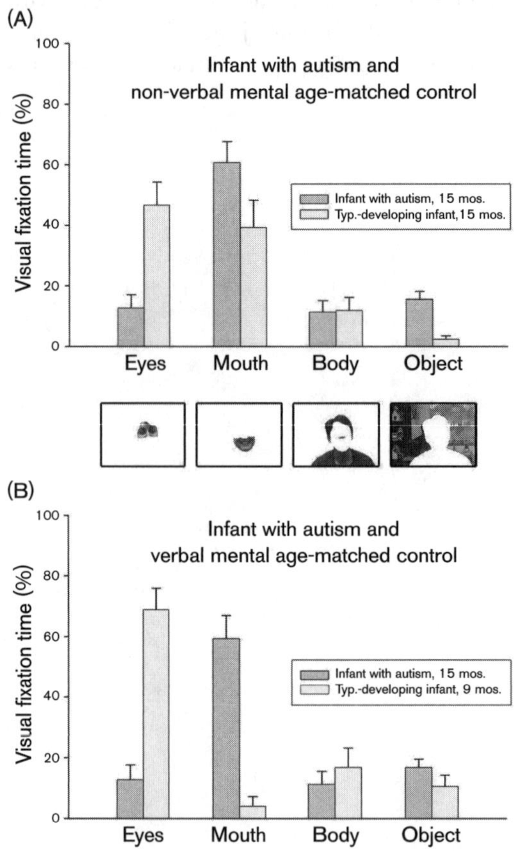

Figure 7.2 Visual fixation while watching scenes of a caregiver. Data from infant with autism in comparison to a nonverbal mental age-matched control (A) and in comparison to a verbal mental-age matched control (B).

age-matched toddler (Figure 7.2A). Some fixation on the mouth region (although still less than on the eye region) would be expected in toddlers learning to speak given the bimodal (auditory and visual) perception of speech acquisition (Kuhl & Meltzoff, 1982). We would expect this to be a stronger phenomenon in the older, nonverbal mental age-matched toddler than in the younger, verbal mental age-matched baby, given each child's stage of speech acquisition (in the midst of, versus preceding, the state of *word explosion*). In accord with this expectation, the difference in percentage of fixation time on the mouth region was even greater for the comparison of the toddler with autism and the younger child (Figure 7.2B). From these results, the landscape of relative salience—what attracts the attention of a developing child—seems fundamentally altered by the age of 15 months in this child with autism.

We followed up on this case study with a case-control series of two-year-olds with ASD and two control groups: a typically developing (TD) group and a developmentally delayed (DD) but not autistic group, matched on nonverbal mental age and on verbal mental age, respectively. Experimental procedures (see Jones et al., 2008) mirrored those reported for the 15-month-old toddler with autism. As shown in Figure 7.3, there were marked differences in percent of visual fixation time on the eye and mouth regions between the ASD group and each of the two control groups (TD and DD). Results for the TD and DD groups did not differ significantly. The ASD group fixated significantly less on the eye region (30.04% of the time) relative to the TD group (54.16%) and DD group (54.68%; $p < .001$). The ASD group also fixated significantly more

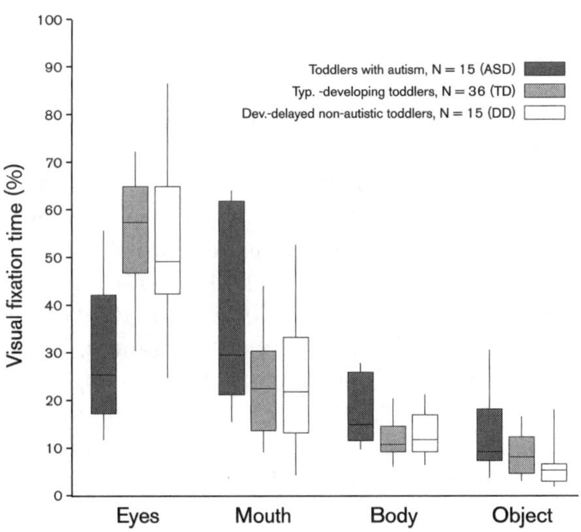

Figure 7.3 Median visual fixation by two-year-olds watching scenes of a caregiver. Boxplots represent percentage of total visual fixation time.

on the mouth region (39.05%) relative to the TD group (23.66%) and DD group (24.73%; $p < .006$). Percent fixation on the body region was comparable across the three groups (17.88% [ASD]; 13.07% [TD]; and 14.29% [DD]), whereas percent fixation on the object region was comparable for the ASD and TD groups but differed significantly between the ASD and DD groups, with the ASD group showing increased fixation on objects (13.02% [ASD]; 9.10% [TD]; and 6.95% [DD]; $p < .033$).

The most powerful predictor of group membership was fixation on the eye region, with minimal overlap in distributions (Cohen's $d = 1.56$ and $d = 1.40$ for the comparisons of ASD vs. TD and ASD vs. DD groups, respectively). The striking similarity in fixation patterns to the eye and mouth regions between the DD and TD control groups attests to the early emergence of preferential visual fixation on the eyes of others, as this was unrelated to developmental (nonverbal or verbal) stage. The specificity of these results to the ASD group suggests that the breakdown of social-affective interaction may in part be predicated on the lack of spontaneous search for the eyes, in turn leading to atypical formation and specialization of the social mind and social brain (Johnson, 2001; Klin et al., 2003; Schultz, 2005).

We then explored the association between fixation on regions-of-interest and level of autistic symptomatology (scores on the socialization domain of the Autism Diagnostic Observation Schedule; Lord, Rutter, DiLavore, & Risi, 1999). Our experimental measures of visual fixation were strong predictors of social disability in these individuals' real lives, a rather unique finding in a field in which experimental findings have historically failed in this regard (Volkmar et al., 2004). Specifically, there was a strong correlation ($r = -.669$, $p < .01$) between levels of eye fixation and levels of social disability, such that lower percent fixation on the eyes predicted greater level of social impairment (Jones et al., 2008).

The visual fixation data for toddlers with ASD present a direct contrast to the sensitivities and visual preferences towards conspecifics that are evident, as noted, in typical development from the first months of life. Similar visual preferences exist in newborn chimpanzees (Myowa-Yamakoshi, Tomonaga, Tanaka, & Matsuzawa, 2003), suggesting that these sensitivities are highly conserved mechanisms in evolution. Likewise, for humans and for chimpanzees, the importance of mutual gaze for both early social development (Bard et al., 2005; Brooks & Meltzoff, 2002; de Waal, 2003; Emery, 2000; Kampe, Frith, Dolan, & Frith, 2001) and social adaptation throughout the lifespan (de Waal, 2003; Emery, 2000; Kampe et al., 2001) indicates that fixation on the eyes of others plays a critical role in socialization. Our results suggest that preferential attention to conspecifics and fixation on the eyes is altered in young children with autism.

ATTENTION TO CONSPECIFICS IN TYPICAL DEVELOPMENT AND IN INFANTS AND TODDLERS WITH ASD: PREFERENTIAL ORIENTATION TO BIOLOGICAL MOTION

Preferential attention to biological motion (i.e., the movement patterns of living beings) is a fundamental mechanism facilitating adaptive interaction with conspecifics (Johnson, 2006). As noted, it is present throughout a wide range of species, from birds (Omori & Watanabe, 1996) to monkeys (Oram & Perrett, 1996) to humans (Fox & McDaniel, 1982; Johansson, 1973). Developmentally, it can be found in newly hatched chicks (Vallortigara, Regolin, & Marconato, 2005) and in human infants as young as two days of age (Simion et al., 2008). This ability is believed to be critical for filial attachment and for detection of predators (Johnson, 2006). The neural underpinnings of biological motion perception (Allison, Puce, & McCarthy, 2000) are overlapping with brain regions involved in perception of other basic social signals, such as facial expression (Carter & Pelphrey, 2008) and gaze direction (Pelphrey, Morris, Michelich, Allison, & McCarthy, 2005; Wicker, Michel, Henaff, & Decety, 1998), and preferential attention to biological motion is seen as a precursor of Theory of Mind skills (Frith & Frith, 1999). Each of these aspects suggests ready benefits for adaptive interaction with other living beings: following the movements of a conspecific; looking at others to entreat or avoid interaction; learning by imitation; or directing preferential attention to cues that build on biological motion, such as facial expression and gaze direction (Klin et al., 2009).

Strikingly, problems with many of those same behaviors have also been noted in children with autism: deficits in social interaction; diminished eye contact and reduced looking at others; problems with imitation; deficits in recognizing facial expressions; and difficulties following another's gaze (Chawarska et al., 2008). In a serendipitous observation (Klin & Jones, 2008), we found that the same 15-month-old toddler described above also failed to recognize point-light displays of biological motion but was instead highly sensitive to the presence of a non-social, physical contingency that occurred within the stimuli by chance. In a case-control series that followed up that case study (Klin et al., 2009), we showed that two-year-olds with autism fail to orient towards point-light displays of biological motion and that their viewing behavior when watching these displays can be explained instead as a response to non-social, physical contingencies that are disregarded by control children.

In this study, the toddlers were presented with five counter-balanced pairs of point-light animations. The animations consisted of children's games, such as playing peek-a-boo or pat-a-cake, and were created with live actors and motion-capture technology and simultaneous audio recording. The experimental task was a preferential looking paradigm (Figure 7.4A) in which a point-light animation of biological motion was presented on one half of a computer

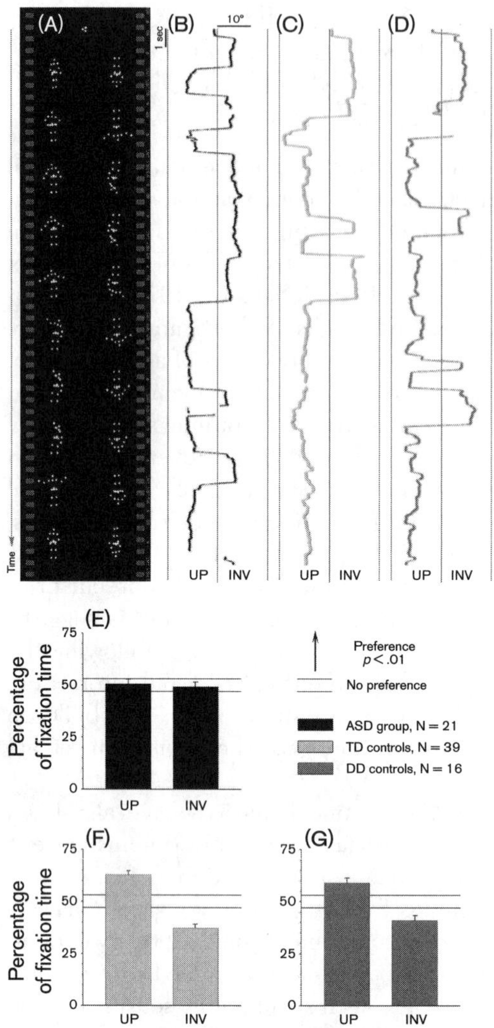

Figure 7.4 Two-year-olds with autism exhibit no preferential attention to biological motion, while control children show significant preferences. (A) Example still images, from point-light biological motion stimuli, show the centering cue at start. Each animation showed an upright (UP) and inverted (INV) figure with accompanying soundtrack matching the actions of the upright figure. The upright figure enacted childhood games. Figures were identical except that the inverted figure was rotated 180 degrees and its movements were played in reverse order. In (B), (C), and (D), visual scanning data of individual children are plotted as horizontal location by time. Breaks in data occur for blinks or offscreen fixations. (B) Visual scanning data from one toddler with autism (ASD) for one animation. (C) Data from one typically developing (TD) toddler. (D) Data from one developmentally delayed (DD) but non-autistic toddler.

screen together with the audio soundtrack of the actor's vocalizations. On the other half of the screen, the same animation was presented, but that point-light figure was inverted in orientation (shown upside-down) and played in reverse (the frames of animated action played from the end of the sequence until its beginning). Only one (forward) audio soundtrack was presented. Inverted presentation disrupts perception of biological motion in young children (Pavlova & Sokolov, 2000) and is processed by different neural circuits in infants as young as eight months of age (Reid, Hoehl, & Striano, 2006). Also, by playing the inverted animation backwards, its relative levels of motion complexity, speed, and gestalt coherence were preserved, but its motion was not an exact mirror of the upright. Each animation lasted an average of 30.5 seconds. Order of presentation was randomized, and presentation of the upright figure was counter-balanced to appear on the left side of the screen as often as on the right. Evidence for recognition and preferential attention to biological motion was measured by the child's viewing patterns: Increased looking towards the upright figure indicated preferential attention to normal biological motion (Simion et al., 2008) and the perceptual matching of a human voice with a mental template of human action (Klin et al., 2003). Visual scanning was measured with eye-tracking equipment (Figure 7.4B–7.4D).

Seventy-six children with a mean chronological age of 2.05 years (SD = 0.62) participated. These children comprised the same three groups as in the study reported above (Jones et al., 2008) with 21 toddlers with ASD, 39 who were TD, and 16 who were DD. Results are plotted in Figures 7.4E and 7.4F. When viewing point-light displays of human biological motion, two-year-olds with ASD were random in their looking patterns: 50.7% of fixation time was spent on the upright figure vs. 49.3% on the inverted (Figure 7.4E). In contrast, both control groups demonstrated significant preferential attention to the upright animations: 62.7% of the time for the TD group, and 58.9% of the time for the DD group (Figures 7.4F–7.4G). Comparison across groups was significantly different ($p < .001$). In pairwise comparisons, looking by the ASD group differed significantly from that of each control group ($p < .001$ in com-

(E) For the ASD group, fixation to upright and inverted biological motion occurs at chance levels. (F) TD toddlers give preferential attention to upright animations. (G) DD toddlers also give preferential attention to upright animations. Horizontal guidelines denote percentages not significantly different from chance. Error bars are SEM. * = p < .05; ** = p < .01; *** = p < .001. Figure based on Figure 1 of Klin, A., Lin, D. J., Gorrindo, P., Ramsay, G., & Jones, W. (2009). Two-year-olds with autism fail to orient towards human biological motion but attend instead to non-social, physical contingencies. Nature, 459, 247–261.

parison with the TD group, and $p = .0185$ relative to the DD group). The two control groups did not differ significantly from one another ($p = .27$).

Results in Figure 7.4 are for four of the five types of animations originally presented. In our earlier research (Klin & Jones, 2008), we found that one of the animations contained a confound. While four animations presented only moving point-lights with accompanying human voice, one animation included a different sound. The actor in that animation played pat-a-cake, and the sound of clapping was heard at the same time that two point-lights, the actor's hands, collided. The collision of point-lights and the resulting clapping sound created a causal physical contingency: Rather than merely co-occurring (as with the speech sounds and movements in the other animations), the movements of the point-light hands in this case actually *caused* a noise to occur. In the earlier research, we found that the 15-month-old with autism was very sensitive to the occurrence of this clapping: Her preferential looking went from random during other animations to 93.1% upright during the pat-a-cake animation (Klin & Jones, 2008).

During the clapping, the causal physical contingency only existed on the upright side. The single audio track played normally (forward) matched the upright movements, but the action of the inverted figure, played in reverse, did not move in time to the clapping sounds. When analyzed independently (Figure 7.5), the toddlers with ASD showed a significant preference for the upright clapping figure: 65.9% upright during the pat-a-cake animation. This was significantly increased relative to other animations: 65.9% upright during pat-a-cake vs. only 50.7% in the other four animations ($p = .02$). Behavior of the TD and DD groups was unchanged: They continued to give preferential attention to the upright figure: 58.6% upright during pat-a-cake vs. 62.7% in the other four animations for TD ($p = .44$); and 54.4% vs. 58.9% for DD ($p = .51$). Overall, on the pat-a-cake animation, results for the three groups did not differ significantly ($p = .52$).

Following this observation, we questioned whether the presence of more subtle synchronies might have played an unanticipated role in the viewing of all animations—that is, whether visual scanning that had appeared random by the toddlers with ASD might actually be related to audiovisual synchronies less obvious than clapping. To test this, we quantified levels of audiovisual synchrony (AVS) in all animations. Details on this quantification methodology are provided elsewhere (Driver & Spence, 2000). In the pat-a-cake animation, when the point-light hands collide and a clapping sound occurs, an abrupt change in motion coincides with a large change in sound amplitude. We measured audiovisual synchrony in our stimuli to match this case: the synchronous occurrence of change in motion and change in sound. By summing the AVS signals of all point-lights over time, we generated cumulative maps of audiovisual synchrony for each animation. From the cumulative maps, we calculated the difference between maximum audiovisual synchrony on the upright side and maximum synchrony on the inverted side (as a percentage difference to normalize across animations).

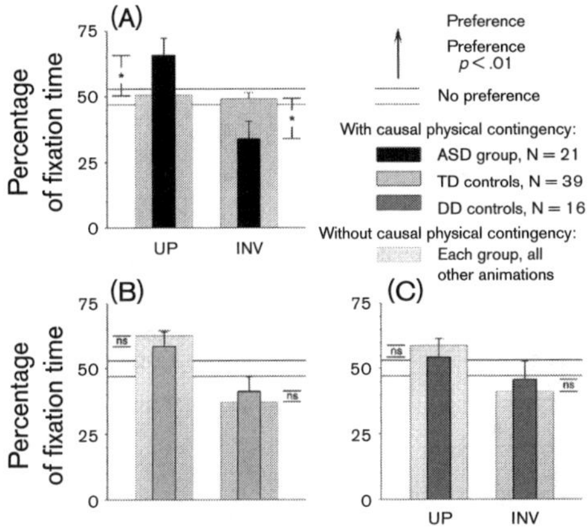

Figure 7.5 When the animation contains a physical contingency, two-year-olds with autism do show significant viewing preferences. (A) During other biological motion animations, ASD toddlers show no preference, but when a physical contingency is present on the upright side, these toddlers show significant preference for the upright figure (different from chance [p < .01] and different from their viewing behavior in other animations [p = .044]). While other animations presented only moving point-lights and human voices, one type of animation contained an additional cue: As two point-lights, representing the actor's hands, collided, the sound of clapping could be heard (playing pat-a-cake). The collision of point-light "hands" actually caused a noise (the clap) to occur, localized to the upright figure and absent from the inverted (the inverted figure's movements were not synchronous with the claps). (B) TD toddlers show no significant change in preferential viewing. (C) DD toddlers also show no significant change in preferential viewing. Horizontal guidelines denote percentages not significantly different from chance. Error bars are SEM. * = p < .05. Figure based on Figure 2 of Klin, A., Lin, D. J., Gorrindo, P., Ramsay, G., & Jones, W. (2009). Two-year-olds with autism fail to orient towards human biological motion but attend instead to non-social, physical contingencies. Nature, 459, 257–261.

Using regression analysis, this measure of upright versus inverted synchrony was tested as a predictor of preferential attention for each version of the video clips (Figure 7.6, below). For the ASD group, preferential looking was significantly and strongly correlated with level of audiovisual synchrony ($r^2 = .90$, $p = .01$) (Figure 7.6A). In the TD and the DD groups, there was no significant correlation between viewing and audiovisual synchrony ($r^2 = .29$ and $r^2 = .17$, respectively) (Figures 7.6B–7.6C). Correlation coefficients for the three groups were significantly different from one another ($\chi^2 = 7.24$, $p < .05$), with the ASD group significantly differing from the TD group ($z = 2.41$, $p < .05$) and

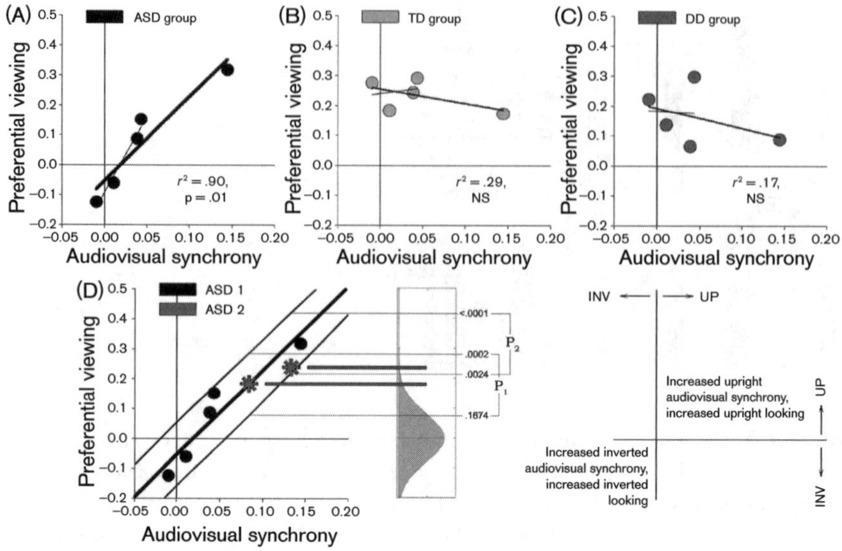

Figure 7.6 Level of audiovisual synchrony is highly correlated with preferential viewing in two-year-olds with autism; is uncorrelated with viewing in control children; and can predict ASD viewing patterns in novel animations. (A) Preferential viewing is significantly correlated with audiovisual synchrony in ASD toddlers. Plots pair preferential viewing and audiovisual synchrony. When the animation with greatest upright audiovisual synchrony (i.e., pat-a-cake) is withheld from analysis, audiovisual synchrony is still significantly correlated with viewing behavior in ASD toddlers ($r^2 = .95$, $p = .018$, plotted as thin regression line through remaining four data points). (B) Preferential viewing by TD toddlers is uncorrelated with audiovisual synchrony, across either four or five animations. (C) Preferential viewing by DD toddlers is also uncorrelated with audiovisual synchrony. (D) To test whether audiovisual synchrony could predict looking behavior in new animations, we created two additional animation types. The regression from the original data, with weighted binomial prediction intervals, provided a model for expected behavior. P_1 and P_2 denote prediction intervals for the new animations. Probability of obtaining results in these intervals is noted to the right of the regression plot. For an independent cohort of toddlers with autism, matched to the original cohort, preferential viewing was predicted on the basis of audiovisual synchrony ($p = .0004$). In all plots, axis Y shows preferential viewing as a difference score (percentage of fixation time to upright [UP] minus percentage of fixation time to inverted [INV]). Positive values indicate greater percentage of time spent looking at the upright animation. Likewise, axis X shows audiovisual synchrony as synchrony of the upright (as percentage of total synchrony) minus synchrony of the inverted (also as percentage of the total). Positive values indicate greater synchrony

the DD group ($z = -2.25, p < .05$). The two control groups did not differ significantly. The pat-a-cake animation had greatest upright audiovisual synchrony. When we withheld that animation and re-analyzed, the correlation between preferential viewing and audiovisual synchrony remained significant for the ASD group ($r^2 = .95, p = .018$), but was still not significant for the other groups ($r^2 = .04$ for TD and $r^2 = .001$ for DD).

The results from this post hoc quantification of audiovisual synchrony and preferential viewing indicated that the viewing patterns of toddlers with ASD, which were random relative to social content, showed a marked reliance on audiovisual synchrony. This one measure accounted for 90% of the autism group's variance in preferential viewing. In contrast, the looking patterns of typically developing children and of developmentally delayed children who did not have autism showed no relationship with levels of audiovisual synchrony. The control children gave preferential attention to biological motion, disregarding audiovisual synchrony in favor of more socially relevant signals.

To test whether audiovisual synchrony could predict looking behavior in new animations, we designed a follow-up experiment (Figure 7.6D). We created two new recordings with increased levels of audiovisual synchrony, filling the gap in synchrony signal strength of our original stimuli. We recruited an additional cohort of toddlers with autism and used our original results to build a predictive model for expected behavior, creating weighted binomial prediction intervals around the original regression line (Von Collani & Dräger, 2001) with specific predictions for each animation. The probability of both results falling within their respective prediction intervals is equal to the probability of obtaining a value in one interval multiplied by the probability of obtaining a value within the other ($p = [.1674 - .0002] \times [.0024 - 0]$). Preferential viewing by this second cohort of toddlers with autism fit the predictions based on audiovisual synchrony, a result with chance likelihood of $p = .0004$. Overall, these results indicate that a skill present in two-day-old, typically developing infants (Simion et al., 2008), as well as in chronologically, nonverbally, and verbally matched control children (the TD and DD groups herein), is not functioning properly in children with autism at the age of two.

---

in the upright figure. Figure based on Figure 4 of Klin, A., Lin, D. J., Gorrindo, P., Ramsay, G., & Jones, W. (2009). Two-year-olds with autism fail to orient towards human biological motion but attend instead to non-social, physical contingencies. Nature, 459, 257–261.

HETEROGENEITY AND HOMOGENEITY ACROSS THE AUTISM SPECTRUM: THE ROLE OF DEVELOPMENT

In a recent commentary (Jones & Klin, 2009), we asked a question that has been somewhat neglected in autism research: Given the multiplicity of possible causes, and the phenotypic expression of so many "autisms," where does the homogeneity of autism arise? Among clinicians, there is strong consensus on core diagnostic features, autism-specific diagnostic instruments have strong sensitivity and specificity (Volkmar et al., 2004), and, among experienced clinicians at least, agreement in diagnostic assignment is typically high (Klin, Lang, Cicchetti, & Volkmar, 2000). These factors highlight homogeneity of basic features in spite of the wide range of genomic causes and varying outcomes.

In an effort to understand the link between vast genotypic and phenotypic heterogeneity on the one hand, and common manifestations of core disability on the other, one important factor is development. The studies reviewed in this chapter point to early disruptions of highly conserved mechanisms of social development, but more importantly, they point to early departures from normative processes. Following from the experience-expectant model of child development (Johnson & Karmiloff-Smith, 2004), in which the genetically determined schedule of neural maturation matches the timing of adaptive tasks, disruptions of socialization processes occurring at different times are likely to result in different outcomes. Thus we suggest that the homogeneity of autism may originate from shared failings in the process of socialization as a whole, a near-universal process among humans that is closely tied to evolutionarily based, survival tasks. Following this reasoning, the heterogeneity may stem from variable timing in the onset of individual disruptions: The earlier the "lesion," the more severe the outcome (Figure 7.7). This parallels the notion that activation or de-activation of the same gene at different embryological phases can result in extremely different phenotypes (DiCicco-Bloom et al., 2006).

This approach emphasizes the *development* in neurodevelopmental disorders. There is vast clinical variability in the expression and severity of symptoms displayed by individuals with autism, spanning the entire IQ and language spectrum of abilities and a wide range of social, communication, and behavioral disabilities (Volkmar et al., 2004). This is one of the greatest obstacles in the identification of discrete causes of autism (Happé, Ronald, & Plomin, 2006). Indeed, despite being the most strongly genetic among the psychiatric disorders, with a heritability estimated to be over 90%, geneticists have been baffled by such a vast phenotypic heterogeneity (Grice & Buxbaum, 2006). Yet, an experienced clinician is likely to recognize a child with ASD upon a few minutes of direct observation and interaction. By emphasizing the disruption of a universal process, rather than the variable profile of symptoms and outcomes resulting from the disruption of this process, we question efforts to link specific symptoms or clusters of symptoms directly to genes or molecular genetic

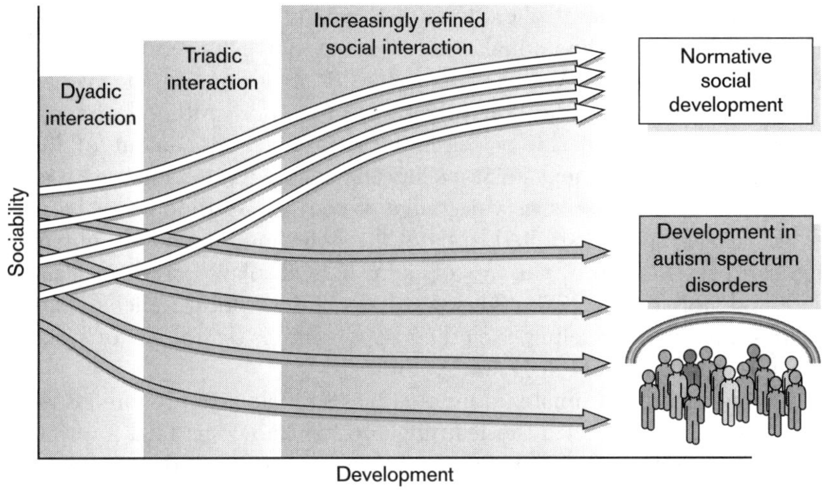

Figure 7.7 Adaptive action in response to environmental demand constrains typical development towards increasingly refined forms of social interaction. In contrast, development in autism spectrum disorders, with a lack of preferential attention to socially relevant stimuli, leads to increasingly atypical behaviors. The homogeneity of autism spectrum disorders may originate from shared failings in the process of socialization as a whole, whereas the heterogeneity may stem from variable timing in the onset of individual disruptions. Figure based on Figure 1 of Jones, W., & Klin, A. (2009). Heterogeneity and homogeneity across the autism spectrum: The role of development. Journal of the American Academy of Child and Adolescent Psychiatry, 48, 471–473.

processes because the gap between the two is vast. The distance between genes that code for proteins, which go on to realize neural circuitries meant to realize adaptive skills, and the endpoint of interaction between faulted adaptive skills and the social-environmental demands of socialization that give rise to autistic symptomatology, are several steps removed from straightforward, causative neurobiological processes. Our proposal is to intersperse a bridging factor between neurobiology and symptomatology: the quantified study of evolutionarily highly conserved, and developmentally early-emerging, mechanisms of socialization.

CREATING BETTER BEHAVIORAL ASSAYS FOR ANIMAL MODELING IN AUTISM RESEARCH

We argued previously that more successful targets for animal models of autism should comply with three principles: a general focus on adaptive or survival skills which are more (a) proximal to genetic expression; (b) central to the expression of the behavioral phenotype of the condition; and (c) relevant to the adaptive survival of the animal used in the model (DiCicco-Bloom et al., 2006; Jones & Klin, 2009). We can exemplify this suggestion by means of the research on preferential attention to biological motion outlined above. As noted, biased attention to biological motion (i.e., the movement of living beings) is a fundamental mechanism facilitating adaptive interaction with conspecifics and is present across a wide range of species. Methodologically, and across the various species studied to date, the behavioral assays are obtained through the presentation of variants of point-light displays based on Johansson's method (Johansson, 1973). This, in turn, creates opportunities for novel approaches in animal modeling, including opportunities that allow for systems biology and multilevel and integrated syntheses.

For example, in birds, innate attentional bias to biological motion has been linked to filial attachment via the learning process known as filial imprinting (Bolhuis, 1999; Johnson, 1999, 2006). Since the original descriptions by Konrad Lorenz (Lorenz, 1937), filial imprinting has become an important paradigm for the study of the neural mechanisms of learning and memory (Horn, 1998). In a series of studies employing autoradiographic, biochemical, lesion, and electrophysiological techniques to study imprinting in newly hatched chicks, Horn and colleagues established that a localized region of the chick forebrain, the intermediate and medial part of the hyperstriatum ventrale (IMHV), is crucially involved in visual imprinting (Horn, Nicol, & Brown, 2001). The IMHV exhibits a variety of changes as a function of imprinting, including increases in synaptic density and elevated glutamate binding (Rose, 2000). Although the avian forebrain lacks the layered structure of mammalian cortex, the relation of the forebrain to subcortical structures is similar, following a basic higher vertebrate brain design (Nauta & Karten, 1970). The mammalian homologue to the IMHV is thought to be prefrontal and cingulated cortices (Horn, 1998). More recent advances have substantially increased knowledge of the basic science of filial attachment using the young chick as a model system to study pertinent gene expression and biochemical and morphological processes (Rose, 2000).

There are several avenues of exploration opened up by such a model. For example, Fos-like immunoreactivity is positively correlated with strength of imprinting in the IMHV (McCabe & Horn, 1994). Neural cell adhesion molecules expressed in the IMHV play a time-dependent role in the learning process of imprinting (Solomonia, McCabe, & Horn, 1998). Increases in the amount of these molecules serve to stabilize the synaptic changes associated with a particular memory by strengthening pre- to postsynaptic adhesion, and by more strongly interconnecting the cytoskeletal frameworks of the dendritic spine and the synaptic terminal (Horn, 1998). Collectively, this effort suggests the promise of bringing two decades of basic science research of filial attachment to bear on developmental neurobiology research of autism. Such a programmatic effort would leverage juvenile chicks as a laboratory for molecular and neuronal mechanisms with a view to examine the earliest expressions of social orientation and disruptions thereof in autism, particularly if behavioral assays are found to be adaptively comparable (i.e., they trigger orientation to and engagement with a conspecific).

Some comparisons are appealing. For example, chicks that receive exposure to increased amounts of species-typical embryonic vocalizations before hatching show accelerated patterns of species-typical visual responsiveness in early imprinting (Lickliter & Stoumbos, 1991). A similar process has been suggested for the innate orientation of human infants to their caregivers' eyes (Locke, 1992). Intrauterine exposure to maternal voice may encourage attachment between the newborn child and the person who is his or her primary source of sustenance and care. The newborn's preference for the voice of his or her mother (DeCasper & Fifer, 1980) selectively orients visual attention to the source of that voice (Farroni et al., 2002; Locke, 1992). Similarly, two recent genetic discoveries (Glessner et al., 2009; Wang et al., 2009) based on genome-wide association scans pointed to several locations in the genome at or near genes that encode cadherins and other cell-adhesion proteins. While there is a need to resist any simplistic cross-species comparison or overinterpretation of unlocalized expressions of proteins, pertinent comparative assays can serve as a platform for animal modeling. Bridging the gaps between gene–brain–behavior discoveries is sorely needed (Crawley, 2007; Jones & Klin, 2009; Varki et al., 2008). Because the processing of social information (e.g., caregiver, gender, kin, social status) is essential for reproduction and survival, it seems likely that specialized neural mechanisms have evolved for this purpose, defining the circuitry of a social brain with ancestral, though foundational, implications for understanding disruptions of social development in humans (Insel & Fernald, 2004). These various promises underlie the current work of our lab. Our goal is to advance research on behavioral assays known to be (a) critical in human social-cognitive development; (b) disrupted in infants and toddlers with ASD; and (c) a promising strategy for basic neuroscience studies of filial attachment.

FUTURE RESEARCH

Intriguing as the recent experimental results outlined in this chapter are in suggesting a developmental pathway to autism, they still refer to data on two-year-olds. By that time, typically developing children are already accomplished social interactionists, and most children with autism already display symptoms of the condition and can be diagnosed. Our frontier is the infancy period, the period of greatest neuroplasticity and change, and also the period of emergence of the syndrome. The exemplified mechanisms of social engagement are online from the first weeks of life. Thus our goal is to quantify departures from normative development from as early as they are detectable and to map their timing and consequences to subsequent social-cognitive growth and syndrome expression. In this way, we hope to establish early detection of autism on firm, quantifiable ground. We also hope for increased synergy between genetic and developmental social neuroscience investigations. Social behavior has long been a target in genetic investigations, albeit primarily in simpler organisms than humans (Robinson, Fernald, & Clayton, 2008). If the confluence of these various disciplines were to be the process of development and its disruptions, we believe that the results of such an enterprise might provide sorely needed guidance to ventures into the sea of genomic variability in search of autism-associated genes.

REFERENCES

Abrahams, B. S., & Geschwind, D. H. (2008). Advances in autism genetics: On the threshold of a new neurobiology. *Nature Reviews: Genetics, 9*, 341–355.

Allison, T., Puce, A., & McCarthy, G. (2000). Social perception from visual cues: Role of the STS region. *Trends in Cognitive Sciences, 4*, 267–278.

Anokhin, P. K. (1964). Systemogenesis as a general regulator of brain development. *Progress in Brain Research, 9*, 54–105.

Bard, K. A., Costall, A., Myowa-Yamakoshi, M., Tomonaga, M., Tanaka, M., & Matsuzawa, T. (2005). Group differences in the mutual gaze of chimpanzees (*Pan Troglodytes*). *Developmental Psychology, 41*, 616–624.

Baron-Cohen, S. (1997). Are children with autism superior at folk physics? *New Directions for Child Development, 75*, 45–54.

Baron-Cohen, S., Leslie, A. M., & Frith, U. (1986). Does the autistic child have a "theory of mind"? *Cognition, 21*, 37–46.

Bates, E. (1979). On the evolution and development of symbols. In E. Bates (Ed.), *The emergence of symbols: Cognition and communication in infancy* (pp. 1–32). New York: Academic Press.

Blake, R. (1993). Cats perceive biological motion. *Psychological Science, 4*, 54–57.

Bolhuis, J. J. (1999). Early learning and the development of filial preferences in the chick. *Behavioral Brain Research, 98*, 245–252.

Brooks, R., & Meltzoff, A. N. (2002). The importance of eyes: How infants interpret adult looking behavior. *Developmental Psychology, 38*, 958–966.

Carter, E. J., & Pelphrey, K. A. (2008). School-aged children exhibit domain-specific responses to biological motion. *Social Neuroscience, 1*, 396–411.

Chawarska, K., Klin, A., & Volkmar, F. R. (2003). Automatic attention cueing through eye movement in 2-year-old children with autism. *Child Development, 74*, 1108–1122.

Chawarska, K., Paul, R., Klin, A., Hannigen, S., Dichtel, L. E., & Volkmar, F. R. (2007). Parental recognition of developmental problems in toddlers with autism spectrum disorders. *Journal of Autism and Developmental Disorders, 37*, 62–72.

Chawarska, K., Volkmar, F. R., & Klin, A. (Eds.). (2008). *Autism spectrum disorders in infants and toddlers: Diagnosis, assessment, and treatment.* New York: Guilford Press.

Collani, E. von, & Dräger, K. (2001). *Binomial distribution handbook for scientists and engineers*. Boston: Birkhäuser.

Crawley, J. N. (2007). Testing hypotheses about autism. *Science, 318*, 56–57.

Dawson, G., Meltzoff, A. N., Osterling, J., Rinaldi, J., & Brown, E. (1998). Children

with autism fail to orient to naturally occurring stimuli. *Journal of Autism and Developmental Disorders, 28*, 479–485.
DeCasper, A. J., & Fifer, W. P. (1980). Of human bonding: Newborns prefer their mothers' voices. *Science, 208*, 1174–1176.
de Waal, F. X. (2003). Darwin's legacy and the study of primate visual communication. *Annals of the New York Academy of Sciences, 1000*, 7–31.
DiCicco-Bloom, E., Lord, C., Zwaigenbaum, L., Courchesne, E., Dager, S. R., Schmitz, C.,... Young, L. J. (2006). The developmental neurobiology of autism spectrum disorder. *Journal of Neuroscience, 26*, 6897–6906.
Driver, J., & Spence, C. (2000). Multisensory perception: Beyond modularity and convergence. *Current Biology, 10*, R731–R735.
Emery, N. J. (2000). The eyes have it: The neuroethology, function, and evolution of social gaze. *Neuroscience and Biobehavioral Reviews, 24*, 581–604.
Farroni, T., Csibra, G., Simion, F., & Johnson, M. H. (2002). Eye contact detection in humans from birth. *Proceedings of the National Academy of Sciences, 99*, 9602–9605.
Fox, R., & McDaniel, C. (1982). The perception of biological motion by human infants. *Science, 218*, 486–487.
Frith, C. D., & Frith, U. (1999). Interacting minds: A biological basis. *Science, 286*, 1692–1695.
Glessner, J. T., Wang, K., Cai, G., Korvatska, O., Kim, C. E., Wood, S.,... Hakonarson, H. (2009). Autism genome-wide copy number variation reveals ubiquitin and neuronal genes. *Nature, 7246*, 569–573.
Grice, D. E., & Buxbaum, J. D. (2006). The genetics of autism spectrum disorders. *Neuromolecular Medicine, 8*, 451–460.
Grigorenko, E. L., Klin, A., & Volkmar, F. (2003). Annotation: Hyperlexia: Disability or superability? *Journal of Child Psychology and Psychiatry, 44*, 1079–1091.
Haith, M. M., Bergman, T., & Moore, M. J. (1977). Eye contact and face scanning in early infancy. *Science, 198*, 853–855.
Happé, F., Ronald, A., & Plomin, R. (2006). Time to give up on a single explanation for autism. *Nature Neuroscience, 9*, 1218–1220.
Horn, G. (1998). Visual imprinting and the neural mechanisms of recognition memory. *Trends in Neurosciences, 21*, 300–305.
Horn, G., Nicol, A. U., & Brown, M. W. (2001). Tracking memory's trace. *Proceedings of the National Academy of Sciences of the United States of America, 98*, 5282–5287.
Insel, T. R., & Fernald, R. D. (2004). How the brain processes social information: Searching for the social brain. *Annual Review of Neuroscience, 27*, 697–722.
Johansson, G. (1973). Visual perception of biological motion and a model for its analysis. *Perception and Psychophysics, 14*, 201–211.
Johnson, M. H. (1999). Ontogenetic constraints on neural and behavioral plasticity: Evidence from imprinting and face processing. *Canadian Journal of Experimental Psychology, 53*, 77–91.
Johnson, M. H. (2001). Functional brain development in humans. *Nature Reviews: Neuroscience, 2*, 475–483.
Johnson, M. H. (2006). Biological motion: A perceptual life detector? *Current Biology, 16*, R376–R377.
Johnson, M. H., & Karmiloff-Smith, A. (2004). Neuroscience perspectives on infant development. In G. Bremner, & A. Slater (Eds.), *Theories of infant development* (pp. 121–141). Malden, MA: Blackwell.

Jones, W., Carr, K., & Klin, A. (2008). Absence of preferential looking to the eyes of approaching adults predicts level of social disability in 2-year-olds with autism. *Archives of General Psychiatry, 65*, 946–954.

Jones, W., & Klin, A. (2009). Heterogeneity and homogeneity across the autism spectrum: The role of development. *Journal of the American Academy of Child and Adolescent Psychiatry, 48*, 471–473.

Kampe, K. K. W., Frith, C. D., Dolan, R. J., & Frith, U. (2001). Reward value of attractiveness and gaze. *Nature, 413*, 589–590.

Karmiloff-Smith, A. (2002). Development itself is the key to understanding developmental disorders. In M. H. Johnson, Y. Munakata, & R. O. Gilmore (Eds.), *Brain development and cognition: A Reader* (2nd ed.) (pp. 375–391). Malden, MA: Blackwell Publishers.

Klin, A. (1991). Young autistic children's listening preferences in regard to speech: A possible characterization of the symptom of social withdrawal. *Journal of Autism and Developmental Disorders, 21*, 29–42.

Klin, A. (1992). Listening preferences in regard to speech in four children with developmental disabilities. *Journal of Child Psychology and Psychiatry, 33*, 763–769.

Klin, A., Chawarska, K., Paul, R., Rubin, E., Morgan, T., Wiesner, L., & Volkmar, F. R. (2004). Autism in a 15-month-old child. *American Journal of Psychiatry, 161*, 1–8.

Klin, A., Chawarska, K., & Volkmar, F. R. (2008). Opportunities for research: Concepts and future directions. In K. Chawarska, F. R. Volkmar, & A. Klin (Eds.), *Autism in Infancy* (pp. 327–336). New York: Guilford Press.

Klin, A., Danovitch, J. H., Merz, A. B., Dohrmann, E. H., & Volkmar, F. R. (2007). Circumscribed interests in higher-functioning individuals with autism spectrum disorders: An exploratory study and a theory. *Research and Practice for Persons with Severe Disabilities, 32*, 89–100.

Klin, A., & Jones, W. (2006). Attributing social and physical meaning to ambiguous visual displays in individuals with higher functioning autism spectrum disorders. *Brain and Cognition, 61*, 40–53.

Klin, A., & Jones, W. (2008). Altered face scanning and impaired recognition of biological motion in a 15 month-old infant with autism. *Developmental Science, 11*, 40–46.

Klin, A., Jones, W., Schultz, R., & Volkmar, F. (2003). The enactive mind, or from actions to cognition: Lessons from autism. *Philosophical Transactions of the Royal Society B: Biological Sciences, 358*, 345–360.

Klin, A., Jones, W., Schultz, R., Volkmar, F., & Cohen, D. (2002a). Visual fixation patterns during viewing of naturalistic social situations as predictors of social competence in individuals with autism. *Archives of General Psychiatry, 59*, 809–816.

Klin, A., Jones, W., Schultz, R., Volkmar, F., & Cohen, D. (2002b). Defining and quantifying the social phenotype in autism. *American Journal of Psychiatry, 159*, 895–908.

Klin, A., Lang, J., Cicchetti, D. V., & Volkmar, F. R. (2000). Interrater reliability of clinical diagnosis and DSM-IV criteria for autistic disorder: Results of the DSM-IV autism field trial. *Journal of Autism and Developmental Disorders, 30*, 163–167.

Klin, A., Lin, D. J., Gorrindo, P., Ramsay, G., & Jones, W. (2009). Two-year-olds with autism fail to orient towards human biological motion but attend instead to non-social, physical contingencies. *Nature, 459*, 257–261.

Kuhl, P. K., & Meltzoff, A. N. (1982). The bimodal perception of speech in infancy. *Science, 218*, 1138–1141.

Lickliter, R., & Stoumbos, J. (1991). Enhanced prenatal auditory experience facilitates species-specific visual responsiveness in bobwhite quail chicks (*Colinus virginianus*). *Journal of Comparative Psychology, 105*, 89–94.

Locke, J. L. (1992). Thirty years of research on developmental neurolinguistics. *Pediatric Neurology, 8*, 245–250.

Lord, C., Rutter, M., DiLavore, P. C., & Risi, S. (1999). *Autism Diagnostic Observation Schedule – WPS (ADOS-WPS)*. Los Angeles, CA: Western Psychological Services.

Lorenz, K. (1937). Imprinting. *Auk, 54*, 245–273.

McCabe, B. J., & Horn, G. (1994). Learning-related changes in Fos-like immunoreactivity in the chick forebrain after imprinting. *Proceedings of the National Academy of Sciences of the United States of America, 24*, 11417–11421.

Meltzoff, A. N., & Moore, M. K. (1992). Early imitation within a functional framework: The importance of person identity, movement, and development. *Infant Behavior and Development, 15*, 479–505.

Morrow, E. M., Yoo, S., Flavell, S. W., Kim, T., Lin, Y., Hill, R. S.,... Walsh, C. A. (2008). Identifying autism loci and genes by tracing recent shared ancestry. *Science, 321*, 218–223.

Mundy, P., & Neal, R. (2000). Neural plasticity, joint attention, and autistic developmental pathology. In L. Glidden (Ed.), *International review of research in mental retardation, volume 23* (pp. 141–168). New York: Academic Press.

Myowa-Yamakoshi, M., Tomonaga, M., Tanaka, M., & Matsuzawa, T. (2003). Preference for human direct gaze in infant chimpanzees (*Pan troglodytes*). *Cognition, 89*, 53–64.

Nauta, W. J. H., & Karten, H. J. (1970). A general profile of the vertebrate brain, with sidelights on the ancestry of cerebral cortex. In F. O. Schmitt (Ed.), *The neurosciences: Second study program* (pp. 7–26). New York: Rockefeller University Press.

Oliver, A., Johnson, M. H., Karmiloff-Smith, A., & Pennington, B. (2000). Deviations in the emergence of representations: A neuroconstructivist framework for analyzing developmental disorders. *Developmental Science, 3*, 1–23.

Omori, E., & Watanabe, S. (1996). Discrimination of Johansson's stimuli in pigeons. *International Journal of Comparative Psychology, 9*, 92.

Oram, M. W., & Perrett, D. I. (1996). Integration of form and motion in the anterior superior temporal polysensory area (STPa) of the macaque monkey. *Journal of Neurophysiology, 76*, 109–129.

O'Shea, A. G., Fein, D. A., Cillessen, A. H. N., Klin, A., & Schultz, R. T. (2005). Source memory in children with autism spectrum disorders. *Developmental Neuropsychology, 27*, 337–360.

Osterling, J. A., Dawson, G., & Munson, J. A. (2002). Early recognition of 1-year-old infants with autism spectrum disorder versus mental retardation. *Development and Psychopathology, 14*, 239–251.

Pavlova, M., & Sokolov, A. (2000). Orientation specificity in biological motion perception. *Perception and Psychophysics, 62*, 889–899.

Pelphrey, K. A., Morris, J. P., Michelich, C. R., Allison, T., & McCarthy, G. (2005). Functional anatomy of biological motion perception in posterior temporal cortex: An fMRI study of eye, mouth, and hand movements. *Cerebral Cortex, 15*, 1866–1876.

Regolin, L., Tommasi, L., & Vallortigara, G. (2000). Visual perception of biological motion in newly hatched chicks as revealed by an imprinting procedure. *Animal Cognition, 3*, 53–60.

Reid, V. M., Hoehl, S., & Striano, T. (2006). The perception of biological motion by infants: An event-related potential study. *Neuroscience Letters, 395*, 211–214.

Robinson, G. E., Fernald, R. D., & Clayton, D. F. (2008). Genes and social behavior. *Science, 322*, 896–900.

Rose, S. P. R. (2000). God's organism? The chick as a model system for memory studies. *Learning and Memory, 7*, 1–17.

Rutter, M. (2005). Genetic influences and autism. In F. R. Volkmar, R. Paul, A. Klin, & D. J. Cohen (Eds.), *Handbook of autism and pervasive developmental disorders* (3rd ed.) (pp. 425–452). New York: Wiley.

Schultz, R. T. (2005). Developmental deficits in social perception in autism: The role of the amygdala and fusiform face area. *International Journal of Developmental Neuroscience, 23*, 125–141.

Sebat, J., Lakshmi, B., Malhotra, D., Troge, J., Lese-Martin, C., Walsh, T.,… Wigler, M. (2007). Strong association of de novo copy number mutations with autism. *Science, 316*, 445–449.

Simion, F., Regolin, L., & Bulf, H. (2008). A predisposition for biological motion in the newborn baby. *Proceedings of the National Academy of Sciences, 105*, 809–813.

Solomonia, R. O., McCabe, B. J., & Horn, G. (1998). Neural cell adhesion molecules, learning, and memory in the domestic chick. *Behavioral Neuroscience, 3*, 646–655.

Tager-Flusberg, H., Paul, R., & Lord, C. (2005). Communication in autism. In F. Volkmar, A. Klin, R. Paul, & D. Cohen (Eds.), *Handbook of autism and pervasive developmental disorders* (3rd ed.) (pp. 335–364). New York: Wiley & Sons.

Tomasello, M., & Carpenter, M. (2007). Shared intentionality. *Developmental Science, 10*, 121–125.

Vallortigara, G., Regolin, L., & Marconato, F. (2005). Visually inexperienced chicks exhibit spontaneous preference for biological motion patterns. *PLoS Biology, 3*, 208.

Varki, A., Geschwind, D. H., & Eichler, E. E. (2008). Explaining human uniqueness: Genome interactions with environment, behaviour and culture. *Nature Reviews: Genetics, 9*, 749–763.

Volkmar, F., Lord, C., Bailey, A., Schultz, R. T., & Klin, A. (2004). Autism and pervasive developmental disorders. *Journal of Child Psychology and Psychiatry, 45*, 135–170.

Volkmar, F. R., & Pauls, D. (2003). Autism. *Lancet, 362*, 1133–1141.

Volkmar, F. R., Stier, D. M., & Cohen, D. J. (1985). Age of recognition of pervasive developmental disorder. *American Journal of Psychiatry, 142*, 1450–1452.

Wang, K., Zhang, H., Ma, D., Bucan, M., Glessner, G. T., Abrahams, B. S.,… Hakonarson, H. (2009). Common genetic variants on 5p14.1 associate with autism spectrum disorders. *Nature, 459*, 528–533.

Weiss, L. A., Shen, Y., Korn, J. M., Arking, D. E., Miller, D. T., Fossdal, R.,… Daly, M. J. (2008). Association between microdeletion and microduplication at 16p11.2 and autism. *New England Journal of Medicine, 358*, 667–675.

Werner, E., Dawson, G., Osterling, J., & Dinno, H. (2000). Recognition of autism spectrum disorder before one year of age: A retrospective study based on home videotapes. *Journal of Autism and Developmental Disorders, 30*, 157–162.

Wicker, B., Michel, F., Henaff, M. A., & Decety, J. (1998). Brain regions involved in the perception of gaze: A PET study. *NeuroImage, 8*, 221–227.

Zwaigenbaum, L., Bryson, S., Rogers, T., Roberts, W., Brian, J., & Szatmari, P. (2005).

Behavioral manifestations of autism in the first year of life. *International Journal of Developmental Neuroscience, 23*, 143–152.

Zwaigenbaum, L., Thurm, A., Stone, W., Baranek, G., Bryson, S., Iverson, J.,… Sigman, M. (2007). Studying the emergence of autism spectrum disorders in high-risk infants: Methodological and practical issues. *Journal of Autism and Developmental Disorders, 37*, 466–480.

Section IV

Neural Systems in Social and Emotional Processes

8

Brain Mechanisms for Social Perception Dysfunction in Autism

KEVIN A. PELPHREY
Yale Child Study Center, Yale University, New Haven, CT

SUSAN B. PERLMAN
University of Pittsburgh, Pittsburgh, PA

BRENT C. VANDER WYK
Yale Child Study Center, Yale University, New Haven, CT

INTRODUCING THE SOCIAL BRAIN

Social perception refers to "the initial stages in the processing of information that culminates in the accurate analysis of the dispositions and intentions of other individuals" (Allison, Puce, & McCarthy, 2000, p. 1). Additionally, we view social perception as an ontogenetic and phylogenetic prequel to more sophisticated aspects of social cognition, including Theory of Mind (Premack & Woodruff, 1978). While neuroscientists have only recently focused on identifying the neural substrates of social perception, the construct has been of interest to psychologists for decades. For example, a major focus of Fritz Heider's (1944, 1958) work was the description of cognitive mechanisms for the perception of social objects. In collaboration with Mary-Ann Simmel, he provided elegant experimental demonstrations of the ways in which the perception of people differs from the perception of objects, particularly with regard to the attributions we make for each category of visual stimulus (Heider & Simmel, 1944). Psychological scientists commonly divvy up human cognitive abilities into memory, attention, reasoning, perception, etc. Our textbooks help to consecrate these categories. Yet nature has not always respected these boundaries. Humans are, at their core, social and affective beings, but these essential characteristics have often been treated as sources of noise to be excluded from controlled experiments in the laboratories of cognitive psychologists. This point of view will soon become extinct, owing in large part to remarkable new discoveries that have provided strong evidence for the need for an "apocryphal" chapter regarding the unique ways in which social information is processed by the brain.

Neuroscientists became deeply interested in social perception when it was discovered that neurons within the temporal cortex and amygdaloidal complex of monkeys were sensitive to and selective for social objects (e.g., faces and hands) and complex social stimuli (actions in a social context and direction of gaze) (Brothers & Ring, 1993; Brothers, Ring, & Kling, 1990; Desimone, 1991; Desimone, Albright, Gross, & Bruce, 1984; Perrett, Rolls, & Caan, 1979, 1982; Perrett et al., 1984, 1985; Rolls, 1981, 1995). On the basis of these seminal findings, the field began to think seriously about the possibility of a network of brain regions dedicated to processing social information. The label *the social brain* was coined by Leslie Brothers (1990), and it served to capture elegantly the core, emerging idea. The social brain is defined as the complex network of areas that enables us to recognize other individuals and to evaluate their mental states (e.g., intentions, dispositions, desires, and beliefs). The key idea is that human beings, in response to the unique computational demands of their highly social environments, have evolved cognitive mechanisms and an associated, dedicated neural system supporting such abilities as recognizing other agents and their actions, individuating others, perceiving the emotional states of others, analyzing the intentions and dispositions of others, sharing attention with one another, and representing another person's perceptions and beliefs.

In an early and influential model of the social brain, Brothers (1990) emphasized the contributions of the superior temporal sulcus (STS), amygdala, orbital frontal cortex (OFC), and fusiform gyrus (FFG) to social perception. In humans, the STS region, particularly the posterior STS in the right hemisphere, analyzes biological motion cues, including eye, hand, and other body movements, to interpret and predict the actions and intentions of others (e.g., Bonda, Petrides, Ostry, & Evans, 1996; Pelphrey, Morris, Michelich, Allison, & McCarthy, 2005). The FFG, located in the ventral occipitotemporal cortex, contains a region termed the *fusiform face area* (FFA), which has been implicated in face detection (identifying a face as a face) and face recognition (identifying one's friend versus a stranger) (e.g., Kanwisher, McDermott, & Chun, 1997; Puce, Allison, Asgari, Gore, & McCarthy, 1996). The OFC has been strongly implicated in social reinforcement and reward processes more broadly (e.g., Rolls, 2000, 2009). Finally, the amygdala, a complex structure that is highly interconnected with cortical (including the STS and FFG) and other subcortical brain structures, has been implicated in helping to recognize the emotional states of others through analysis of facial expressions (e.g., Morris et al., 1996), as well as in multiple aspects of the experience and regulation of emotion (e.g., Davis & Whalen, 2001; Klüver & Bucy, 1997; LeDoux, 2000).

To understand social brain function, we must be as attentive to the interconnections of neuroanatomical structures as we are to their individual contributions. Currently, in humans, much is known about the roles played by the individual brain regions, but very little is known about the ways in which they are interconnected, and thus even less is known about how they interact functionally. However, we can take some initial guidance from the monkey brain. Here, it is known that the STS region has reciprocal connections to the amygdala (Amaral, Price, Pitkanen, & Carmichael, 1992). The amygdala, in turn, is connected to the OFC (Amaral et al., 1992), and the STS is also connected with the OFC (Barbas, 1988). The OFC is connected to the prefrontal cortex (Pandya & Yeterian, 1996), which is connected to the motor cortex and the basal ganglia, thus completing what Allison and colleagues (2000) described as a pathway from perception to action.

AUTISM: "DISTURBANCES OF AFFECT CONTACT"

Autism is a behaviorally defined, pervasive neurodevelopmental disorder characterized by a distinctive developmental course with an onset no later than the first two to three years of life, as well as a triad of deficits: (1) impairments in social interactions; (2) delays in and absences of communicative skills; and (3) restricted interests and stereotyped, repetitive behaviors (American Psychiatric Association [APA], 1994). While all children with autism exhibit these features, there is a vast amount of heterogeneity within each symptom domain.

The social deficits were particularly emphasized in Kanner's (1943) original descriptions of children with "autistic disturbances of affective contact." He described the children as lacking the necessary skills for normal social functioning, with a particular impairment in emotional interactions. He wrote, "We must, then, assume that these children have come into the world with innate inability to form the usual, biologically-provided affective contact with other people, just as other children come into the world with innate physical or intellectual handicaps" (p. 250). The social deficits appear to be unique, pathognomic features of autism (Kanner, 1943; Wing & Gould, 1979). For instance, although repetitive behaviors and restricted interests as well as language deficits are seen in other disorders (e.g., obsessive-compulsive disorder and specific language impairment, respectively), only autism presents with a set of deficits that includes social dysfunction. Given the centrality of the social deficits to this neurodevelopmental disorder, the study of autism and the study of the social brain are inextricably intertwined.

My laboratory employs functional magnetic resonance imaging (fMRI), eye tracking, and virtual reality stimuli in experiments designed to identify the development of the brain mechanisms involved in various aspects of social perception. Having identified these mechanisms, we use this knowledge to explore the brain basis of social perception dysfunction in individuals with autism. We are keenly interested in the social brain because we believe that an understanding of it will reveal fundamental insights into the origins of autism. These insights, in turn, will improve the diagnosis, treatment, and prevention of autism spectrum disorders. This chapter is organized to mirror the approach we have taken in our research program. We begin by describing studies that have examined specific aspects of social perception in typically developing or "neurotypical" adults. Having provided sufficient background on the normative functioning of the social brain, we then present recent findings from studies of the social brain in individuals with autism.

BRAIN MECHANISMS FOR SOCIAL PERCEPTION IN TYPICALLY DEVELOPING ADULTS

Detecting Animate Beings

A critical component of social perception is the detection and recognition of other people in the environment. In particular, social animals must distinguish between living, dynamic, animate beings, with which there is a potential for social interaction, and static, lifeless objects that require a different mode of reasoning and interaction (Johnson, 2006). How might the human brain perform this task? People move in a fashion very different from lifeless objects. These differences in movement patterns provide an incredibly rich source of information to facilitate the recognition of other individuals. Specifically, people exhibit biological motion. We use the term *biological motion* to refer to the visual perception of a living entity engaged in a recognizable activity (Pelphrey & Morris, 2006). This definition includes the observation of humans walking and making eye and mouth movements, but the term can also refer to the mammalian visual system's ability to recover information about a person's motion from sparse input. The latter is well-illustrated by the discovery that point-light displays (moving images created by placing lights on the major joints of a walking person and filming them in the dark), though relatively impoverished stimuli, contain the information necessary to identify the agent of motion and the kind of motion produced by the agent (Johansson, 1973). As Johansson originally demonstrated, humans readily distinguish between biological and non-biological motion, and this ability is present remarkably early in development (e.g., Simion, Regolin, & Bulf, 2008). Given the existence of a cognitive mechanism for distinguishing between biological and non-biological motion, what might be its neural basis?

Numerous early functional neuroimaging studies implicated the STS region of the human brain in the perception of biological motion. Indeed, a meta-analysis summarized overwhelming evidence for the involvement of this neuroanatomical structure in distinguishing between biological and non-biological motion (Allison et al., 2000). However, most of the prior studies had used as non-biological comparison stimuli point-light displays conveying random or meaningless/unnameable motions. This led to uncertainty about whether the STS region was specialized for the perception of biological motion, or if it were broadly engaged in processing any complex, nameable motion. To address this issue, we used virtual reality animation techniques to generate four types of visual motion. These were a walking robot, a grandfather clock, a disjointed mechanical figure, and a walking human. Using fMRI, we recorded brain activity in a sample of typically developing adults as they viewed these stimuli (Pelphrey, Mitchell, et al., 2003). We demonstrated that the STS responds more strongly to biological motion (as conveyed by a walking robot or walking human) than it does to non-meaningful but complex non-biological motion (a disjointed mechanical figure) or to complex and meaningful non-biological motion (the movements of a grandfather clock). It was noteworthy that the nearby and well-characterized motion-processing area V5 (e.g., Zeki et al., 1991) responded strongly and equivalently to all four movements. Thus, it is not likely that the results from the STS can be accounted for by lower-level differences in the attentional value of the stimuli or by differences in the amount of movement inherent in each stimulus. We concluded that the STS region is involved in signaling the presence of another agent in the environment and is capable of distinguishing between the movements of another person versus the complex motions of an inanimate but nameable machine.

Perceiving the Intentions and Dispositions of Other People

The initial pattern of findings greatly increased our interest in the STS region as a component of the social brain. We had identified a region that we were confident was involved in recognizing biological versus non-biological motion. Given this capacity, we argued that this region could represent the actions of other individuals and also serve to facilitate the detection of other entities with which there were opportunities for interaction. Given this starting point, we next wondered whether this region was involved in simply representing biological motion as such, or if it was more broadly involved in deriving higher-level mentalistic descriptions from motion for use in action interpretation and other inferences regarding the goals and intentions underlying observed actions. To answer this question, we conducted a study in which participants viewed the face of a virtual female character that was present on the screen throughout the fMRI experiment (Pelphrey, Singerman, Allison, & McCarthy, 2003). As shown in Figure 8.1, at the beginning of a trial, a checkerboard would appear within the character's field of view. She would then make an eye gaze shift towards or away from the checkerboard. In this context, a gaze shift towards the checkerboard was consistent with the expectation that another person would look at a target appearing in her visual field. We called these trials *congruent*. A shift away from the checkerboard would be inconsistent with this expectation and would demand additional processing from regions involved in processing the intentions of actions. We called these trials *incongruent*. We observed that the STS region, particularly the posterior portion of this region in the right hemisphere, responded more strongly to an eye gaze when it was incongruent with the participant's expectations about what a person ought to do in this particular context. We concluded that the STS does not merely represent the surface features of biological motion, but also participates in integrating biological motion, or actions, with the social and/or physical context, and thereby plays a role in analyzing and interpreting the intentions underlying observed biological motions.

These conclusions were bolstered by other findings regarding a role for the posterior STS region in analyzing the intentions and dispositions of others as conveyed by biological motion (e.g., Brass, Schmitt, Spengler, & Gergely, 2007; Castelli, Happé, Frith, & Frith, 2000; Pelphrey, Morris, & McCarthy, 2004; Pelphrey, Viola, & McCarthy, 2004; Saxe, Xiao, Kovacs, Perrett, & Kanwisher, 2004). However, potential limitations in the experimental designs employed by our group and others left the findings open to an alternative interpretation. Corbetta, Patel, and Shulman (2008) argued that the prior results could be more parsimoniously explained by uncontrolled stimulus differences in demands for shifting attention. After all, the posterior STS region is known to be involved in the allocation of spatial attention in response to visual cues (e.g., Hopfinger, Buonocore, & Mangun, 2000). When we scrutinized our own study involving congruent and incongruent eye gaze shifts, we recognized that our two conditions might differ in the number of attention shifts evoked (see Figure 8.1). Assuming that participants begin a trial looking at the eye region of the face, the flashing checkerboard in the periphery of their visual field is a powerful attractor that should elicit a shift of attention to the checkerboard. Then, once attention is focused on the flashing checkerboard, an eye gaze shift occurs. In the congruent condition, this gaze shift, another powerful elicitor of an attentional shift, simply reinforces the prior attentional shift towards the flashing checkerboard. However, in the incongruent case, attention might be directed by the gaze shift to a new location in space. In the congruent case, there is one shift of attention. In the incongruent case, there are two shifts of attention.

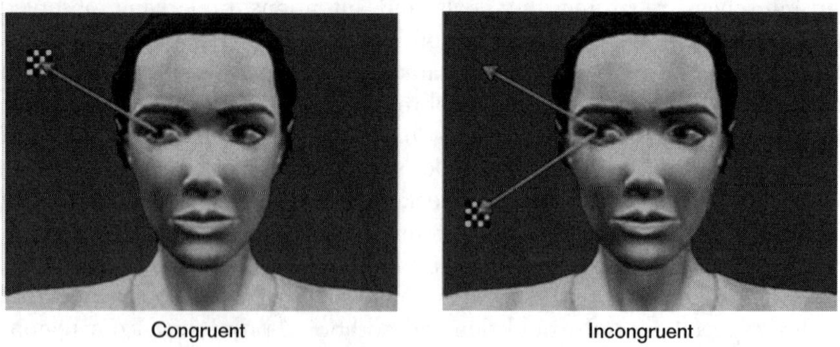

Figure 8.1 The design of a study to examine intention understanding in the human brain. Arrows illustrate hypothesized shifts of attention.

Thus, our manipulation of congruency was potentially confounded with the number of attention shifts evoked by the stimuli.

We conducted a follow-up study that directly addressed this concern (Vander Wyk, Hudac, Carter, Sobel, & Pelphrey, 2009). We reasoned that, if the posterior STS region participates in integrating actions with the social and physical context, it would need to be sensitive to environmental or cognitive sources of information that affect this context. An especially salient component of context is perceived emotion, particularly when emotion indicates a preference for or against an object or event. We examined whether the STS exhibits differences in activity that are dependent on the previous emotional context related to understanding another's preferences, which would inform the viewer about that person's underlying intentions. This experiment used a paradigm, adapted from Phillips, Wellman, & Spelke (2002), in which participants observed an actress on video express positive or negative regard towards one of two objects. She then reached and picked up that same object or the other one. Viewing the actress's emotional expression allowed the participant to attribute an intention to her: Positive expressions towards an object warranted the attribution of the intent to pick up the object, while negative expressions warranted the opposite attribution. The subsequent reaching gesture was then interpreted as being either congruent or incongruent with the intention. By using both positive and negative emotions directed towards an object, we ensured that the number of attention shifts was fully balanced between congruent and incongruent trials.

Our results indicated that one brain region, localized to the right posterior STS, exhibited significantly more activity for the incongruent trials than for the congruent trials. This finding indicated that the activity of the right posterior STS region to a given biological motion is sensitive to prior emotional context. Specifically, the STS showed a greater response when participants viewed a reach incongruent with a prior emotional expression (i.e., when the actress reached for the object not targeted by a prior positive expression or when she reached for the object targeted by a prior negative expression) than when they viewed a reach congruent with the actress's expression. In both cases in which positive and negative emotions set up these expectations about the actress's future behaviors towards an object, the response in the posterior STS was greater upon viewing unanticipated actions. This finding was very much in accord with the prior research arguing for a role of the posterior STS in doing more than simply representing the current state of biological motion.

Critically, the pattern of findings we observed in this study contradicted fully the argument that, in the earlier findings, increased activity in the posterior STS region while viewing unexpected actions was related to additional shifts in attention required when observed movements differ from expectations (Corbetta et al., 2008). The attention-reorienting account predicts greater activity for the positive–incongruent than for the negative–incongruent condition because the former requires the participant to reorient attention twice and the latter only once. Likewise, the positive–congruent condition would be expected to involve only one shift in attention, while the negative–congruent condition should demand two shifts in attention (i.e., shifting attention to the cup at which the actress directed negative regard and then shifting attention to the cup picked up by the actress). This attention account would therefore predict equivalent activation in the positive–incongruent and negative–congruent conditions and equivalent activity in the positive–congruent and negative–incongruent conditions. We observed a very different pattern of effects: Within the STS, the incongruent condition was greater than the congruent condition, regardless of the affect—a pattern of effects that an attention-reorienting account cannot explain.

Connectivity among Brain Regions Supporting Social Perception

Having obtained a clearer picture of the role of the STS region in social perception, we recognized that it was very important to map connectivity among the posterior STS and regions representing other aspects of social perception. Such a map of the functional interactions would allow us to better understand the mechanisms underlying the observed activity differences in the posterior STS region. We have taken an initial step towards this goal by employing Granger Causality Mapping, a relatively new (in fMRI) and very powerful technique for assessing functional connectivity. Granger Causality (Granger, 1969) is a concept developed within the field of economics, for which Clive W. J. Granger received the 2003 Nobel Prize in Economics. As applied to fMRI data, this technique seeks to find directional influence between two time courses of blood oxygenation level dependent (BOLD) contrast, typically an average time course of activity of a region of interest and a set of voxels. This process adopts the underlying logical assumption that, if region A causes the activity of region B, then A must temporally precede B, and information about A ought to improve the ability to predict B over and above other information we have about B. This means that, by using past measures of A, one ought to improve the predictions of future measures of B after taking into account past measures of B itself (since the past of B is a source of information we can use to predict the future measures of B).

Granger Causality values can be computed as the linear, directed influence of the vector of volume measures from brain region A on the vector of residual volume measures of brain region B shifted by one time point, after regressing out information from the latter region's past (Geweke, 1982). If, at a moment in time, nothing can be predicted about the measure of region B by taking into account the past of the region A, then there is no linear dependence, and thus we would claim no causality. Since directed causality values can be computed independently from region A to region B and vice versa, the difference between the computed values gives the dominant direction of causality

(Roebroeck, Formisano, & Goebel, 2005). The statistical significance of a given computed causality can be calculated from an empirically derived distribution via a bootstrap method (Efron & Tibshirani, 1993) using methods to control the false discovery rate (Genovese, Lazar, & Nichols, 2002).

We applied Granger Causality Mapping to the data reported by Vander Wyk and colleagues (2009). The seed region was the area of 301 voxels in the posterior STS shown to have greater activity to reaches to a target that were incongruent with a previous emotional expression (as described above). The dominant direction of causality was computed between the average time course of the seed region and every other voxel in the brain for the set of time points that extended one volume prior to the onset of the expression, to two volumes after the completion of the reach (seven volumes, 14 seconds total). Separate values were computed for congruent and incongruent trials.

The results of this analysis are summarized in Figure 8.2. Regions are shown that both were active during the task and showed a significant causal relationship with the posterior STS. During congruent trials, a number of brain regions in both frontal and posterior cortical areas were shown to be causal of the posterior STS activity. These regions included the medial prefrontal cortex (mPFC), the right dorsal lateral and ventral lateral prefrontal cortex (dl-PFC and vl-PFC), the right inferior parietal lobule (IPL), and the right anterior superior temporal sulcus (aSTS). The posterior STS was shown

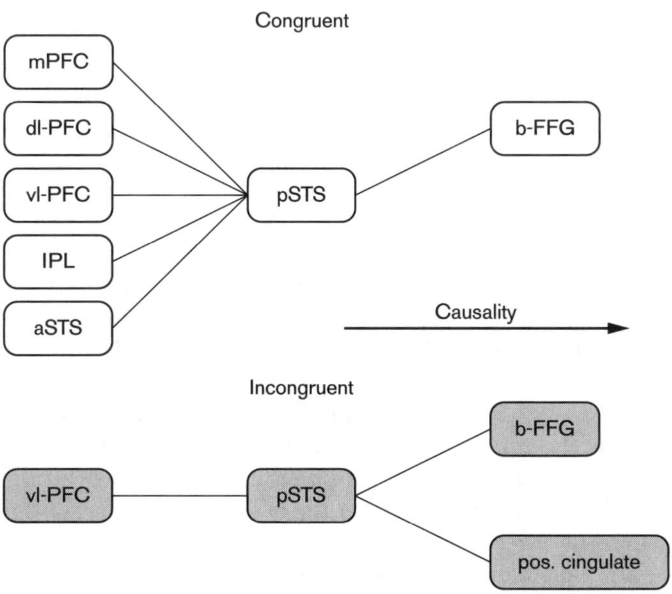

Figure 8.2 Charted are networks of brain regions that cause or are caused by activity in the posterior STS region as a function of congruency.

to cause activity in the FFG, in and around the expected location of the FFA, bilaterally. The causal network was quite different for the incongruent trials. Specifically, only the right vl-PFC was causal of the posterior STS, and in turn, the posterior STS was causal of activity in the posterior cingulate cortex.

This analysis allowed us to identify a significant causal network to and from a region of the posterior STS that we had shown repeatedly to be involved in the analysis of the intentions and dispositions of other individuals. Furthermore, this technique allowed us to show that the composition of the network of brain regions recruited during this important aspect of social perception varies from trial to trial as a function of experimental manipulation. In particular, a number of regions that are predictive of the activity in the posterior STS during the congruent trials are not predictive during incongruent trials. At the same time, the posterior STS also appears to drive activity in the FFG. However, during incongruent trials, it also drives activity in the posterior cingulate. This suggests two modes of operation. In the first, a number of regions serve to inform and constrain the ongoing activity of the posterior STS. In turn, the posterior STS continues to modulate processing in the FFG, potentially related to processing of face and body information. However, a second mode appears to be engaged upon the detection of the incongruent reach, where the posterior STS decouples from many of the previously informative regions, and now activates only the posterior cingulate, a region associated with anticipation of attention shifts (Small et al., 2003), thus potentially helping the system to prepare for the deployment of attention in response to potential further unexpected information as signaled by the observed incongruent reach.

NEURAL BASIS OF SOCIAL PERCEPTION DYSFUNCTION IN AUTISM

Armed with a much richer understanding of the neural basis of social perception, we were in a position to begin using this knowledge to make forward progress in our understanding of the social perception deficits that are core characteristics of autism. A striking and very well-replicated finding in the autism literature is that affected individuals look at faces differently than do typically developing individuals (e.g., Klin, Jones, Schultz, Volkmar, & Cohen, 2002; Pelphrey et al., 2002). When presented with a face, typically developing adults direct most of their attention to the core features of the face (i.e., eyes, nose, and mouth) and spend very little time on other areas. In stark contrast, individuals with autism do not look at the eyes or the other core features of the faces. Instead, they scan the faces in a seemingly random fashion. Such findings suggest a failure to understand the significance of the features for social understanding and could represent a mechanism leading to a failure to develop the normal specialization of some brain regions for processing social information.

When individuals with autism do look at the eyes, they often fail to connect the eye gaze with its mentalistic significance. This point is elegantly demonstrated by an experiment conducted by Simon Baron-Cohen (1995). They presented to children with autism, children who were developmentally delayed but did not have autism, and typically developing children a picture of "Charlie." Charlie was a simple schematic face. Positioned in the four corners around Charlie were four different pictures of various kinds of candy. Charlie's eyes gazed to one of the four pictures. Children were then asked one of two questions: "At which candy is Charlie looking?" and "Which candy does Charlie want?" All children studied, including those with and without autism, could answer the first question, correctly identifying the object of Charlie's gaze. This demonstrated that autism is not characterized by a deficit in the identification of gaze direction. Responses to the second question revealed a striking deficit that was specific to the children with autism: They could not tell the experimenter which candy Charlie wanted, failing to make the mentalistic connection that Charlie's gaze could inform them of his desires. Instead, the children with autism guessed as to which candy Charlie might want or they picked the candy they would prefer. On the other hand, both typically developing children and children who were developmentally delayed but did not have autism could easily make this connection. They reliably selected the candy to which Charlie directed his eye gaze. These two observations—a lack of attention to the eye region and the failure to understand the mentalistic significance of eye gaze—have served as two of the focal points for our research efforts in the area of autism.

The Neural Basis of Intention Understanding Deficits in Autism

We first tackled the issue of eye gaze and intention understanding. Given the natural history of eye-gaze processing deficits in autism, we hypothesized that STS dysfunction was involved. Based on our prior findings and knowledge of these deficits, we decided to explore the role of the STS in gaze processing dysfunction in autism (Pelphrey, Morris, & McCarthy, 2005). To do so, we used our checkerboard paradigm (Pelphrey, Singerman, et al., 2003) (see Figure 8.1). As expected, our sample of typically developing individuals exhibited an increased response for incongruent versus congruent gaze shifts in the posterior STS region, replicating our prior findings (Mosconi, Mack, McCarthy, & Pelphrey, 2005; Pelphrey, Singerman, et al., 2003; Pelphrey, Morris, et al., 2004). However, although we found activity in the STS region in individuals with autism, we did not see differential activity as a function of congruency. This indicated an absence of contextual influence on the STS region and a lack of sensitivity to the intentional and goal-directed structure of actions. We concluded that this was a brain mechanism underlying the gaze processing deficits reported behaviorally in autism. This lack of processing of intentions and dispositions could explain why individuals with autism fail to link the perceptual representation of eyes moving and the concurrent representation regarding a character's goals, motives, and desires (i.e., the contents of the actor's mind) to determine the intentions of another person.

Dysfunction in the STS region was strongly and specifically correlated with the level of social impairment exhibited by individual participants. As a group, activity in the STS region in the participants with autism did not differ significantly for incongruent and congruent gaze shifts. However, just as autism is heterogeneous in severity, there were clear individual differences in the degree of STS dysfunction. To explore whether these individual differences were related to the severity of autism, we computed correlations between the scores on several algorithmic domains of the Autism Diagnostic Interview—Revised (ADI-R; Lord, Rutter, & Le Couteur, 1994), which is used to support the clinical diagnosis of autism, and the magnitude of the incongruent versus congruent differentiation in the right STS region. We assumed that lower levels of incongruent versus congruent differentiation (i.e., incongruent minus congruent scores) in the STS region would indicate greater cortical dysfunction. Higher scores on aspects of the ADI-R can indicate greater severity of autism. The magnitude of the incongruent versus congruent difference score was strongly negatively correlated with scores in the Reciprocal Social Interaction Domain ($R^2 = .78$, $p = .004$), but was not significantly correlated with impairments in the Communication Domain or with the Restricted, Repetitive, and Stereotyped Patterns of Behavior Domain, nor was the measure of STS dysfunction correlated with levels of general intellectual function (as measured by an IQ test). These findings suggest that the degree of neurofunctional impairment in the right STS region is related to the severity of specific core features of the autism phenotype.

Seeing a Face as a Face: Searching for Mechanisms Underlying the Lack of Eye Contact

Our search for the brain mechanisms underlying abnormal scanpaths began similarly to other neuroimaging studies of individuals with autism: by examining activity in the face processing system. In comparison to typically developing participants, hypoactivation of both the amygdalae (e.g., Baron-Cohen et al., 1999; Ogai et al., 2003; Pelphrey, Morris, McCarthy, & LaBar, 2007) and the FFA (e.g., Critchley et al., 2000; Pelphrey et al., 2007; Schultz et al., 2000) has often been observed in people with autism. However, the question of whether or not hypoactivation in these regions is an aspect of the brain phenotype in autism remains open and widely debated.

We recently conducted a literature search that revealed 17 studies of the face processing system in individuals with autism published between 1999 and 2008. Of those 17 studies, 14 reported data from the FFG and 11 reported data from the amygdalae. Ten (Critchley et al., 2000; Dalton et al., 2005; Hubl et al., 2003; Humphreys, Hasson, Avidan, Minshew, & Behrmann, 2008; Koshino et al., 2008; Pelphrey et al., 2007; Pierce, Müller, Ambrose, Allern, & Courchesne, 2001; Piggot et al., 2004; Schultz et al., 2000; Wang, Dapretto, Hariri, Sigman, & Bookheimer, 2004) out of the 14 studies of the FFG reported hypoactivation in participants with autism compared to neurotypical participants, while four reported equivalent FFG activity (Bookheimer, Wang, Scott, Sigman, & Dapretto, 2008; Hadjikhani et al., 2004; Pierce, Haist, Sedaghat, & Courchesne, 2004; Pierce & Redcay, 2008) in participants with and without autism. Eight (Ashwin, Baron-Cohen, Wheelwright, O'Riordan, & Bullmore, 2007; Baron-Cohen et al., 1999; Bookheimer et al., 2008; Critchley et al., 2000; Pelphrey et al., 2007; Pierce et al., 2004; Pierce et al., 2001; Wang et al., 2004) of the 11 studies of the amygdalae reported hypoactivation of the amygdale in participants with autism as compared to typically developing participants. Two reported equivalent amygdalae activity in affected and unaffected individuals (Pierce et al., 2004; Piggot et al., 2004). One study reported left amygdala hyperactivation (Dalton et al., 2005) in participants with autism relative to typically developing participants.

Critical methodological differences exist between those studies that have reported hypoactivation versus equivalent activity in the FFG. The majority of studies reporting FFG hypoactivation involved free viewing and/or very modest task demands. In contrast, two of the four studies reporting equivalent activation in the FFG constrained the viewing patterns of the participants by placing a fixation cross in the center of the stimulus (e.g., on the bridge of the nose between the eyes) (Hadjikhani et al., 2004; Pierce et al., 2004). A third study reporting equivalent FFG activation involved a relatively demanding face recognition task in the context of upright and inverted faces (Bookheimer et al., 2008). Finally, Pierce and Redcay (2008) observed equivalent FFG activity in children with and without autism when the children viewed highly familiar and salient pictures of their mothers. It is possible that the underlying connection between these studies is a task manipulation that increased visual attention to the face, and particularly the eyes, either by requiring participants to maintain a fixation placed between the eyes (Hadjikhani et al., 2004; Pierce et al., 2004), thereby removing the confound of altered visual scanpaths directly; by increasing the salience of the face (Pierce & Redcay, 2008); or by increasing the relevance of the core facial features to the task at hand (Bookheimer et al., 2008).

All of the prior studies can be criticized, albeit on different grounds, for the approaches they have taken to the issue of potentially confounding differences in overt visual attention (Klin, 2008). Studies that have involved free viewing can be criticized for ignoring known differences in visual attention in individuals with autism. The two studies that have controlled for differences in visual scanpaths by constraining fixation to a central cross may be criticized because their design does not allow us to evaluate experimentally the exact mechanism underlying the observed outcome. That is, it is possible that constraining visual fixation to the center of the face inadvertently alters the task for the typically developing participants, who are forced to attend to a fixation point that, in turn, may reduce their experiences of faces as such. In this circumstance, the observed lack of FFG abnormalities in individuals with autism might actually reflect reduced FFG activation in neurotypical participants relative to what would be seen during free viewing rather than increased activity in participants with autism.

Relevant to the last point above, Morris and McCarthy (2006) experimentally manipulated typically developing subjects' scanpaths as they viewed a fixation cross in separate runs on one of three background images: a face, a flower, or a uniform gray field. Participants followed a small fixation cross as it made discrete jumps within the background image every 500 ms. They were thus required to make a saccade to the cross's new location and fixate. A block design was used that alternated small central scanpaths with large, spatially extensive scanpaths of the same background image. The authors demonstrated that large saccades evoked substantially more activation within the FFG and other portions of ventrolateral occipital temporal cortex than small saccades for all background images. Furthermore, activation within the predefined FFA was greater when participants were making large saccades over a face than when making small saccades over a face (the small saccades condition was indeed very similar to the study by Hadjikhani et al., 2004) or large saccades over a flower or gray field. This study therefore established that the magnitude of saccades can differentially influence category-specific activity in the FFA and nearby cortical regions.

A second study (Morris, Pelphrey, & McCarthy, 2007a) manipulated visual scanpaths, but this time addressed whether the precise features of scanpaths composed of saccades of similar magnitude can also influence FFA activity. Participants visually tracked a small crosshair moving across a static face. When the crosshair followed an *atypical* scanpath (landing on eyes less than 12% of the time), decreased FFA activation was observed as compared to that recorded during a *typical* scanpath (landing on eyes approximately 80% of the time). The results showed that the pattern of fixations and saccades used by a subject in viewing a face image strongly influences the amplitude and spatial extent of activation in the ventral occipital temporal cortex generally, and the predefined FFA in particular. Typical scanpaths, with frequent fixations on the eyes, evoked significantly more activity than atypical scanpaths with far fewer such fixations. This difference occurred despite the overall equivalence in average Euclidian distance of saccades in both conditions. This study demonstrates that, by making typically developing individuals scan the eyes less, we can actually reduce their levels of FFA activity.

These findings from typically developing individuals are generally consistent with the conclusions drawn by Dalton and colleagues (2005), who reported a strong, positive correlation in participants with autism between the number of fixations upon the eyes of faces and the level of activation in the FFG, suggesting a link between visual scanpaths and hypoactivation in this component of the face processing system. The two studies described above experimentally manipulated the scanpath within typically developing individuals, and thus strengthen the conclusions drawn by Dalton and colleagues (2005), which were based upon correlational evidence in individuals with autism. Critically, for the purposes of identifying mechanisms underlying abnormal scanpaths, the association they observed could mean that individuals with more FFG activity are the ones who look more at the eyes of faces. Alternatively, the correlation could reflect that, when subjects with autism happen to look more at the eyes, they in turn exhibit greater activity in the FFG. This latter explanation could indicate that direct eye contact is experienced as aversive for individuals with autism. The available data could not clearly adjudicate between these two plausible mechanisms because scanpaths had not been experimentally manipulated in individuals with autism.

To address these issues, we conducted an fMRI study in which we experimentally manipulated activity in the face processing system of high functioning adults with autism by compelling them to look at the eyes of faces to varying degrees. We hypothesized that requiring individuals with autism to visually scan the eyes of an emotionally expressive face would serve to increase activation in key components of the face processing system. We directly manipulated visual scanpaths during fMRI across four incremental experimental conditions: free viewing and low, medium, or high amounts of fixating on the eyes of a single fearful face in full color from the NimStim set of facial expressions (Tottenham et al., 2009) in a group of high-functioning adults with autism and a group of IQ- and age-matched typically developing adults (Perlman, Hudac, Pegors, Minshew, & Pelphrey, 2010).

We first identified a region localized to the right lateral FFG (consistent with the expected location of the FFA) and bilateral amygdalae that were significantly more active in the typically developing participants than in individuals with autism during free viewing. We then examined how, for the group of individuals with autism, our manipulation of eye contact influenced levels of activity. A comparison of the high and free viewing conditions revealed regions within the right lateral FFG and left amygdala in which participants with autism demonstrated significant high > free viewing activity. To further investigate the form of this effect, we computed the average *t*-score for each participant with autism within each region of high > free viewing activity. Activation in these regions increased from negative during free viewing to strongly positive during the high condition. Positive activity in the left amygdala was only observed during the high condition.

These results revealed the striking discovery that, by simply manipulating the amount of visual attention to the eyes, we were able to *normalize* activity in components of the face processing system in individuals with autism as compared to the level of activity in the same participants during free viewing, and the level of normalization was tightly coupled with the amount of time spent viewing the eyes. Furthermore, we demonstrated that the effect of eye contact on activity in the right FFG and left amygdala of individuals with autism is a true effect that is specific to the group of participants with autism. That is, our findings from the free viewing condition revealed that the effect is not attributable to decreases in activity in the FFG of our neurotypical participants as a function of artificially constraining their visual scanpaths.

These findings offer some preliminary insights into the mechanisms by which the common clinical practice of encouraging eye contact might serve to shape the development of the social brain. Requiring individuals with autism, even high-functioning adults, to fixate on the eyes appears to normalize activity temporarily within previously silent components of the face processing system. The results may also speak to the question of whether the previously observed correlation between fixations upon the eyes and the level of activation in the FFG and left amygdala (Dalton et al., 2005) should be interpreted as reflecting that individuals with more FFG and amygdala activity are the ones who look more at the eyes of faces, or if looking at the eyes causes increased activation in these components of the face processing system in people with autism because they are experiencing these stimuli as aversive. It is tempting to interpret the greater-than-normal (defined here as the level of activity observed in typically developing participants during free viewing) amount of activity observed in the high condition as reflecting hyperactivity resulting from the experience of mild aversion upon being compelled to spend a high percentage of the time inspecting the eyes. However, in the absence of within-subject corroborating data (e.g., increases in skin-conductance response or self-reports of finding the stimuli aversive when compelled to look more at the eyes), we can only speculate about this possibility.

Finally, these findings point to important repercussions for theoretical debates concerning the nature of the FFA. Some researchers have argued that the FFA is not specialized for faces per se, but rather that the seemingly selective response to faces reflects the development of a high level of visual *expertise* for faces, relative to other categories of objects, in typically developing individuals (Gauthier, Behrmann, & Tarr, 1999; Tarr & Gauthier, 2000). This theoretical camp has seized upon the findings of FFA hypoactivation in autism as evidence in favor of their theory of visual processing (e.g., Grelotti, Gauthier, & Schultz, 2002). Specifically, they argue that a lack of attention to the eyes leads to a failure to develop a FFA in individuals with autism. Our results are not easily reconciled with the expertise view of face processing deficits in autism. We do find that the FFA is hypoactive in individuals with autism, but we show here that this hypoactivation can be reversed with a simple manipulation of fixation to the eyes. It appears that an FFA is present in individuals who presumably lack the necessary expertise and experience with faces to have developed such a region.

So what do these findings mean for our understanding of the FFA in autism and our understanding of mechanisms underlying abnormal visual scanpaths in affected individuals? With regard to the first part of this question, it is tempting to conclude from the available fMRI studies that the often-replicated finding of hypoactivation in the FFA region is, in the absence of good control over fixations and scanpaths, secondary to systematic differences in scanpaths. With regard to the second part of this question, if our conclusion regarding the mechanism underlying FFA dysfunction is veridical, it would follow that the FFA and amygdala dysfunctions are not important causes of the observed differences in scanpaths. However, there is simply too much evidence suggesting structural differences in both the FFG (e.g., Neeley et al., 2007; van Kooten et al., 2008) and the amygdalae (e.g., Aylward et al., 1999; Bauman & Kemper, 1995; Howard et al., 2000; Schumann & Amaral, 2006; Schumann et al., 2004) of individuals with autism that would have to be ignored in order to readily accept these conclusions. We therefore believe that these conclusions are quite premature and instead propose here an alternative account that casts doubt on firm conclusions regarding the brain and its dysfunction in autism from any one single neuroimaging technique. Specifically, a reconciliation of the available findings points towards an inherent limitation in the available fMRI data: its lack of temporal resolution.

Morris, Pelphrey, and McCarthy (2007b) conducted an fMRI study in which they presented typically developing participants with masked (i.e., subliminally presented) and unmasked faces and objects. Analyses revealed a highly focal region of the right FFG, which was selectively activated by both masked and unmasked faces. They demonstrate that the initial response from the FFG is capable of discriminating faces from other objects even when trials occur outside of conscious awareness. These results support the notion that automatic processes in the FFG reflect the operations of a face detector that is necessary for rapid discrimination between faces and non-face objects (McCarthy, 1999).

More evidence for the early response of the FFG representing face detection comes from electrophysiological recordings made by Gregory McCarthy and his colleagues from subdural electrodes in the FFG of humans. They identified a field potential with a peak latency of about 200 ms (N200) that responds selectively to faces (Allison, McCarthy, Nobre, Puce, & Belger, 1994). The N200 shows little or no habituation to repeated faces, appears unaffected by the affective qualities of stimuli, and is unaffected by attention, eye movements, emotional context, familiarity, priming, or learning (McCarthy, Puce, Belger, & Allison, 1999; Puce, Allison, & McCarthy, 1999). However, FFG activations measured in functional neuroimaging studies are strongly influenced by top-down processes, including attention (Clark et al., 1996; Haxby et al., 1994; Wojciulik, Kanwisher, & Driver, 1998), emotional content (Vuilleumier, Armony, Driver, & Dolan, 2001), and familiarity (Henson, Shallice, & Dolan, 2000). Morris and colleagues (2007b) suggested that the discrepancies in the literature for the face-specific N200 directly recorded from the FFG and for functional neuroimaging activations in this same region reflect the fact that the latter integrates the blood oxygenation correlates of brain activity that persists over a long temporal interval.

Thus, neuroimaging activations may be more sensitive to sustained and recurrent activation evoked by task-related and strategic processing that occur subsequent to the recognition that a face is in the visual field. This interpretation is consistent with intracranial evoked response potential (ERP) recordings showing that, while the N200 is insensitive to attention and task demands, longer latency components may be modulated by top-down processing (Puce et al., 1999). Given this logic, we speculate that the BOLD activation observed in the FFG of individuals in the study by Perlman and colleagues (2010), in which we manipulated overt visual attention to the eyes, reflects sustained and recurrent activation evoked by the task of attending to the face and scanning it in atypical fashion. This activation would normally occur subsequent to recognizing that a face is in the visual field. By manipulating scanpaths, we removed the need for the participants with autism to recognize that a face was in their visual field and instead directly engaged the recurrent activation. If this speculation is correct, it could have strong implications for our understanding of the origin of the abnormal scanpaths observed in autism. Below, we propose a working model to better specify the proposed mechanisms. This is our initial working model and our first attempt to explain the origins of abnormal scanpaths in autism.

As illustrated in Figure 8.3A, in the neurotypical brain during free viewing, when a face appears in the visual field, it is processed in early visual cortices and the results of this processing are passed on to the extrastriate ventral-temporal cortices, including the FFA (step 1 in this figure). Within the FFA, there is an initial response that occurs at approximately 200 ms post stimulus onset. This response reflects the structural encoding of a face as a face and thereby differentiates faces from other objects in the visual field. In step 2 of our model, we record the effects of this response as a change in BOLD activity (via fMRI) or a local field potential (via intracranial ERP) as the FFA sends out the results of its initial processing. Here, we are emphasizing the flow of information regarding the presence of a face from the FFA to the amygdala, although we recognize that the information from the FFA does travel to other regions as well. In step 3, we hypothesize that the information regarding the presence of the face is passed from the amygdala to regions in the prefrontal and frontal cortices involved in the execution of eye movements. The signal from the amygdala engages these centers to execute a scanpath that facilitates the inspection of a face with regard to its social significance, with the majority of the scanning time spent on the eyes and other core facial features (step 4). As the typical scanpath unfolds, additional information is gathered from the face in an efficient fashion (e.g., data regarding identity, emotional expression, familiarity, and simple mental states). This information is fed back into the FFA via the early visual cortices (step 5 in our model) and is measured as additional BOLD activity with fMRI or later modulation of electrical potentials via intracranial ERP.

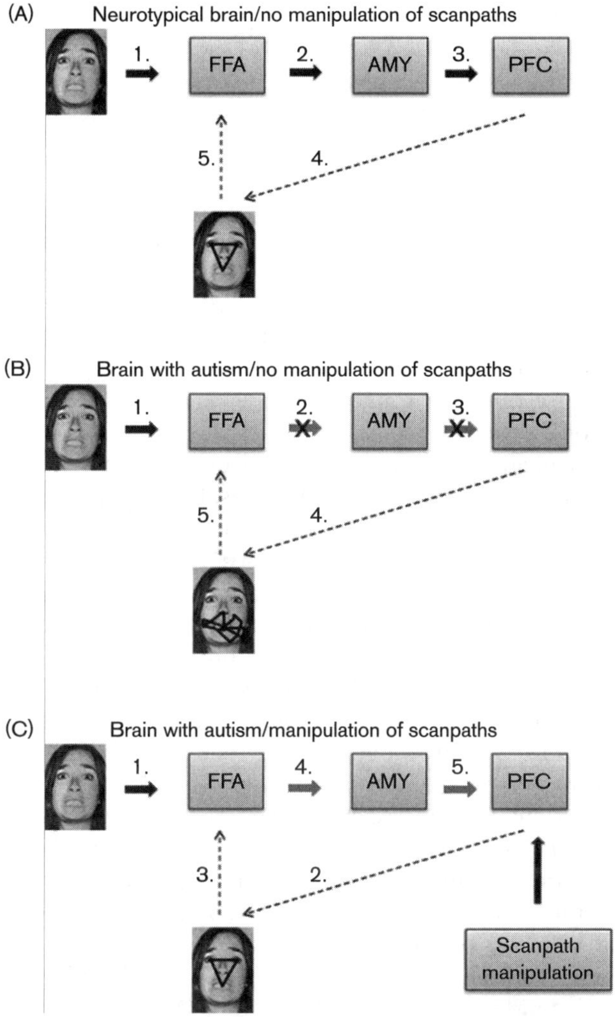

Figure 8.3 A working model of the process by which manipulation of scanpaths influences activity in the FFA.

As portrayed in Figure 8.3B, the sequence of events is altered in the brain of individuals with autism during free viewing. Here, in step 1, the early visual cortices are unaffected and pass a representation of the face to the FFA. However, we hypothesize that the FFA fails to execute the processing that would signal this stimulus as a face versus any other object. As such, the normal steps 2 and 3 fail to occur. Information is not passed from the FFA to the amygdala, and the amygdala fails to signal the prefrontal cortices. In turn, the prefrontal cortices fail to initiate the motor planning needed to execute a typical scanpath (step 4). Note, however, that in the eye-tracking literature on autism there is a growing consensus that individuals do not scan in a random fashion. They fail to look at the eyes, but they also spend an abnormally high amount of time looking at the mouth, particularly if the stimuli are dynamic (Klin et al., 2002). We suggest that this pattern reflects the input of other, unaffected influences on activity in the prefrontal cortices. That is, in the absence of normal signaling from the amygdala, other normal influences are dominant in shaping the resultant scanpath. Given the recent findings regarding the importance of audiovisual synchrony in shaping the visual scanpaths of toddlers in response to point-light displays (Klin, Lin, Gorrindo, Ramsay, & Jones, 2009; also see Chapter 7 in this volume), we hypothesize that the movement of the mouth and accompanying, synchronous sounds serve as powerful influences over the visual behavior of individuals with autism during the inspection of faces. With the execution of an abnormal scanpath, the fusiform receives a suboptimal signal for recurrent processing to occur. As a result, we hypothesize that the hypoactivation commonly observed in functional neuroimaging studies of individuals with autism reflects two underlying processes. First, failure of the initial encoding of a face as a face gives rise to the subsequent failure for a typical scanpath to occur. Secondary to these initial failures, recurrent processing and sustained activation do not occur, and hypoactivation is observed.

What evidence is there for a lack of an initial response in the FFA of individuals with autism? Intracranial data are not currently available to address this question. However, there is a growing literature comparing the face-specific N170 component response recorded from the surface of the scalp in individuals with and without autism. The exact neural generators responsible for the N170 remain a matter of active debate, but it is widely believed that the FFA is one of the neuroanatomical structures involved (Shibata et al., 2002). Studies examining this component in children and adults have consistently reported increased latencies of the N170 response in individuals with autism as compared to age- and IQ-matched neurotypical controls (McPartland, Dawson, Webb, Panagiotides, & Carver, 2004; Webb, Dawson, Bernier, & Panagiotides, 2006). These findings indicate that individuals with autism have abnormal N170 responses, reflecting an abnormal pattern of brain responses to faces and objects from an early age, and this is a life-long characteristic of the brain phenotype.

How then does our experimental manipulation of visual scanpaths fit into this scheme? As shown in Figure 8.3C, we propose that our manipulation allows us to effectively bypass the normal, early processing that would occur in the FFA and amygdala, as well as the early scanpath initial signaling of the amygdala to the prefrontal cortices. By directing scanpaths, we also serve to inhibit the influence of other sources of information on the activity of the prefrontal cortices. In this scheme, step 1 remains the early visual processing of the face, while step 2 is the execution of a scanpath by the prefrontal cortex, which is now under experimental control. Step 3 represents the input through the early visual cortices of information that effectively activates the FFA. This recurrent, sustained activation is measured as the normalized signal via fMRI. At this point, we hypothesize that the FFA sends the results of its processing to the amygdala (step 4), and we indeed register amygdala activation during our experiment. The amygdalae, in turn, begin to signal the prefrontal cortex. We speculate that it is possible for the normal cycle of activity to be engaged at this point. The missing piece, we hypothesize, is the initial response of the FFA to signal the presence of a face (and its social significance) in the visual field. Interestingly, this model seems to fit well with one of Kanner's (1943) original observations regarding children with autism:

> Objects that do not change their appearance and position, that retain their sameness and never threaten to interfere with the child's aloneness, are readily accepted. … The children's relation to people is altogether different. Every one of the children, upon entering the office, immediately went after blocks, toys, or other objects, without paying the least attention to the persons present.
>
> (p. 246)

Are there more general implications that can be drawn from a better understanding of the mechanisms underlying a lack of eye contact in autism? As reviewed above, a deficit in eye contact is among the most striking and consistent of the social impairments in autism and, therefore, is one of the diagnostic criteria for the disorder (APA, 1994). This deficit appears to be among the earliest behavioral manifestations of autism. For example, in a study of first birthday videos, looking at others was found to be among four social behaviors that differentiated children who would go on to be diagnosed with autism later in childhood (Osterling & Dawson, 1994). Furthermore, eye-tracking studies have served to quantify and characterize the developmental nature of the eye-to-eye gaze impairment (Jones, Carr, & Klin, 2008; Klin et al., 2002; Pelphrey et al., 2002). For instance, Warren Jones, Ami Klin, and their colleagues (2008) measured looking to the eyes of others in two-year-old children with autism (currently the earliest possible point of reliable diagnosis), typically developing children, and developmentally delayed children without autism. They found that looking at the eyes of others was significantly decreased, while looking at mouths was increased in two-year-olds with autism, compared with typically developing and developmentally delayed but non-autistic children. As Jones and colleagues (2008) concluded, "diminished and aberrant eye contact is a lifelong hallmark of disability" (p. 946). The lack of eye contact therefore deeply reflects the core social dysfunction. The brain of the individual with autism, unlike the typically developing brain, does not seem to contain some of the basic mechanisms for preparing the individual to interact in a social world. We hope that a better understanding of this specific deficit, and then others, will provide single scientific threads that can then be followed experimentally and ultimately used to disentangle a number of the mysteries currently facing those of us interested in identifying causes of autism.

ACKNOWLEDGMENTS

The research reviewed in this chapter was supported by grants from the National Institute of Mental Health, the National Institute of Child Health and Development, the John Merck Scholars Fund, the Simons Foundation, the Veterans Affairs Administration, Autism Speaks, and the National Institute for Neurological Disorders and Stroke. Kevin Pelphrey was supported by a Career Development Award from the National Institutes of Health (NIMH Grant MH071284). We gratefully acknowledge our collaborators, especially Gregory McCarthy, James Morris, and Truett Allison. We are deeply grateful to the families and children who participate in our research.

REFERENCES

Allison, T., McCarthy, G., Nobre, A., Puce, A., & Belger, A. (1994). Human extrastriate visual cortex and the perception of faces, words, numbers, and colors. *Cerebral Cortex, 4*, 544–554.

Allison, T., Puce, A., & McCarthy, G. (2000). Social perception from visual cues: Role of the STS region. *Trends in Cognitive Sciences, 4*, 267–278.

Amaral, D. G., Price, J. L., Pitkanen, A., & Carmichael, S. T. (1992). Anatomical organization of the primate amygdaloid complex. In J. P. Aggleton (Ed.), *The amygdala: Neurobiological aspects of emotion, memory, and mental dysfunction* (pp. 1–66). New York: Wiley-Liss.

American Psychiatric Association (1994). *Diagnostic and statistical manual of mental disorders* (4th ed.). Washington, DC: American Psychiatric Press.

Ashwin, C., Baron-Cohen, S., Wheelwright, S., O'Riordan, M., & Bullmore, E. T. (2007). Differential activation of the amygdale and the "social brain" during fearful face-processing in Asperger syndrome. *Neuropsychologia, 45*, 2–14.

Aylward, E. H., Minshew, N. J., Goldstein, G., Honeycutt, N. A., Augustine, A. M., Yates, K. O.,… Pearlson, G. D. (1999). MRI volumes of amygdala and hippocampus in non–mentally retarded autistic adolescents and adults. *Neurology*, 53, 2145.

Barbas, H. (1988). Anatomic organization of basoventral and mediodorsal visual recipient prefrontal regions in the rhesus monkey. *Journal of Comparative Neurology*, 276, 313–342.

Baron-Cohen, S. (1995). *Mindblindness: An essay on autism and theory of mind*. Cambridge, MA: MIT Press.

Baron-Cohen, S., Ring, H. A., Wheelright, S., Bullmore, E. T., Brammer, M. J., Simmons, A., & Williams, S. C. R. (1999). Social intelligence in the normal and autistic brain: An fMRI study. *European Journal of Neuroscience, 11*, 1891–1898.

Bauman, M. L., & Kemper, T. L. (1995). Neuroanatomic observations of the brain in autism. In M. L. Bauman, & T. L. Kemper (Eds.), *The neurobiology of autism* (pp. 119–145). Baltimore, MD: Johns Hopkins University Press.

Bonda, E., Petrides, M., Ostry, D., & Evans, A. (1996). Specific involvement of human parietal systems and the amygdala in the perception of biological motion. *Journal of Neuroscience, 16*, 3737–3744.

Bookheimer, S. Y., Wang, A. T., Scott, A., Sigman, M., & Dapretto, M. (2008). Frontal contributions to face processing differences in autism: Evidence from fMRI of inverted face processing. *Journal of the International Neuropsychological Society, 14*, 922–932.

Brass, M., Schmitt, R. M., Spengler, S., & Gergely, G. (2007). Investigating action understanding: Inferential processes versus action simulation. *Current Biology, 17*, 2117–2121.

Brothers, L. (1990). The social brain: A project for integrating primate behavior and neurophysiology in a new domain. *Concepts in Neuroscience, 1*, 27–51.

Brothers, L., & Ring, B. (1993). Mesial temporal neurons in the macaque monkey with responses selective for aspects of social stimuli. *Behavioural Brain Research, 57*, 53–61.

Brothers, L., Ring, B., & Kling, A. (1990). Response of neurons in the macaque amygdala to complex social stimuli. *Behavioural Brain Research, 41*, 199–213.

Castelli, F., Happé, F., Frith, U., & Frith, C. (2000). Movement and mind: A functional imaging study of perception and interpretation of complex intentional movement patterns. *NeuroImage, 12*, 314–325.

Clark, V. P., Keil, K., Maisog, J. M., Courtney, S., Ungerleider, L. G., & Haxby, J. V. (1996). Functional magnetic resonance imaging of human visual cortex during face matching: A comparison with positron emission tomography. *NeuroImage, 4*, 1–15.

Corbetta, M., Patel, G., & Shulman, G. L. (2008). The reorienting system of the human brain: From environment to theory of mind. *Neuron, 58*, 306–324.

Critchley, H. D., Daly, E. M., Bullmore, E. T., Williams, S. C. R., Van Amelsvoort, T., Robertson, D. M.,... Murphy, D. G. M. (2000). The functional neuroanatomy of social behavior: Changes in cerebral bloodflow when people with autistic disorder process facial expressions. *Brain, 123*, 2203–2212.

Dalton, K. M., Nacewicz, B. M., Johnstone, T., Schaefer, H. S., Gernsbacher, M. A., Goldsmith, H. H.,... Davidson, R. J. (2005). Gaze fixation and the neural circuitry of face processing in autism. *Nature Neuroscience, 8*, 519–526.

Davis, M., & Whalen, P. J. (2001). The amygdala: Vigilance and emotion. *Molecular Psychiatry, 6*, 13–34.

Desimone, R. (1991). Face-selective cells in the temporal cortex of monkeys. *Journal of Cognitive Neuroscience, Special Issue: Face Perception, 3*, 1–8.

Desimone, R., Albright, T. D., Gross, C. G., & Bruce, C. (1984). Stimulus-selective properties of inferior temporal neurons in the macaque. *Journal of Neuroscience, 4*, 2051–2062.

Efron, B., & Tibshirani, R. J. (1993). *An introduction to the bootstrap: Monographs on statistics and applied probability*. New York: Chapman & Hall.

Gauthier, I., Behrmann, M., & Tarr, M. J. (1999). Can face recognition really be dissociated from object recognition? *Journal of Cognitive Neuroscience, 11*, 349–370.

Genovese, C. R., Lazar, N. A., & Nichols, T. (2002). Thresholding of statistical maps in functional neuroimaging using the false discovery rate. *NeuroImage, 15*, 870–878.

Geweke, J. (1982). Measurement of linear dependence and feedback between time series. *Journal of the American Statistical Association, 79*, 304–324.

Granger, C. W. J. (1969). Investigating causal relation by econometric and cross-sectional method. *Econometrica, 37*, 424–438.

Grelotti, D. J., Gauthier, I., & Schultz, R. T. (2002). Social interest and the development of cortical face specialization: What autism teaches us about face processing. *Developmental Psychobiology, 40*, 213–225.

Hadjikhani, N., Joseph, R. M., Snyder, J., Chabris, C. F., Clark, J., Steele, S.,… Tager-Flusberg, H. (2004). Activation of the fusiform gyrus when individuals with autism spectrum disorder view faces. *NeuroImage, 22*, 1141–1150.

Haxby, J. V., Horwitz, B., Ungerleider, L. G., Maisog, J. M., Pietrini, P., & Grady, C. L. (1994). The functional organization of human extrastriate cortex: A PET–rCBF study of selective attention to faces and locations. *Journal of Neuroscience, 14*, 6336–6353.

Heider, F. (1958). *The psychology of interpersonal relations*. New York: John Wiley & Sons.

Heider, F., & Simmel, M. (1944). An experimental study of apparent behavior. *American Journal of Psychology, 57*, 243–259.

Henson, R., Shallice, T., & Dolan, R. (2000). Neuroimaging evidence for dissociable forms of repetition priming. *Science, 287*, 1269–1272.

Hopfinger, J. B., Buonocore, M. H., & Mangun, G. R. (2000). The neural mechanisms of top-down attentional control. *Nature Neuroscience, 3*, 284–291.

Howard, M. A., Cowell, P. E., Boucher, J., Broks, P., Mayes, A., Farrant, A., & Robert, N. (2000). Convergent neuroanatomical and behavioural evidence of an amygdala hypothesis of autism. *NeuroReport, 11*, 2931–2935.

Hubl, D., Bölte, S., Feineis-Matthews, S., Lanfermann, H., Federspiel, A., Strik, F.,… Dierks, T. (2003). Functional imbalance of visual pathways indicates alternative face processing strategies in autism. *Neurology, 61*, 1232–1237.

Humphreys, K., Hasson, U., Avidan, G., Minshew, N., & Behrmann, M. (2008). Cortical patterns of category-selective activation for faces, places, and objects in adults with autism. *Autism Research, 1*, 52–63.

Johansson, G. (1973). Visual perception of biological motion and a model for its analysis. *Perception & Psychophysics, 14*, 201–211.

Johnson, M. H. (2006). Biological motion: A perceptual "life detector?" *Current Biology, 16*, 376–377.

Jones, W., Carr, K., & Klin, A. (2008). Absence of preferential looking to the eyes of approaching adults predicts level of social disability in 2-year-old toddlers with autism spectrum disorder. *Archives of General Psychiatry, 65*, 946–954.

Kanner, L. (1943). Autistic disturbances of affective contact. *The Nervous Child, 2*, 217–250.

Kanwisher, N., McDermott, J., & Chun, M. M. (1997). The fusiform face area: A module in human extrastriate cortex specialized for face perception. *Journal of Neuroscience, 17*, 4302–4311.

Klin, A. (2008). Three things to remember if you are a functional magnetic resonance imaging researcher of face processing in autism spectrum disorders. *Biological Psychiatry, 64*, 549–551.

Klin, A., Jones, W., Schultz, R. T., Volkmar, F. R., & Cohen, D. J. (2002). Visual fixation patterns during viewing of naturalistic social situations as predictors of social competence in individuals with autism. *Archives of General Psychiatry, 59*, 809–816.

Klin, A., Lin, D. J., Gorrindo, P., Ramsay, G., & Jones, W. (2009). Two-year-olds with autism fail to orient towards human biological motion but attend instead to non-social, physical contingencies. *Nature, 459*, 257–261.

Klüver, H., & Bucy, P. C. (1997). Preliminary analysis of functions of the temporal lobes in monkeys. *Journal of Neuropsychiatry Clinical Neuroscience, 9*, 606–620.

Koshino, H., Kana, R. J., Keller, T. A., Cherkassky, V. L., Minshew, N. J., & Just, M. A. (2008). fMRI investigation of working memory for faces in autism: Visual coding underconnectivity with frontal areas. *Cerebral Cortex, 18*, 289–300.

LeDoux, J. E. (2000). Emotion circuits in the brain. *Annual Review of Neuroscience, 23*, 155–184.

Lord, C., Rutter, M., & Le Couteur, A. (1994). Autism diagnostic interview-revised: A revised version of a diagnostic interview for caregivers of individuals with possible pervasive developmental disorders. *Journal of Autism and Developmental Disorders, 24*, 659–685.

McCarthy, G. (1999). Event-related potentials and functional MRI: A comparison of localization in sensory, perceptual, and cognitive tasks. *Electroencephalography and Clinical Neurophysiology, 49*, 3–12.

McCarthy, G., Puce, A., Belger, A., & Allison, T. (1999). Electrophysiological studies of human face perception. II: Response properties of face-specific potentials generated in occipitotemporal cortex. *Cerebral Cortex, 9*, 431–444.

McPartland, J., Dawson, G., Webb, S. J., Panagiotides, H., & Carver, L. J. (2004). Event-related brain potentials reveal anomalies in temporal processing of faces in autism spectrum disorder. *Journal of Child Psychology and Psychiatry, 45*, 1235–1245.

Morris, J. P., & McCarthy, G. (2006). Guided saccades modulate object and face-specific activity in the fusiform gyrus. *Human Brain Mapping, 28*, 691–702.

Morris, J. P., Pelphrey, K. A., & McCarthy, G. (2007a). Controlled scanpath variation alters fusiform face activation. *Social Cognitive and Affective Neuroscience, 2*, 31–38.

Morris, J. P., Pelphrey, K. A., & McCarthy, G. (2007b). Face processing without awareness in the right fusiform gyrus. *Neuropsychologia, 45*, 3087–3091.

Morris, J. S., Frith, C. D., Perrett, D. I., Rowland, D., Young, A. W., Calder, A. J., & Dolan, R. J. (1996). A differential neural response in the human amygdala to fearful and happy facial expressions. *Nature, 383*, 812–815.

Mosconi, M. W., Mack, P. B., McCarthy, G., & Pelphrey, K. A. (2005). Taking an "intentional stance" on eye-gaze shifts: A functional neuroimaging study of social perception in children. *NeuroImage, 27*, 247–252.

Neeley, E. S., Bigler, E. D., Krasny, L., Ozonoff, S., McMahon, W., & Lainhart, J. E. (2007). Quantitative temporal lobe differences: Autism distinguished from controls using classification and regression tree analysis. *Brain and Development, 29*, 389–399.

Ogai, M., Matsumoto, H., Suzuki, K., Ozawa, F., Fukuda, R., Uchiyama, I., . . . Takei, N. (2003). fMRI study of recognition of facial expression in high-functioning autistic patients. *NeuroReport, 14*, 559–563.

Osterling, J., & Dawson, G. (1994). Early recognition of children with autism: A study of first birthday home videotapes. *Journal of Autism and Developmental Disorders, 24*, 247–257.

Pandya, D. N., & Yeterian, E. H. (1996). Morphological correlations of human and monkey frontal lobe. In A. R. Damasio, H. Damasio, & Y. Christen (Eds.), *Neurobiology of decision making* (pp. 13–46). New York: Springer.

Pelphrey, K. A., Mitchell, T. V., McKeown, M. J., Goldstein, J., Allison, T., & McCarthy, G. (2003). Brain activity evoked by the perception of human walking: Controlling for meaningful coherent motion. *Journal of Neuroscience, 23*, 6819–6825.

Pelphrey, K. A., & Morris, J. P. (2006). Brain mechanisms for interpreting the actions of others from biological-motion cues. *Current Directions in Psychological Science, 15*, 136–140.

Pelphrey, K. A., Morris, J. P., & McCarthy, G. (2004). Grasping the intentions of others: The perceived intentionality of an action influences activity in the superior temporal sulcus during social perception. *Journal of Cognitive Neuroscience, 16*, 1706–1716.

Pelphrey, K. A., Morris, J. P., & McCarthy, G. (2005). Neural basis of eye gaze processing deficits in autism. *Brain, 128*, 1038–1048.

Pelphrey, K. A., Morris, J. P., McCarthy, G., & LaBar, K. S. (2007). Perception of dynamic changes in facial affect and identity in autism. *Social Cognitive and Affective Neuroscience, 2*, 140–150.

Pelphrey, K. A., Morris, J. P., Michelich, C. R., Allison, T., & McCarthy, G. (2005). Functional anatomy of biological motion perception in posterior temporal cortex: An FMRI study of eye, mouth, and hand movements. *Cerebral Cortex, 15*, 1866–1876.

Pelphrey, K. A., Sasson, N. J., Reznick, J. S., Paul, G., Goldman, B. D., & Piven, J. (2002). Visual scanning of faces in autism. *Journal of Autism and Developmental Disorders, 32*, 249–261.

Pelphrey, K. A., Singerman, J. D., Allison, T., & McCarthy, G. (2003). Brain activation evoked by perception of gaze shifts: The influence of context. *Neuropsychologia, 41*, 156–170.

Pelphrey, K. A., Viola, R. J., & McCarthy, G. (2004). When strangers pass: Processing of mutual and averted social gaze in the superior temporal sulcus. *Psychological Science, 15*, 598–603.

Perlman, S. B., Hudac, C. M., Pegors, T., Minshew, N. J., & Pelphrey, K. A. (2010). Experimental manipulation of activity in the fusiform gyrus of individuals with autism. *Social Neuroscience, 27*, 1–9.

Perrett, D. I., Rolls, E. T., & Caan, W. (1979). Temporal lobe cells of the monkey with visual responses selective for faces. *Neuroscience Letters*, S358.

Perrett, D. I., Rolls, E. T., & Caan, W. (1982). Visual neurons responsive to faces in the monkey temporal cortex. *Experimental Brain Research, 47*, 329–342.

Perrett, D. I., Smith, P. A. J., Potter, D. D., Mistlin, A. J., Head, A. S., Milner, A. D., & Jeeves, M. A. (1984). Neurones responsive to faces in the temporal cortex: Studies of functional organization, sensitivity to identity, and relation to perception. *Human Neurobiology, 3*, 197–208.

Perrett, D. I., Smith, P. A. J., Potter, D. D., Mistlin, A. J., Head, A. S., Milner, A. D., & Jeeves, M. A. (1985). Visual cells in the temporal cortex sensitive to face view and gaze direction. *Proceedings of the Royal Society of London Series, 223*, 293–317.

Phillips, A. T., Wellman, H. M., & Spelke, E. S. (2002). Infants' ability to connect gaze and emotional expression to intentional action. *Cognition, 85*, 53–78.

Pierce, K., Haist, F., Sedaghat, F., & Courchesne, E. (2004). The brain response to personally familiar faces in autism: Findings of fusiform activity and beyond. *Brain, 127*, 2703–2716.

Pierce, K., Müller, R. A., Ambrose, J., Allern, G., & Courchesne, E. (2001). Face processing occurs outside the fusiform "face area" in autism: Evidence from functional MRI. *Brain, 124*, 2059–2073.

Pierce, K., & Redcay, E. (2008). Fusiform function in children with an autism spectrum disorder is a matter of "who." *Biological Psychiatry, 64*, 552–560.

Piggot, J., Kwon, H., Mobbs, D., Blasey, C., Lotspeich, L., Menon, V.,... Reiss, A. L. (2004). Emotional attribution in high-functioning individuals with autistic spectrum disorder: A functional imaging study. *Journal of American Academy of Child and Adolescent Psychiatry, 43*, 473–480.

Premack, D., & Woodruff, G. (1978). Does the chimpanzee have a theory of mind? *Behavioral and Brain Science, 4*, 515–526.

Puce, A., Allison, T., Asgari, M., Gore, J. C., & McCarthy, G. (1996). Differential sensitivity of human visual cortex to faces, letterstrings, and textures: A functional MRI study. *The Journal of Neuroscience, 16*, 5205–5215.

Puce, A., Allison, T., & McCarthy, G. (1999). Electrophysiological studies of human face perception. III: Top-down processing on face-specific potentials. *Cerebral Cortex, 9*, 445–458.

Roebroeck, A., Formisano, E., & Goebel, R. (2005). Mapping directed influence over the brain using Granger causality and fMRI. *NeuroImage, 25*, 230–242.

Rolls, E. T. (1981). Responses of amygdaloid neurons in the primate. In Y. Ben-Ari (Ed.), *The amygdaloid complex* (pp. 383–393). Amsterdam: Elsevier.

Rolls, E. T. (1995). Central taste anatomy and neurophysiology. In R. L. Doty (Ed.), *Handbook of olfaction and gestation* (pp. 549–573). New York: Dekker.

Rolls, E. T. (2000). The orbitofrontal cortex and reward. *Cerebral Cortex, 10*, 284–294.

Rolls, E. T. (2009). Prefrontal contributions to reward encoding. In L. R. Squire (Ed.), *Encyclopedia of neuroscience* (pp. 895–903). Oxford: Academic Press.

Saxe, R., Xiao, D. K., Kovacs, G., Perrett, D. I., & Kanwisher, N. (2004). A region of right posterior superior temporal sulcus responds to observed intentional actions. *Neuropsychologia, 42*, 1435–1446.

Schultz, R. T., Gauthier, I., Klin, A., Fulbright, R. K., Anderson, A. W., Volkmar, F.,... Gore, J. C. (2000). Abnormal ventral temporal cortical activity during face discrimination among individuals with autism and Asperger syndrome. *Archives of General Psychiatry, 57*, 331–340.

Schumann, C. M., & Amaral, D. G. (2006). Stereological analysis of amygdala neuron number in autism. *The Journal of Neuroscience, 26*, 7674–7679.

Schumann, C. M., Hamstra, J., Goodlin-Jones, B. L., Lotspeich, L. J., Kwon, H., Buonocore, M. H.,... Amaral, D. G. (2004). The amygdala is enlarged in children but not adolescents with autism; the hippocampus is enlarged at all ages. *The Journal of Neuroscience, 24*, 6392–6401.

Shibata, T., Nishijo, H., Tamura, R., Miyamoto, K., Eifuku, S., Endo, S., & Ono, T. (2002). Generators of visual evoked potentials for faces and eyes in the human brain as determined by dipole localization. *Brain Topography, 15*, 51–63.

Simion, F., Regolin, L., & Bulf, H. (2008). A predisposition for biological motion in the newborn baby. *Proceedings of the National Academy of Sciences, 105*, 809–813.

Small, D. M., Gitelman, D. R., Gregory, M. D., Nobre, A. C., Parrish, T. B., & Mesulam, M. M. (2003). The posterior cingulate and medial prefrontal cortex mediate the anticipatory allocation of spatial attention. *NeuroImage, 18*, 633–641.

Tarr, M. J., & Gauthier, I. (2000). FFA: A flexible fusiform area for subordinate-level visual-processing automatized by expertise. *Nature Neuroscience, 3*, 764–769.

Tottenham, N., Tanaka, J. W., Leon, A. C., McCarry, T., Nurse, M., Hare, T. A.,... Nelson, C. (2009). The NimStim set of facial expressions: Judgments from untrained research participants. *Psychiatry Research, 168*, 242–249.

Vander Wyk, B. C., Hudac, C. M., Carter, E. J., Sobel, D. M., & Pelphrey, K. A.

(2009). Action understanding in the superior temporal sulcus region. *Psychological Science, 20*, 771–777.

van Kooten, I. A. J., Palmen, S. J. M. C., von Cappeln, P., Steinbusch, H. W. M., Korr, H., Heinsen, H.,... Schmitz, C. (2008). Neurons in the fusiform gyrus are fewer and smaller in autism. *Brain, 131*, 987–999.

Vuilleumier, P., Armony, J. L., Driver, J., & Dolan, R. J. (2001). Effects of attention and emotion on face processing in the human brain: An event-related fMRI study, *Neuron, 30*, 829–841.

Wang, A. T., Dapretto, M., Hariri, A. R., Sigman, M., & Bookheimer, S. (2004). Neural correlates of facial affect processing in children and adolescents with autism spectrum disorder. *Journal of American Academy of Child and Adolescent Psychiatry, 43*, 481–490.

Webb, S. J., Dawson, G., Bernier, R., & Panagiotides, H. (2006). ERP evidence of atypical face processing in young children with autism. *Journal of Autism and Developmental Disorders, 36*, 881–890.

Wing, L., & Gould, J. (1979). Severe impairments of social interaction and associated abnormalities in children: Epidemiology and classification. *Journal of Autism and Developmental Disorders, 9*, 11–29.

Wojciulik, E., Kanwisher, N., & Driver, J. (1998). Covert visual attention modulates face-specific activity in the human fusiform gyrus: fMRI study. *Journal of Neurophysiology, 79*, 1574–1578.

Zeki, S., Watson, J. D., Lueck, C. J., Friston, K. J., Kennard, C., & Frackowiak, R. S. (1991). A direct demonstration of functional specialization in human visual cortex. *Journal of Neuroscience, 11*, 641–649.

9

Neural Representations of Self versus Other

Lessons from Autism

RAJESH K. KANA
UAB Department of Psychology, Birmingham, AL

CHRISTOPHER L. KLEIN
Marietta College, Marietta, OH

LAURA GROFER KLINGER
Department of Psychology, University of Alabama, Tuscaloosa, AL

BRITTANY G. TRAVERS
University of Wisconsin-Madison, WI

MARK R. KLINGER
Department of Psychology, University of Alabama, Tuscaloosa, AL

Social cognition broadly refers to the way people make sense of others and themselves (Fiske & Taylor, 1991), the way people construct representations of the relation between self and other, and the way people flexibly use such representations to guide social behavior (Adolphs, Sears, & Piven, 2001). Human social interactions require the ability to relate self with others, as well as the ability to distinguish self from others. However, a key question is at what stage in development do we begin to differentiate others from ourselves, and what role does this distinction play in the development of critical social-cognitive functions, such as Theory of Mind (ToM), action understanding, embodiment, social evaluation, and empathizing? Indeed, these social-cognitive functions appear to be interrelated, as ToM refers to the ability to understand that mental states can cause, explain, and predict others' behavior (Premack & Woodruff, 1978), and action understanding, and embodiment may be basic to mental state attribution.

Although embodiment and empathizing are mechanisms that are thought to allow us to see others as "like me" (Meltzoff, 2007), it is possible that the development of the concept of "me" facilitates the development of embodiment and empathizing, and that an atypical representation of "me" inhibits these processes, thus inhibiting ToM. Therefore, a second question pertains to learning the nature of typical functions from the dysfunctions in disabled populations, such as neurodevelopmental disorders. For instance, autism spectrum disorders (ASD) have been found to be characterized by extreme withdrawal to oneself, complete self-focus, or extreme egocentrism (Kanner, 1943; Asperger, 1944; Frith & de Vignemont, 2005). Examining the neural correlates of self in individuals with ASD may help us gain insight into important social-cognitive functions like ToM, social evaluation, and empathy. To this end, we will examine the integrity of three neural systems (cortical midline structures, the mirror neuron system, and the Theory of Mind network) thought to underlie self-related thinking and related aspects of social cognition and social functioning. Then, we will examine how these neural systems are possibly altered in individuals with ASD.

For self-understanding, we will examine cortical midline structures (CMS), a set of regions in the midline of the cortex arching around the corpus callosum. The CMS (constituting the medial prefrontal cortex, the anterior, middle and posterior cingulate cortices, and the precuneus) are thought to functionally integrate self-related thought and planning (see Northoff et al., 2006). The CMS seem to attenuate their activity when participants engage in explicit, attention-demanding, and goal-directed cognitive tasks. These structures are also called the default mode network of the brain, which may be the psychological baseline of brain functioning (Raichle, 2001; Gusnard & Raichle, 2001; Fox & Raichle, 2007). The activity of this network has been linked to task-unrelated mental processes (Giambra, 1995). Such thoughts are usually autobiographical in nature, which would naturally have strong associations with the self. fMRI and positron-emission tomography (PET) studies have implicated the CMS in self-referential processing compared to non self-referential tasks (see Northoff et al., 2006, for a meta-analysis of brain activation in several studies on self-processing). In addition to playing an active role in tasks that focus on self, most of the CMS regions have been found to be active during resting state, when people tend to reflect on themselves and their actions (Raichle et al., 2001; Gusnard & Raichle, 2001; Fox & Raichle, 2007; Raichle & Snyder, 2007). In autism, resting state fMRI studies have revealed altered neural response during self-referential thinking (Cherkassky, Kana, Keller, & Just, 2006; Kennedy, Redcay, & Courchesne, 2006), which, in addition to the behavioral evidence of abnormalities in the development of self-concept, provide a compelling case to study self in persons with ASD.

For Theory of Mind, we will examine the ToM network, composed of the temporoparietal junction (TPJ) (Saxe & Wexler, 2005) and the medial prefrontal cortex (MPFC) (Castelli, Frith, Happé, & Frith, 2002; Kana, Keller, Cherkassky, Minshew, & Just, 2009), which is involved in understanding the intentions of others. Despite the participation of other regions, such as the amygdala, anterior paracingulate, orbitofrontal cortex, and temporal pole, in ToM tasks, the debate in ToM literature has focused more on the relative role of TPJ and MPFC (Gallagher & Frith, 2003; Saxe & Wexler, 2005). While the MPFC has been found to play an active role in resting state as well as in ToM tasks involving self-reflection, transcranial magnetic stimulation (TMS) studies of TPJ reveal out-of-body experience (OBE) (Blanke & Arzy, 2005). Research on OBE as well as other related functions have established the role of TPJ in perception of body parts (Bonda, Petrides, Ostry, & Evans, 1995), perception of the entire body (Downing, Jiang, Shuman, & Kanwisher, 2001; Astafiev, Stanley, Shulman, & Corbetta, 2004), and mental imagery with respect to one's own body (Zacks, Ollinger, Sheridan, & Tversky, 2002; Blanke, 2004), suggesting the importance of this region in body perception and in forming bodily self.

For embodiment, we will examine the mirror neuron system (MNS), consisting primarily of the inferior parietal lobule (IPL) and the inferior frontal gyrus (IFG), thought to be involved in simulating the actions of oneself and others (Rizzolatti & Craighero, 2004). The MNS seems to form the connecting link between self and other by translocating the self to the other and vice versa. In a typically developing individual, the MNS plays an important role in both empathy and imitation (Iacoboni & Dapretto, 2006); and empathy is not only involved in responding to others, but also necessary for making a distinction between the "self" and the "other" (Greimel et al., 2010). As the understanding of the self and other develop, children begin to adjust their actions to the needs of others around them (Hobson & Meyer, 2005). It has been hypothesized that people with ASD may have an aberrant mirror neuron functioning (Williams, Whiten, Suddendorf, & Perrett, 2001; Williams, 2008).

We speculate that these three systems (CMS, ToM, and MNS) may function in an integrated fashion to form the basic foundation for creating as well as for understanding socially meaningful interactions. Since "self" and "other" form two critical nodes in social interactions, what orchestrates the interaction between these nodes may be these three systems. We hypothesize that the CMS may mediate the evaluative and self-reflective aspects of the self, ToM may help understand the mental states of oneself and others, and MNS may help the self simulate the actions of the other to understand goals and intentions. In clinical populations, such as persons with ASD, the functional synchrony between the three systems or within a given system may be impaired, thus having cascading social and cognitive effects. Below we discuss in detail how different systems mediate self–other understanding and how, if at all, this is altered in individuals with ASD.

SELF-CONCEPT AND CMS

Development of Self in Individuals with Typical Development

Children with typical development begin to show signs of developing a sense of self around the age of two through their ability to recognize themselves in mirrors, use their names to self-reference, point to themselves to self-reference, and express their personal emotions (Bullock & Lutkenhaus, 1990; Kagan, 1981; Lewis & Brooks-Gunn, 1979; Lewis & Ramsay, 2004; Lewis, Sullivan, Stanger, & Weiss, 1989; Stipek, Gralinski, & Kopp, 1990). However, the idea of self may not develop as a singular entity (Kagan, 1991) but may be comprised of both objective and subjective components (James, 1890). While subjective self-awareness may be a state of consciousness in which attention is focused on events external to the individual's consciousness, personal history, or body, the objective self-awareness may be the exact opposite state (Duval & Wicklund, 1972).

At the neural level, self–other representations may involve the integration of information from subcortical structures (brain stem, colliculi, periaqueductal gray [PAG], and hypothalamus involved with bodily self), CMS (involved with the creation of mental self), and higher cortical structures (e.g., the lateral prefrontal cortex involved with the creation of the autobiographical and narrative selves) (see Northoff et al., 2006, for a review). Thus, the interaction among cortical and subcortical midline structures and lateral prefrontal cortex may be critical in creating a mental self. Evidence from imaging studies has shown problems in the connections between different regions in the CMS and between CMS and other regions in individuals with ASD. Altered resting state connectivity in people with autism has been reported by a handful of previous studies (Cherkassky et al., 2006; Kennedy et al., 2006; Murias, Webb, Greenson, & Dawson, 2007). While Cherkassky et al. (2006) found lower functional connectivity between specific regions of interest within the CMS (especially between the anterior and posterior areas) in ASD during rest, Kennedy et al. (2006) found an abnormal pattern of deactivation and connectivity in individuals with ASD. The study by Murias et al. (2007) used EEG coherence methods, the findings of which support alterations in functional connectivity during rest in individuals with ASD. These findings of altered spontaneous fluctuations of the brain in ASD may be indicative of the problems in their default brain state, which can have a telling influence on their concept of self.

Self in Persons with ASD

In her fascinating book *Pretending to be Normal: Living with Asperger's Syndrome*, Liane Willey writes, "My own conversations and thoughts were always my best friends. I was happy spending time with only me, happy to talk to myself, and happy to entertain myself" (1999, p. 35). These words underscore the aloofness and extreme withdrawal to oneself documented in people with autism in Kanner's (1943) initial description of the disorder and in subsequent reports. Difficulties in the representation of the concepts of self and other have been reflected in several functions in people with ASD, especially in linguistic and social modalities. In the linguistic domain, pronoun reversal has been reported in children with autism (Lord & Paul, 1997), although linguistically advanced children overcome pronoun reversal as they get older (Tager-Flusberg, 1994). Pronoun reversal in autism has been attributed to echolalia (Kanner, 1943); to linguistic and information processing demands for shifting and making reference, such as deixis (Rice, Oetting, & Marquis, 1994); to difficulties in conceptualizing the notions of self and other (Lee, Hobson, & Chiat, 1994; Tager-Flusberg, 1993); and to difficulties in conceptual perspective-taking (Loveland, 1984). Prolonged use of reversed pronouns may be an indication of the atypical representation of self and other in children and adolescents with ASD, as switching between "I" and "you" may involve more than linguistic demands.

Another area where problems in self–other representation may be manifested in ASD is in imitation tasks, since imitating the actions of others involves a one-to-one mapping of that action in one's mind. Deficits in imitation, a key feature of social dysfunction in children with ASD, may be related to a core problem in self–other representations (Gallese, 2006). It has been debated both ways: A lack of imitation may lead to development of very different self–other representation or a deficit in appropriate self–other representation may lead to a lack of imitation (Freitag, Kleser, & von Gontard, 2006; Rogers & Pennington, 1991). Williams, Massaro, Peel, Bosseler, and Suddendorf (2004) suggest that typically developing individuals will unconsciously use the same neural systems for actions of both self and other, which is the basis of their ability to imitate. Individuals with autism, however, lack the ability to create this social representation of self, leading not only to an inability to imitate but also to a host of other impairments.

THEORY OF MIND

The development of Theory of Mind (ToM) in children is characterized by their ability to distinguish belief and appearance from reality, to understand that the mental world is distinct from the physical world, and to understand that other people can have beliefs and desires that are different from one's own. In the first few months of life itself, infants are able to imitate the facial expressions of their caregivers (Caron, Caron, & Myers, 1982) and track their intentions (Gergely, Nádasdy, Csibra, & Bíró, 1995). Although children may begin to refer to themselves as "I," and are able to talk about the mental states of others by two years of age (Bretherton & Beeghly, 1982), higher-order ToM tasks, such as false belief, are not processed effectively until the child is older.

False belief tasks, although directed at the mind of the "other," also require the development and understanding of the "self." Studies show that these two substrates develop in series; in order for one to pass the "other" question, they first have to pass the "self" question (Happé, 2003).

Evidence from developmental studies indicates that the neural network underlying ToM processing changes throughout childhood and adolescence. This network includes the superior temporal sulcus, the medial prefrontal cortex, and the temporal poles (Blakemore, den Ouden, Choudhury, & Frith, 2007; Blakemore, 2008; Kobayashi, Glover, & Temple, 2007; Moriguchi et al., 2007; Pfeifer, Lieberman, & Dapretto, 2007). The most consistent findings have indicated a decrease of the activity in the MPFC (Blakemore, 2008) and in the precuneus (Kobayashi, Glover, & Temple, 2008) as one ages. A recent study by Greimel et al. (2010) found increased activity in inferior frontal gyri depending on whether the subject was performing a "self" or an "other" task. When performing a self task, the study found decreased activation in the right parietal cortex with increase in age.

It has been repeatedly shown that children with ASD have marked disabilities with ToM tasks. They have difficulties in understanding the emotional states and intentions of others, as well as fully understanding the "self." One study on self–other tasks shows that children with autism do not use their own body as a reference when trying to talk about another person's body (Hobson & Meyer, 2005). The children with typical development would point to themselves to tell the researcher where to put a sticker on the researcher's body. The children with autism never pointed to themselves; they pointed to the tester instead. This finding is similar to those found when looking at ASD performance on false belief tasks (Baron-Cohen, 1989). False belief tasks require that one be able to consider the knowledge of another and hold that knowledge separate from one's own knowledge. As mentioned before, one must understand the "self" before they are able to understand "others." Children with ASD may lack the ability to understand their own actions. Therefore, they may have a low self-awareness that causes them to perform as poorly on "self" tasks as they tend to do on the "other" tasks (Perner, Frith, Leslie, & Leekam, 1989).

MIRROR NEURON SYSTEM

Mirror neurons were first discovered when neurons dedicated to the visual processing of the actions of one's self and the actions of others were identified in area F5 and in area PF of non-human primates (Gallese, Fadiga, Fogassi, & Rizzolatti, 1996; Rizzolatti et al., 1996; Rizzolatti & Craighero, 2004). Subsequently, studies have found evidence of a human homologue of the monkey mirror neuron system (MNS) (Iacoboni & Dapretto, 2006), with the human inferior frontal gyrus (IFG) loosely corresponding to the monkey F5, and the human inferior parietal lobule (IPL) to the monkey PF. Within the specialized areas of the MNS, research in humans suggests that the IPL plays a role in interpreting the goals of an action (e.g., Tunik, Frey, & Grafton, 2005; Buxbaum, Kyle, & Menon, 2005), and the IFG in interpreting more specific action properties (e.g., Pobric & Hamilton, 2006; Urgesi, Candidi, Ionta, & Aglioti, 2007). By decoding both the action's goals and specific motor properties, many researchers believe that the MNS directly influences imitation (Iacoboni et al., 1999; Koski et al., 2002; Koski, Iacoboni, Dubeau, Woods, & Mazziotta, 2003; Heiser, Iacoboni, Maeda, Marcus, & Mazziotta, 2003).

Representing others' actions and matching it with that of the self may be critical in imitation, and this process may be mediated by mirror neurons. Problems related to imitation in autism have been documented widely (Rogers, 1999; Rogers & Williams, 2006; Smith & Bryson, 1994; Williams, Whiten, & Singh, 2004). A comprehensive review by Rogers & Pennington (1991) suggested that impairments in self–other matching in autism might be the underlying factor of their problems in imitation. They suggested that a biological impairment in autism restricted the capacity of the infant to "form and coordinate social representations of self and other at increasingly complex levels via amodal or cross-modal representational processes." They hypothesized that a primary deficit in such a capacity would lead to a cascade of effects, including impaired imitation, social, communicative, and affective skills, and that a deficit of praxis involving the prefrontal–limbic neural system could form the basis for this impairment (see Williams, 2008, for a review). Research in persons with ASD has suggested that a disruption in the MNS early in development may be able to account for many of the symptoms of ASD (Oberman & Ramachandran, 2007; Williams et al., 2001). Indeed, the "mirror neuron dysfunction hypothesis of autism" has received widespread attention, with quite a few studies suggesting atypicalities of the MNS in persons with autism contributing to autism symptomatology (for recent reviews, see Williams, 2008; Bernier & Dawson, 2009; Kana, Wadsworth, & Travers, 2011).

Mirror neuron-related impairments found in autism may be manifested cognitively and behaviorally in multiple ways, leading to problems in self–other matching, in simulation, and in empathizing. A handful of studies have also examined reflex-like imitation, such as yawn contagion in children with ASD (Helt, Eigsti, Snyder, & Fein, 2010; Senju et al., 2007). They found that children with ASD yawned less in response to seeing other people yawning compared to children with typical development. This result suggests that persons with ASD may not exhibit automatic yawn contagion, which is thought to be a type of reflex-like imitation. Similarly, McIntosh, Reichmann-Decker, Winkielman, and Wilbarger (2006) found that participants with ASD were able to effortfully mimic pictures of faces as well as participants with typical development. However, when simply shown pictures of faces, participants with ASD exhibited less reflex-like face mimicry (measured by electromyography [EMG]). On the other hand, there may be evidence for instances of increased reflex-like imitation (i.e., echolalia). In this respect, Hamilton (2008) suggested that difficulties associated with ToM in persons with ASD may affect the activation of the direct pathway that codes for mimicry (between the superior temporal sulcus [STS] and IFG). This disruption is then thought to make reflex-like imitation appear either hyperactive (e.g., echolalia) or hypoactive (i.e., lack of social mirroring). However, with automatic imitation, it is also possible that the MNS-mediated reflex-like imitation may also set the stage for later ToM development. Specifically, if people with ASD do not automatically mirror the actions of others, this may prevent them from developing a sense of a causal link between the actions of self and the actions of others.

There is also strong evidence that mirror neurons may be involved in empathizing with others (Decety & Chaminade 2005; Gallese, 2005; Iacoboni, 2005; Iacoboni et al., 1999; Rizzolatti, 2005). In typically developing children, Pfeifer, Iacoboni, Mazziotta, and Dapretto (2008) found that the activation of the IFG was significantly correlated with self-reported empathy during both action observation and imitation, suggesting a link between MNS function and empathic reactions. In persons with ASD, Minio-Paluello, Baron-Cohen, Avenanti, Walsh, and Aglioti (2009) examined motor-evoked potentials in persons with ASD during the observation of another's pain and found less motor-evoked potentials in ASD compared to participants with typical development, suggesting that participants with ASD lacked an automatic motor representation of the pain they were observing in another. The authors suggested that this lack of a response may be due to difficulties with empathy in ASD. Because MNS function is thought to underlie motor-evoked potentials in response to observed action, this study suggests a link between MNS activity in persons with ASD and their ability to empathically respond to others. Furthermore, the embodiment of the emotions of another person, which is supposedly mediated by the MNS, may serve as a foundation from which we begin to better understand the intentions and behaviors of another, thus facilitating ToM development. However, if the MNS is impaired, this may create difficulties for developing ToM and for developing a coherent sense of self.

IS "SELF" A UNIQUE COGNITIVE STRUCTURE?

Several studies have documented that self-referential processing, the ability to consider information accompanied by self-awareness and self-memory, enhances word memory relative to other semantic forms of word processing (Symons & Johnson, 1997). Does self-referential processing have a privileged status in the brain or is it functionally equivalent to semantic processing of other classes of stimuli (Maki & McCaul, 1985; Markus, 1977)? If it does hold a special status in the brain, how is it different in the ASD population and what are the neural correlates of such differences? Self-referential processing has been linked to several brain areas in typically developing individuals, such as the dorsal medial prefrontal cortex, left inferior frontal cortex, and the anterior cingulate cortex (Craik et al., 1999; Kelley et al., 2002). Additionally, activation in these regions has been correlated with deficits in social communication related to ToM in persons with ASD (Ohnishi et al., 2000). Previous research has indicated that impairments in self-referential processing in ASD may contribute to deficits in social learning in general and joint attention in particular (Frith & Happé, 1999; Mundy, 2003).

The goal of a recent study from our lab (Powell et al., in preparation) is to further explore the cerebral correlates of self and other processing in persons with ASD, as well as how they differ from typically developing individuals, using more concrete designations of self-referential encoding and memory. In this fMRI study, 10 high-functioning autistic and 10 matched control adult participants made *yes* or *no* decisions about whether a visually presented adjective (e.g., smart, intelligent, unhappy) described them (self-judgment condition), described their favorite teacher (other-judgment condition), or contained the letter "e" (case-judgment control condition). The experiment was presented in a blocked design format with the order of presentation of blocks counter-balanced across participants. Additionally, participants completed a memory test of 60 words (outside the scanner), half of which they had seen in the scanner, providing a behavioral measure of whether self-related words had a privileged status in memory.

The primary results of this study are two-fold. (1) When self- and other-judgment trials were contrasted with case-judgment trials, there was significantly reduced activation in the left inferior frontal gyrus (LIFG) and left posterior superior temporal gyrus (LSTG) in participants with autism relative to controls (see Figure 9.1A, see plate section), suggesting less semantically complex processing of the words and more shallow or superficial semantic representations; (2) When self-judgment trials were contrasted with case-judgment and other-judgment trials, the participants with autism activated less relative to controls in a key CMS region, the left medial prefrontal cortex (MPFC) ($x=-10$, $y=60$, $z=12$) (see Figure 9.1B). The contrast between other-judgment trials and case-judgment trials also yielded less activation in left MPFC in autism ($x=-10$, $y=60$, $z=4$), although the cluster was smaller than that found in the self condition. These results underscore the role of MPFC in reflecting on one's own mind as well as about others' mind. The MPFC might be associated with evaluating the mental states of self and other (Uddin, Iacoboni, Lange, & Keenan, 2007). This overlapping of functions (self-related processing and other-related processing) associated with MPFC suggests the interrelationship between self–other processes. In other words, MPFC might be the connecting link between the theory of own mind and the theory of other minds.

At the behavioral level, the participants with autism did not show any difference in the number of words recalled in the self condition versus the other condition, whereas the control participants showed a significant increase in the number of words recalled in the self condition compared to that in the other condition. The results here suggest a lack of self-related advantage in semantic memory in autism. The behavioral and neuroimaging results from this study point to semantically weaker and less socially oriented conceptualization of self and other in people with ASD.

Another recent fMRI study (Chiu et al., 2008) examined how the cingulate cortex responded differentially to self- and other-related judgments in people with ASD. Their task involved an interpersonal multi-round trust game played by a participant with a partner while being scanned using a hyperscanning technique. The authors not only found reduced activation in autism in the cingulate cortex while participants made decisions in response to the investor's decisions, but also found that the activation in the cingulate was negatively correlated with ASD symptom severity (operationalized as score on the Autism Diagnostic Interview-Revised [Lord, Rutter, & Le Couteur, 1994]). Unlike the study by Powell et al. (in preparation), where the self was examined in the personal domain, this study investigated the nature of self as a social agent making decisions and responding to others' decisions. Both studies showed hypoactivation of CMS (specifically the cingulate cortex and MPFC) in autism associated with self-related responses.

Similarly, Lombardo and colleagues (2009) examined the functional activation of the middle cingulate cortex and ventromedial prefrontal cortex in ASD in response to judgments about one's self versus judgments about another (e.g., the Queen of England). Whereas persons with typical development activated the middle cingulate in response to thoughts of one's self more than to thoughts of another, the participants with ASD demonstrated the opposite pattern. Additionally, the participants with typical development activated the ventromedial prefrontal cortex more in the self condition compared to the other condition, whereas the participants with ASD showed similar activation of the ventromedial prefrontal cortex in both conditions. These results coincide with those of Chiu et al. (2008) and Powell et al. (in preparation), suggesting not only the role of CMS in self representations but also the atypicalities in the neural representation of self in the CMS of persons with ASD.

Studies focusing on ToM in autism also have found atypical response patterns in the cingulate cortex (Castelli et al., 2002; Kana et al., 2009), significantly reduced glucose metabolism (Haznedar et al., 2000), and abnormal development of Von Economo neurons (Allman, Watson, Tetreault, & Hakeen, 2005). These results suggest that overlapping regions shared by ToM and self-representation may exhibit functional atypicalities in persons with autism across ToM and self–other tasks. There is also converging evidence from magnetic resonance imaging-based morphometry (Abell et al., 1999; Haznedar et al., 2000), diffusion tensor imaging (Barnea-Goraly et al., 2004), PET (Haznedar et al., 1997, 2000), single-photon emission computed tomography (Ohnishi et al., 2000), and postmortem studies (Bauman & Kemper, 1994) that has indicated abnormalities associated with the cingulate cortex in autism. Thus, functional alterations in MPFC and the functional and anatomical abnormalities in the cingulate cortex in autism may have an impact on the representation of one's own as well as that of others' mind in people with ASD. Such atypical representation of self may affect one's ability to integrate self-knowledge with what one observes in others, which may prove vital in social-cognitive development (Mundy & Newell, 2007; Oberman & Ramachandran, 2007). Overall, the findings from these studies suggest that self may not be a unique cognitive construct in autism and hence may not have a privileged status in people with autism.

SELF, MIRROR NEURONS, MINDREADING, AND AUTISM

Attribution of intentions to others, a key aspect of ToM, involves complex information processing (such as representing reality, understanding one's own beliefs and the beliefs of others, and decoupling beliefs from reality) and may be fundamentally disrupted in people with autism (Minshew, Goldstein, & Siegel, 1997). Even though difficulty with ToM in autism has been demonstrated extensively in behavioral studies (e.g., Baron-Cohen, Campbell, Karmiloff-Smith, Grant, & Walker, 1995; Baron-Cohen, Leslie, & Frith, 1985; Leekam & Perner, 1991; Perner et al., 1989; Reed & Peterson, 1990; Swettenham, 1996; Swettenham, Baron-Cohen, Gomez, & Walsh, 1996), only a few neuroimaging studies have explored it (e.g., Kana et al., 2009; Castelli et al., 2002; Happé et al., 1996).

According to the simulation theory of mindreading, others' mental states are represented by adopting their perspective (Goldman, 2006; Gallese & Goldman, 1998). This process may be facilitated by embodiment, which is thought to rely on the MNS. According to Gallese (2006), because of the unique properties of mirror neurons in simulating one's own and others' minds, it can provide a link between self and other, enabling intersubjectivity through an intentional attunement mechanism.

In an ongoing fMRI study (Kana, Libero, Hu, Deshpande, & Colburn, in press), we are examining the contribution of mirror system areas in mentalizing in high-functioning adults with autism using a causal attribution paradigm. Although understanding cause and effect is a skill that most children learn, children with autism are known to have impairments in the development of intentional causality (Baron-Cohen, 1995; Baron-Cohen et al., 1985; Baron-Cohen, Tager-Flusberg, & Cohen, 1993). On the other hand, they have relatively normal or even superior development in their understanding of physical causality (Baron-Cohen, 1997; Baron-Cohen, Leslie, & Frith, 1986; Frith, 1989; Jolliffe & Baron-Cohen, 1997). The stimuli (adapted from Brunet, Sarfati, Hardy-Bayle, & Decety, 2000) consisted of comic-strip vignettes that required either an attribution of intention or the use of knowledge about the physical properties of objects. The participants' task was to view the story presented in the vignette and choose the most logical ending to the story from three alternatives.

This study found significantly less recruitment of two regions in autism during intentional causality: the right posterior superior temporal sulcus (pSTS) at the right temporo-parietal junction (RTPJ) and the right inferior frontal gyrus (RIFG). While pSTS/RTPJ has been previously reported in tasks of perceiving biological actions and ToM (Pelphrey, Morris, Michelich, Allison, & McCarthy, 2005; Castelli et al., 2002; Kana et al., 2009; Saxe & Wexler, 2005), the activation in RIFG may be associated with simulation of the actions and mental states of the protagonist in the scenarios depicted (Dapretto et al., 2006; Hadjikhani, Joseph, Snyder, & Tager-Flusberg, 2007). Thus, the co-activation of pSTS/RTPJ with RIFG may support a strategy based on the principles of the simulation theory of mindreading in control participants, and probably not in autism.

While the results of this study may provide evidence for the role of the anterior part of the mirror neuron system (RIFG) in mentalizing based on characters' actions, the CMS also have been found to be critical in ToM (see Amodio & Frith, 2006, for a review). In a recent fMRI study of mental state attribution (Kana et al., 2009), we used animations involving a larger and a smaller triangle (adapted from Heider, 1944; Heider & Simmel, 1944) to evoke social perception and social attribution in participants. The results showed significantly reduced activation in autism in the medial prefrontal, anterior paracingulate, and anterior cingulate cortices, midline cortical regions that have been previously implicated in tasks of ToM (Castelli et al., 2002; Happé et al., 1996; see Frith & Frith, 2005, for a review). The main differences between the causal attribution study and this study are: (1) While the stimuli consisted of static pictures in the former, the latter included dynamic animations; (2) The former study had protagonists/characters in the story, whereas the latter involved geometric shapes; and (3) The former had shorter duration for each stimulus (11 seconds), whereas the latter involved longer animations (35–40 seconds). It is possible that the longer duration may provide the participants more time for self-reflection and reasoning than the shorter, which might have contributed to the CMS activation in the animation study. On the other hand, the presence of characters performing certain acts in the causal attribution study might have triggered action simulation, contributing to the RIFG activation. Although we do not know with certainty that this is the case, it is worth exploring in future research.

The nature of these tasks and the resulting brain activation patterns suggest that mentalizing may involve reflecting on the mental states of oneself and that of the other, and/or simulating the actions and mental states of the other depending on the nature of the task. On a different note, the MNS might also be playing a key role in the evaluation of one's own self, which involves a sense of introspection, as though you are looking at yourself from another person's vantage point (Ramachandran, 2007). This may be a brief meta-analysis of the self just as one is watching one's own videotaped footage. Thus, while mentalizing might involve watching and mimicking the actions and mental states of others, self-processing might involve watching and evaluating the actions of oneself.

SELF–OTHER REPRESENTATION: A CRITICAL IMPAIRMENT IN AUTISM?

Behavioral studies examining the representation of self in autism have reported phenomena that indicate atypicalities in self–other representation. These include a failure to preferentially recall self-performed compared to experimenter-performed actions (Yamamoto, Saito, & Kamio, 2004); poor memory for self-performed versus peer-performed events (Millward, Powell, Messer, & Jordan, 2000); limited differentiation between drawings of themselves versus others (Lee & Hobson, 2006); deficits in self-relevant memory and decreased self-referential effect in memory (Toichi et al., 2002); and a failure to show standard enhanced processing of self-referential memory in children (Henderson et al., 2009). It is possible that such impairments in the conceptual representation of self and other in autism may be the root of their difficulties in social interactions (Frith & Happé, 1999; Hobson, Chidambi, Lee, & Meyer, 2006; Mundy, 2003; Russell, 1997). For instance, extreme autistic aloneness and aloof nature were reported as key symptoms of autism in Kanner's (1943) seminal paper, and the origin of the term *autism*, from the Greek word *autos*, meaning *self*, perhaps sums up the increased focus on self in this disorder.

At the cognitive level, in order to understand the mental states of others and to empathize with them, we take others' perspective. This switch in perspective may require metarepresentation as well as the translocation of an egocentric viewpoint to an allocentric viewpoint. Individuals with ASD are limited in their ability to attribute mental states to others, perhaps because they often are locked into an egocentric perspective (Frith & de Vignemont, 2005). Extreme egocentrism has been suggested as a diagnostic criterion for autism by some researchers (Gillberg & Gillberg, 1989). Identification and sharing of experiences entails a degree of participation in another's psychological stance so that one achieves an expanded subjective state (Hobson & Hobson, 2007); autism seems to involve a relative failure to adopt the bodily anchored psychological and communicative stance of another person. The basic processes underlying the translocation of the self to other's perspective may be complex, requiring skills such as cognitive flexibility, shifting attention, and coherence, many of which people with autism have demonstrated to have difficulty with. Moreover, such complex functions may necessitate the coordination and communication of different and perhaps distant brain regions, a phenomenon found to be weaker in people with autism (Just, Cherkassky, Keller, & Minshew, 2004; Just, Keller, Cherkassky, Kana, & Minshew, 2007; Kana, Keller, Cherkassky, Minshew, & Just, 2006; Kana, Keller, Minshew, & Just, 2007; Kana et al., 2009).

According to Churchland (2002), one's self-concept is a set of organizational tools for "coherencing" the brain's plans, decisions, and perceptions. From this perspective, self can be conceptualized as the *central executive* of the brain or mind. Central coherence, or binding these thoughts, plans, decisions, and perceptions together, has been found to be weaker in individuals with autism (Frith, 1989; Happé & Frith, 2006). Weak central coherence might manifest in terms of information overload in autism due in part to the limited ability to see the global whole, and to the increased focus on details. Such weak central coherence, at the neural level, is reflected through cortical underconnectivity (lower synchronization of activated brain areas) in autism, especially long-distance connectivity from and to the frontal lobe (Just et al., 2004, 2007; Kana et al., 2006, 2007). Weak central coherence may also manifest as a result of an impairment of temporal binding *between* local networks in the brain, whereas temporal binding *within* local networks is presumed to be intact or possibly even enhanced (Brock, Brown, Boucher, & Rippon, 2002). In terms of the interaction between self and other in autism, the neural and cognitive binding forces that integrate these systems to accomplish social cognition and social functioning may be less effective.

CONCLUSIONS

While self and other seem to form the central nodes of human social interaction, what makes it rich and successful may be our ability to relate to, distinguish from, and attribute mental states to others. The CMS, ToM, and the MNS networks in the brain may act in tandem in order to accomplish complex social functions. While the CMS has a critical role in self-processing (Northoff & Bermpohl, 2004), the MNS is involved in self-recognition (Uddin, Kaplan, Molnar-Szakacs, Zaidel, & Iacoboni, 2005) and social understanding (Gallese, 2004). Moreover, the CMS may be involved in the less bodily grounded self (processing the mental states of self and other), whereas the MNS may be associated with the multimodal embodied self (processing the actions of self and other) (Uddin et al., 2007). Functional (Dapretto et al., 2006) and anatomical (Hadjikhani, Joseph, Snyder, & Tager-Flusberg, 2006) abnormalities of the MNS have been documented in autism. Similarly, CMS hypoactivation (Kennedy et al., 2006) and functional underconnectivity (Cherkassky et al., 2006) have also been found in autism. At least one way of mentalizing may be through simulating other minds possibly mediated by ToM and MNS structures, with CMS providing an evaluative support. It is possible that the processes mediated by the CMS, MNS, and ToM structures may not be perfectly distinct. Perhaps what matters more is the functional synchrony of these structures, where people with autism might falter. Future research should examine the co-activation and coordination of these three systems in typical development and in disorders to shed more light on the interrelationship among them.

REFERENCES

Abell, F., Krams, M., Ashburner, J., Passingham, R., Friston, K., Frackowiak, R., & Frith, U. (1999). The neuroanatomy of autism: A voxel-based whole brain analysis of structural scans. *Neuroreport, 10*, 1647–1651.

Adolphs, R., Sears, L., & Piven, J. (2001). Abnormal processing of social information from faces in autism. *Journal of Cognitive Neuroscience, 13*, 232–240.

Allman, J. M., Watson, K. K., Tetreault, N. A., & Hakeen, A. Y. (2005). Intuition and autism: A possible role for Von Economo neurons. *Trends in Cognitive Sciences, 9*, 367–373.

Amodio, D., & Frith, C. (2006). Meeting of minds: The medial frontal cortex and social cognition. *Nature Reviews Neuroscience, 7*, 268–277.

Asperger, H. (1944). "Autistic psychopathy" in childhood. *Archiv für Psychiatrie und Nervenkrankheiten, 117*, 76–136.

Astafiev, S. V., Stanley, C. M., Shulman, G. L., & Corbetta, M. (2004). Extrastriate body area in human occipital cortex responds to the performance of motor actions. *Nature Neuroscience, 7*, 542–548.

Barnea-Goraly, N., Kwon, H., Menon, V., Eliez, S., Lotspeich, L., & Reiss, A. L. (2004). White matter structure in autism: Preliminary evidence from diffusion tensor imaging. *Biological Psychiatry, 55*, 323–326.

Baron-Cohen, S. (1989). Are autistic children behaviorists? An examination of their mental–physical and appearance–reality distinctions. *Journal of Autism & Developmental Disorders, 19*, 579–600.

Baron-Cohen, S. (1995). *Mindblindness: An essay on autism and theory of mind*. Cambridge, MA: MIT Press/Bradford Books.

Baron-Cohen, S. (1997). Are children with autism superior in folk physics? In H. Wellman, & K. Inagaki (Eds.), *Children's theories* (pp. 45–54). San Francisco, CA: Jossey-Bass Inc.

Baron-Cohen, S., Campbell, R., Karmiloff-Smith, A., Grant, J., & Walker, J. (1995). Are children with autism blind to the mentalistic significance of the eyes? *British Journal of Developmental Psychology, 13*, 379–398.

Baron-Cohen, S., Leslie, A. M., & Frith, U. (1985). Does the autistic child have a "theory of mind"? *Cognition, 21*, 37–46.

Baron-Cohen, S., Leslie, A. M., & Frith, U. (1986). Mechanical, behavioral, and intentional understanding of picture stories in autistic children. *British Journal of Developmental Psychology, 4*, 113–125.

Baron-Cohen, S., Tager-Flusberg, H., & Cohen, D. (1993). *Understanding other minds: Perspectives from autism*. Oxford, England: Oxford University Press.

Bauman, M. L., & Kemper, T. L. (1994). Neuroanatomical observations of the brain in autism. In M. L. Bauman, & T. L. Kemper (Eds.), *The neurobiology of autism* (pp. 119–145). Baltimore, MD: Johns Hopkins University Press.

Bernier, R., & Dawson, G. (2009). The role of mirror neuron dysfunction in autism. In J. Pineda (Ed.), *Mirror neuron systems* (pp. 261–286). Totowa, NJ: Humana Press.

Blakemore, S. J. (2008). The social brain in adolescence. *Nature Reviews Neuroscience, 9*, 267–277.

Blakemore, S. J., den Ouden, H., Choudhury, S., & Frith, C. (2007). Adolescent development of the neural circuitry for thinking about intentions. *Social Cognitive and Affective Neuroscience, 2*, 130–139.

Blanke, O. (2004). Out of body experiences and their neural basis. *BMJ, 329*(7480), 1414–1415.

Blanke, O., & Arzy, S. (2005). The out-of-body experience: Disturbed self-processing at the temporo-parietal junction. *Neuroscientist, 11*(1), 16–24.

Bonda, E., Petrides, M., Ostry, D., & Evans, A. (1995). Neural correlates of the perception of action in the human parietal cortex. *Society for Neuroscience Abstracts, 21*, 695.

Bretherton, I., & Beeghly, M. (1982). Talking about internal states: The acquisition of an explicit theory of mind. *Developmental Psychology, 18*, 906–921.

Brock, J., Brown, C. C., Boucher, J., & Rippon, G. (2002). The temporal binding deficit hypothesis of autism. *Development and Psychopathology, 14*, 209–224.

Brunet, E., Sarfati, Y., Hardy-Bayle, M. C., & Decety, J. (2000). A PET investigation of the attribution of intentions with a nonverbal task. *NeuroImage, 11*, 157–166.

Bullock, M., & Lutkenhaus, P., (1990). Who am I? Self-understanding in toddlers, *Merril-Palmer Quarterly, 36*, 217–238.

Buxbaum, L. J., Kyle, K. M., & Menon, R. (2005). On beyond mirror neurons: Onternal representations subserving imitation and recognition of skilled object-related actions in humans. *Cognitive Brain Research, 25*, 226–239.

Caron, R. F., Caron, A. J., & Myers, R. S. (1982). Abstraction of invariant face expressions in infancy. *Child Development,* 53, 1008–1015.

Castelli, F., Frith, C., Happé, F., & Frith, U. (2002). Autism, Asperger syndrome and brain mechanisms for the attribution of mental states to animated shapes. *Brain, 125*, 1839–1849.

Cherkassky, V. L., Kana, R. K., Keller, T. A., & Just, M. A. (2006). Functional connectivity in a baseline resting-state network in autism. *NeuroReport, 17*, 1687–1690.

Chiu, P. H., Kayali, M. A., Kishida, K. T., Tomlin, D., Klinger, M. R., & Montague, P. R. (2008). Self responses along cingulate cortex reveal quantitative neural phenotype for high-functioning autism. *Neuron, 57*, 463–473.

Churchland, P. S. (2002). Self-representation in nervous systems. *Science, 296*, 308–310.

Craik, F., Moroz, T., Moscovich, M., Stuss, D., Winocur, G., Tulving, E., & Kapur, S. (1999). In search of the self: A positron emission tomography study. *Psychological Science, 10*, 26–34.

Dapretto, M., Davies, M. S., Pfeifer, J. H., Scott, A. A., Sigman, M., Bookheimer, S. Y., & Iacoboni, M. (2006). Understanding emotions in others: Mirror neuron dysfunction in children with autism spectrum disorders. *Nature Neuroscience, 9*, 28–30.

Decety, J., & Chaminade, T. (2005). The neurophysiology of imitation and intersubjectivity. In S. Hurley (Ed.), *Perspectives on imitation: From cognitive neuroscience to social science* (pp. 119–140). Cambridge, MA: MIT Press.

Downing, P. E., Jiang, Y., Shuman, M., & Kanwisher, N. (2001). A cortical area selective for visual processing of the human body. *Science, 293*, 2470–2473.

Duval, S., & Wicklund, R. A. (1972). Effects of objective self-awareness on attribution of causality. *Journal of Experimental Social Psychology, 9*, 17–31.

Fiske, S. T., & Taylor, S. E. (1991). *Social cognition* (2nd edition). New York: McGraw-Hill.

Fox, M. D., & Raichle, M. E. (2007). Spontaneous fluctuations in brain activity observed with functional magnetic resonance imaging. *Nature Reviews Neuroscience, 8*, 700–711.

Freitag, C. M., Kleser, C., & von Gontard, A. (2006). Imitation and language abilities in adolescents with autism spectrum disorder without language delay. *European Child and Adolescent Psychiatry, 15*, 282–291.

Frith, C., & Frith, U. (2005). Theory of mind. *Current Biology, 15*, R644–R645.

Frith, U. (1989). *Autism: Explaining the enigma*. Oxford, England: Blackwell.

Frith, U., & de Vignemont, F. (2005). Egocentrism, allocentrism, and Asperger syndrome. *Consciousness and Cognition, 14*, 719–738.

Frith, U., & Happé, F. (1999). Theory of mind and self consciousness: What is it like to be autistic? *Mind and Language, 14*, 1–22.

Gallagher, H. L., & Frith, C. D. (2003). Functional imaging of "theory of mind." *Trends in Cognitive Sciences, 7*, 77–83.

Gallese, V. (2004). "Being like me": Self–other identity, mirror neurons and empathy. In S. Hurley & N. Chater (Eds.), *Perspectives on imitation: From cognitive neuroscience to social science* (pp. 101–118). Cambridge, MA: MIT Press.

Gallese, V. (2005). Embodied simulation: From neurons to phenomenal experience. *Phenomenology and the Cognitive Sciences, 4*, 23–48.

Gallese, V. (2006). Intentional attunement: A neuro-physiological perspective on social cognition and its disruption in autism. *Brain Research, 1079*, 15–24.

Gallese, V., Fadiga, L., Fogassi, L., & Rizzolatti, G. (1996). Action recognition in the premotor cortex. *Brain, 119*, 593–609.

Gallese, V., & Goldman, A. (1998). Mirror neurons and the simulation theory of mind-reading. *Trends in Cognitive Sciences, 12*, 493–501.

Gergely, G., Nádasdy, Z., Csibra, G., & Bíró, S. (1995). Understanding intentional actions at 12 months of age. *Psychology, 15*, 331–367.

Giambra, L. M. (1995). A laboratory method for investigating influences on switching attention to task-unrelated imagery and thought. *Consciousness and Cognition, 4*, 1–21.

Gillberg, I. C., & Gillberg, C. (1989). Asperger syndrome – some epistemological considerations: A research note. *Journal of Child Psychology and Psychiatry, 30*, 631–638.

Goldman, A. I. (2006). *Simulating minds: The philosophy, psychology, and neuroscience of mindreading*. Oxford, England: Oxford University Press.

Greimel, E., Shulte-Ruther, M., Kircher, T., Kamp-Becker, I., Remschmidt, H., Fink, G. . . . Konrad, K. (2010). Neural mechanisms of empathy in adolescents with autism spectrum disorder and their fathers. *NeuroImage, 49*, 1055–1065.

Gusnard, D. A., & Raichle, M. E. (2001). Searching for a baseline: Functional imaging and the resting human brain. *Nature Reviews Neuroscience, 2*, 685–694.

Hadjikhani, N., Joseph, R. M., Snyder, J., & Tager-Flusberg, H. (2006). Anatomical differences in the mirror neuron system and social cognition network in autism. *Cerebral Cortex, 16*, 1276–1282.

Hadjikhani, N., Joseph, R. M., Snyder, J., & Tager-Flusberg, H. (2007). Abnormal activation of the social brain during face perception in autism. *Human Brain Mapping, 28*, 441–449.

Hamilton, A. (2008). Emulation and mimicry for social interaction: A theoretical approach to imitation in autism. *The Quarterly Journal of Experimental Psychology, 61*, 101–115.

Happé, F. (2003). Theory of mind and the self. *Annals of the New York Academy of Sciences, 1001*, 134–144.

Happé, F. G. E., Ehlers, S., Fletcher, P., Frith, U., Johansson, M., Gillberg, C., . . .

Frith, C. (1996). "Theory of mind" in the brain: Evidence from a PET scan study of Asperger syndrome. *NeuroReport, 8*, 197–201.

Happé, F., & Frith, U. (2006). The weak coherence account: Detail-focused cognitive style in autism spectrum disorders. *Journal of Autism and Developmental Disorders, 36*, 5–25.

Haznedar, M. M., Buchsbaum, M. S., Metzger, M. M., Solimando, A., Spiegel-Cohen, J., & Hollander, E. (1997). Anterior cingulate gyrus volume and glucose metabolism in autistic disorder. *American Journal of Psychiatry, 154*, 1047–1050.

Haznedar, M. M., Buchsbaum, M. S., Wei, T. C., Hof, P. R., Cartwright, C., Bienstock, C. A., & Hollander, E. (2000). Limbic circuitry in patients with autism spectrum disorders studied with positron emission tomography and magnetic resonance imaging. *American Journal of Psychiatry, 157*, 1994–2001.

Heider, F. (1944). Social perception and phenomenal causality. *Psychological Review, 51*, 358–374.

Heider, F., & Simmel, M. (1944). An experimental study of apparent behavior. *The American Journal of Psychology, 57*, 242–259.

Heiser, M., Iacoboni, M., Maeda, F., Marcus, J., & Mazziotta, J. C. (2003). The essential role of Broca's area in imitation. *European Journal of Neuroscience, 17*, 1123–1128.

Helt, M., Eigsti, I., Snyder, P., & Fein, D. (2010). Contagious yawning in autistic and typical development. *Child Development, 81*, 1620–1631.

Henderson, H. A., Zahka, N. E., Kojkowski, N. M., Inge, A. P., Schwartz, C. B., Hileman, C. M.,... Mundy, P. C. (2009). Self-referenced memory, social cognition, and symptom presentation in autism. *Journal of Child Psychology and Psychiatry, 50*, 853–861.

Hobson, J. A., & Hobson, R. P. (2007). Identification: The missing link between imitation and joint attention? *Development and Psychopathology, 19*, 411–431.

Hobson, P. R., Chidambi, G., Lee, A., & Meyer, J. (2006). Foundations for self-awareness: An exploration through autism. *Monographs of the Society for Research in Child Development, 71*, vii–166.

Hobson, P. R., & Meyer, J. A. (2005). Foundations for self and other: A study in autism. *Developmental Science, 8*, 481–491.

Iacoboni, M. (2005). Neural mechanisms of imitation. *Current Opinion in Neurobiology, 15*, 632–637.

Iacoboni, M., & Dapretto, M. (2006). The mirror neuron system and the consequences of its dysfunction. *Nature Reviews Neuroscience, 7*, 942–951.

Iacoboni, M., Woods, R. P., Brass, M., Bekkering, H., Mazziotta, J. C., & Rizzolatti, G. (1999). Cortical mechanisms of human imitation. *Science, 286*, 2526–2528.

James, W. (1890). *The principles of psychology*. New York: Holt.

Jolliffe, T., & Baron-Cohen, S. (1997). Are people with autism and Asperger syndrome faster than normal on the Embedded Figures Test? *Journal of Child Psychology & Psychiatry, 38*, 527–534.

Just, M. A., Cherkassky, V. L., Keller, T. A., & Minshew, N. J. (2004). Cortical activation and synchronization during sentence comprehension in high-functioning autism. *Brain, 127*, 1811–1821.

Just, M. A., Keller, T. A., Cherkassky, V. L., Kana, R. K., & Minshew, N. J. (2007). Functional and anatomical cortical underconnectivity in autism: Evidence from an fMRI study of an executive function task and corpus callosum morphometry. *Cerebral Cortex, 17*, 951–961.

Kagan, J. (1981). *The second year: The emergence of self-awareness*. Cambridge, MA: Harvard University Press.

Kagan, J. (1991). The theoretical utility of constructs of self. *Developmental Review, 11*, 244–250.

Kana, R. K., Keller, T. A., Cherkassky, V. L., Minshew, N. J., & Just, M. A. (2006). Sentence comprehension in autism: Thinking in pictures with decreased functional connectivity. *Brain, 129*, 2484–2493.

Kana, R. K., Keller, T. A., Cherkassky, V. L., Minshew, N. J., & Just, M. A. (2009). Atypical frontal-posterior synchronization of theory of mind regions in autism during mental state attribution. *Social Neuroscience, 4*, 135–152.

Kana, R. K., Keller, T. A., Minshew, N. J., & Just, M. A. (2007). Inhibitory control in high functioning autism: Decreased activation and underconnectivity in inhibition networks. *Biological Psychiatry, 62*, 198–206.

Kana, R. K., Libero, L., Hu, C. P., Deshpande, H. R., & Colburn, J. (in press). Functional brain networks and white matter underlying theory-of-mind in autism. *Social Cognitive and Affective Neuroscience.*

Kana, R. K., Wadsworth, H. M., & Travers, B. G. (2011). A systems level analysis of the mirror neuron system hypothesis and imitation impairments in autism. *Neuroscience & Biobehavioral Reviews, 35*, 894–902.

Kanner, L. (1943). Autistic disturbances of affective contact. *The Nervous Child, 2*, 217–250.

Kelley, W. M., Macrae, C. N., Wyland, C. L., Caglar, S., Inati, S., & Heatherton, T. F. (2002). Finding the self? An event-related fMRI study. *Journal of Cognitive Neuroscience, 14*, 785–794.

Kennedy, D. P., Redcay, E., & Courchesne, E. (2006). Failing to deactivate: Resting functional abnormalities in autism. *Proceedings of the National Academy of Sciences of the United States of America, 103*, 8275–8280.

Kobayashi, C., Glover, G. H., & Temple, E. (2007). Children's and adults' neural bases of verbal and non-verbal Theory of Mind. *Neuropsychologia,* 45, 1522–1532.

Kobayashi, C., Glover, G. H., & Temple, E. (2008). Switching language switches mind: Linguistic effects on developmental neural bases of "Theory of Mind." *Social Cognitive and Affective Neuroscience,* 3, 62–70.

Koski, L., Iacoboni, M., Dubeau, M. C., Woods, R. P., & Mazziotta, J. C. (2003). Modulation of cortical activity during different imitative behaviors. *Journal of Neurophysiology, 89*, 460–471.

Koski, L., Wohlschlager, A., Bekkering, H., Woods, R. P., Dubeau, M. C., Mazziotta, J. C., & Iacoboni, M. (2002). Modulation of motor and premotor activity during imitation of target-directed actions. *Cerebral Cortex, 12*, 847–855.

Lee, A., & Hobson, R. P. (2006). Drawing self and others: How do children with autism differ from those with learning difficulties? *British Journal of Developmental Psychology, 24*, 547–565.

Lee, A., Hobson, R. P., & Chiat, S. (1994). I, you, me, and autism: An experimental study. *Journal of Autism and Developmental Disorders, 24*, 155–176.

Leekam, S., & Perner, J. (1991). Does the autistic child have a metarepresentational deficit? *Cognition, 40*, 203–218.

Lewis, M., & Brooks-Gunn, H. (1979). *Social cognition and the acquisition of self*. New York: Plenum Press.

Lewis, M., & Ramsay, D. (2004). Development of self-recognition, personal pronoun use, and pretend play during the 2nd year. *Child Development, 75*, 1821–1831.

Lewis, M., Sullivan, M., Stanger, C., & Weiss, M. (1989). Self-development and self-conscious emotions. *Child Development, 60*, 146–156.

Lombardo, M., Chakrabarti, B., Bullmore, E., Sadek, S., Pasco, G., Wheelwright, S., . . . Baron-Cohen, S. (2009). Atypical neural self-representation in autism. *Brain, 133*, 611–624.

Lord, C., & Paul, R. (1997). Language and communication in autism. In D. J. Cohen, & F. R. Volkmar (Eds.), *Handbook of autism and pervasive developmental disorders* (pp. 195–225). New York, NY: John Wiley & Sons.

Lord, C., Rutter, M., & Le Couteur, A. (1994). Autism Diagnostic Interview-Revised: A revised version of a diagnostic interview for caregivers of individuals with possible pervasive developmental disorders. *Journal of Autism and Developmental Disorders, 5*, 659–685.

Loveland, K. (1984). Learning about points of view: Spatial perspective and the acquisition of "I/you." *Journal of Child Language, 11*, 535–556.

Maki, R. H., & McCaul, K. D. (1985). The effects of self- versus other-reference on the recall of traits and nouns. *Bulletin of the Psychonomic Society, 23*, 169–172.

Markus, H. (1977). Self-schemas and processing information about the self. *Journal of Personality and Social Psychology, 35*, 63–78.

McIntosh, D. N., Reichmann-Decker, A., Winkielman, P., & Wilbarger, J. L. (2006). When the social mirror breaks: Deficits in automatic, but not voluntary mimicry of emotional facial expressions in autism. *Developmental Science, 9*, 295–302.

Meltzoff, A. N. (2007). "Like me": A foundation for social cognition. *Developmental Science, 10*, 126–134.

Millward, C., Powell, S., Messer, D., & Jordan, R. (2000). Recall for self and other in autism: Children's memory for events experienced by themselves and their peers. *Journal of Autism and Developmental Disorders, 30*, 15–28.

Minio-Paluello, I., Baron-Cohen, S., Avenanti, A., Walsh, V., & Aglioti, S. M. (2009). Absence of "sensorimotor contagion" during pain observation in Asperger syndrome. *Biological Psychiatry, 65*, 55–62.

Minshew, N. J., Goldstein, G., & Siegel, D. J. (1997). Neuropsychologic functioning in autism: Profile of a complex information processing disorder. *Journal of the International Neuropsychological Society, 3*, 303–316.

Moriguchi, Y., Decety, J., Ohnishi, T., Maeda, M., Matsuda, H., & Komaki, G. (2007). Empathy and judging other's pain: An fMRI study of alexithymia. *Cerebral Cortex, 17*, 2223–2234.

Mundy, P. (2003). The neural basis of social impairments in autism: The role of the dorsal medial-frontal cortex and anterior cingulate system. *Journal of Child Psychology and Psychiatry, 44*, 793–809.

Mundy, P. C., & Newell, L. (2007). Attention, joint attention, and social cognition. *Current Directions in Psychological Science, 16*, 269–274.

Murias, M., Webb, S., Greenson, J., & Dawson, G. (2007). Resting state cortical connectivity reflected in EEG coherence in individuals with autism. *Biological Psychiatry, 62*, 270–273.

Northoff, G., & Bermpohl, F. (2004). Cortical midline structures and the self. *Trends in Cognitive Sciences, 8*, 102–107.

Northoff, G., Heinzel, A., de Greck, M., Bermpohl, F., Dobrowolny H., & Panksepp, J.

(2006). Self-referential processing in our brain—a meta-analysis of imaging studies on the self. *NeuroImage, 31*, 440–457.

Oberman, L. M., & Ramachandran, V. S. (2007). The simulating social mind: The role of the mirror neuron system and simulation in the social and communicative deficits of autism spectrum disorders. *Psychological Bulletin, 133*, 310–327.

Ohnishi, T., Matsuda, H., Hashimoto, T., Kunihiro, T., Nishikawa, M., Uema, T., & Sasaki, M. (2000). Abnormal regional blood flow in childhood autism. *Brain, 123*, 1838–1844.

Pelphrey, K., Morris, J., Michelich, C., Allison, T., & McCarthy, G. (2005). Functional anatomy of biological motion perception in posterior temporal cortex: An fMRI study of eye, mouth and hand movements. *Cerebral Cortex, 15*, 1866–1876.

Perner, J., Frith, U., Leslie, A. M., & Leekam, S. (1989). Exploration of the autistic child's theory of mind: Knowledge, belief, and communication. *Child Development, 60*, 689–700.

Pfeifer, J., Iacoboni, M., Mazziotta, J., & Dapretto, M. (2008). Mirroring others' emotions relates to empathy and interpersonal competence in children. *NeuroImage, 39*, 2076–2085.

Pfeifer, J. H., Lieberman, M. D., & Dapretto, M. (2007). "I know you are but what am I?": Neural bases of self- and social knowledge retrieval in children and adults. *Journal of Cognitive Neuroscience*, 19, 1323–1337.

Pobric, G., & Hamilton, A. F. (2006). Action understanding requires the left inferior frontal cortex. *Current Biology, 16*, 524–529.

Powell, P., Klein, C. L., Travers, B. G., Klinger, M. R., Klinger, L. G., & Kana, R. K. (in preparation). Neural bases of self–other processing in autism spectrum disorder.

Premack, D., & Woodruff, G. (1978). Does the chimpanzee have a theory of mind? *Behavioral and Brain Sciences, 1*, 515–526.

Raichle, M. E. (2001). Functional neuroimaging: A historical and physiological perspective. In R. K. Cabeza, & A. Kingstone (Eds.), *Handbook of functional neuroimaging and cognition* (pp. 3–26). Cambridge, MA: MIT Press.

Raichle, M. E., MacLeod, A. M., Snyder, A. Z., Powers, W. J., Gusnard, D. A., & Shulman, G. L. (2001). A default mode of brain function. *PNAS, 98*, 676–682.

Raichle, M. E., & Snyder, A. Z. (2007). A default mode of brain function: A brief history of an evolving idea. *NeuroImage, 37*, 1083–1090.

Ramachandran, V. S. (2007). The neurology of self-awareness. *Edge*, January 8.

Reed, T., & Peterson, C. (1990). A comparative study of autistic subjects' performance at two levels of visual and cognitive perspective taking. *Journal of Autism and Developmental Disorders, 20*, 555–568.

Rice, M. L., Oetting, J. B., & Marquis, J. (1994). Frequency of input effects on word comprehension of children with specific language impairment. *Journal of Speech and Hearing Research, 37*, 106–121.

Rizzolatti, G. (2005). The mirror neuron system and its function in humans. *Anatomy and Embryology, 210*, 419–421.

Rizzolatti, G., & Craighero, L. (2004). The mirror-neuron system. *Annual Review of Neuroscience*, 27, 169–192.

Rizzolatti, G., Fadiga, L., Matelli, M., Bettinardi, V., Paulesu, E., Perani, D., & Fazio, F. (1996). Localization of grasp representations in humans by PET: 1. Observation versus execution. *Experimental Brain Research, 111*, 246–252.

Rogers, S. J. (1999). An examination of the imitation deficit in autism. In J. Nadel, & G.

Butterworth (Eds.), *Imitation in infancy* (pp. 254–283). Cambridge: Cambridge University Press.

Rogers, S., & Pennington, B. (1991). A theoretical approach to the deficits in infantile autism. *Development and Psychopathology, 3*, 137–162.

Rogers, S., & Williams, J. (2006). Imitation in autism. In S. J. Rogers, & J. H. G. Williams (Eds.), *Imitation and the social mind: Autism and typical development* (pp. 277–310). New York: Guilford.

Russell, J. (1997). How executive disorders can bring about an inadequate "theory of mind." In J. Russell (Ed.), *Autism as an executive disorder* (pp. 256–304). Oxford, England: Oxford University Press.

Saxe, R., & Wexler, A. (2005). Making sense of another mind: The role of the right temporoparietal junction. *Neuropsychologia, 43*, 1391–1399.

Senju, A., Maeda, M., Kikuchi, Y., Hasegawa, T., Tojo, Y., & Osanai, H. (2007). Absence of contagious yawning in children with autism spectrum disorder. *Biology Letters, 3*, 706–708.

Smith, I., & Bryson, S. (1994). Imitation and action in autism: A critical review. *Psychological Bulletin, 116*, 259–273.

Stipek, D. J., Gralinski, J. H., & Kopp, C. B. (1990). Self-concept development in the toddler years. *Developmental Psychology, 26*, 972–977.

Swettenham, J. (1996). Can children with autism be taught to understand false belief using computers? *Journal of Child Psychology and Psychiatry, 37*, 157–165.

Swettenham, J., Baron-Cohen, S., Gomez, J. C., & Walsh, S. (1996). What's inside a person's head? Conceiving of the mind as a camera helps children with autism develop an alternative theory of mind. *Cognitive Neuropsychiatry, 1*, 73–88.

Symons, C. S., & Johnson, B. T. (1997). The self-reference effect in memory: A meta-analysis. *Psychological Bulletin, 121*, 371–394.

Tager-Flusberg, H. (1993). What language reveals about the understanding of minds in children with autism. In S. Baron-Cohen, H. Tager-Flusberg, & D. J. Cohen (Eds.), *Understanding other minds: Perspectives from autism* (pp. 138–157). Oxford, England: Oxford University Press.

Tager-Flusberg, H. (1994). Dissociations in form and function in the acquisition of language by autistic children. In H. Tager-Flusberg (Ed.), *Constraints on language acquisition: Studies of atypical children* (pp. 175–194). Hillsdale, NJ: Erlbaum.

Toichi, M., Kamio, Y., Okada, T., Sakihama, M., Youngstrom, E. A., Findling, R. L., & Yamamoto, K. (2002). A lack of self-consciousness in autism. *American Journal of Psychiatry, 159*, 1422–1424.

Tunik, E., Frey, S. H., & Grafton, S. T. (2005). Virtual lesions of the anterior intraparietal area disrupt goal-dependent on-line adjustment of grasp. *Nature Neuroscience, 8*, 505–511.

Uddin, L. Q., Iacoboni, M., Lange, C., & Keenan, J. P. (2007). The self and social cognition: The role of cortical midline structures and mirror neurons. *Trends in Cognitive Sciences, 11*, 153–157.

Uddin, L. Q., Kaplan, J. T., Molnar-Szakacs, I., Zaidel, E., & Iacoboni, M. (2005). Self-face recognition activates a frontoparietal "mirror" network in the right hemisphere: An event-related fMRI study. *NeuroImage, 25*, 926–935.

Urgesi, C., Candidi, M., Ionta, S., & Aglioti, S. M. (2007). Representation of body identity and body actions in extrastriate body area and ventral premotor cortex. *Nature Neuroscience, 10*, 30–31.

Willey, L. H. (1999). *Pretending to be normal: Living with Asperger's syndrome.* London, England: Jessica Kingsley.
Williams, J. H. (2008). Self–other relations in social development and autism: Multiple roles for mirror neurons and other brain bases. *Autism Research, 1*, 73–90.
Williams, J. H. G., Massaro, D. W., Peel, N. J., Bosseler, A., & Suddendorf, T. (2004). Visual-auditory integration during speech imitation in autism. *Research in Developmental Disabilities, 25*, 559–575.
Williams, J. H. G., Whiten, A., & Singh, T. (2004). A systematic review of action imitation in autism spectrum disorder. *Journal of Autism and Developmental Disorders, 34*(3), 285–299.
Williams, J. H. G., Whiten, A., Suddendorf, T., & Perrett, D. I. (2001). Imitation, mirror neurons and autism. *Neuroscience and Biobehavioral Reviews, 25*, 287–295.
Yamamoto, Y., Saito, T., & Kamio, Y. (2004). The self and other-processing in verbal children with pervasive developmental disorders (PDD): Effects of self and other-action on episodic memory. *Japanese Journal of Child and Adolescent Psychiatry, 45*, 17–29.
Zacks, J. M., Ollinger, J. M., Sheridan, M. A., & Tversky, B. (2002). A parametric study of mental spatial transformations of bodies. *NeuroImage, 16*, 857–872.

10

Brain Connectivity and Emotional Processing in Autism

JENNIFER MOSS
Carnegie Mellon University, Pittsburgh, PA

BRUNO WICKER
University of Buenos Aires, Buenos Aires, Argentina

Just as important as what we say is how we act, which critically impacts our understanding of each other. Nonverbal social cues, including facial expressions and body movements, are crucial to interpersonal competence and the regulation of social interactions. Autism is a neurodevelopmental disorder whose symptom cluster includes unique impairments in communication and social interaction (Hobson, 1986), resulting in a dearth of adaptive social behavior. Little is known about the pathobiology supporting aberrant social behavior in autism, although converging evidence from several recent studies suggests that cortex-wide abnormal functional connectivity patterns are more influential than local deficits in specific regions (Belmonte et al., 2004; Courchesne & Pierce, 2005; Wickelgren, 2005).

Studies finding reduced connectivity in autism include those investigating language processing (Just, Cherkassky, Keller, & Minshew, 2004), visuomotor skills (Villalobos, Mizuno, Dahl, Kemmotsu, & Müller, 2005), inhibition (Kana, Keller, Minshew, & Just, 2007), Theory of Mind (Castelli, Frith, Happé, & Frith, 2002), and fixation resting state (Cherkassky, Kana, Keller, & Just, 2006). In addition, several recent studies of white matter structure have reported disordered cortico-cortical connections in autism (Barnea-Goraly et al., 2004; Herbert et al., 2004; Keller, Kana, & Just, 2007). Functional connectivity is defined as the correlation of activation between different brain areas; this measure, though successful in identifying impaired networks, does not shed light on how the brain areas interact with each other. However, effective connectivity, defined as the influence one system exerts over another with respect to a given experimental context (Büchel & Friston, 2000), allows the estimation of the parameters that control brain activity over time such that activity in one area can be expressed in terms of activity in other brain region(s).

With the advent of neuroimaging, studies on emotional and social processing have been able to identify the brain regions that support such tasks. The main brain regions that have been identified as parts of the social-emotional brain include (1) perceptual areas: occipital cortex, fusiform gyrus, and superior temporal sulcus (STS); and (2) emotional processing areas: amygdala, dorsomedial prefrontal cortex (DMPFC), and lateral prefrontal cortex. Each area plays a crucial role in the execution of social-emotional processing. For instance, the amygdala plays a central role in empathy and Theory of Mind understanding. Studies suggest that, in response to increased emotional salience, the amygdala boosts activation towards representational sites of emotional stimuli or events, causing attentional amplification (Phelps & LeDoux, 2005). DMPFC carries emotional information from subcortical limbic regions (including the amygdala) to executive centers in the prefrontal cortex and is involved in top-down regulation of information processing. DMPFC is active in Theory of Mind and state attribution tasks (e.g., Vogeley et al., 2001), during which people with autism consistently demonstrate decreased activation (Happé, 2003). In autism, DMPFC shows minicolumn regulation abnormalities (Casanova, 2004), which Courchesne and Pierce (2005) interpret as local overconnectivity. Lateral prefrontal cortex is a part of the mirror neuron system that is involved in higher-order control processes of cognition and behavior (Dove, Manley, Epstein, & Owen, 2008). It is involved in intention recognition, so an improper functioning will lead to a misunderstanding of others' intentions and emotions. It has been suggested that dorsolateral PFC (dLPFC) recodes information from posterior association areas into a more abstract form, while ventrolateral PFC (vLPFC) subserves the expression of first-order executive processes (i.e., active selection, comparison, judgment of stimuli).

The evidence for perceptual deficits in autism is mixed. Some studies of social-emotional processing have found perceptual impairments in autism when compared to controls (Dalton et al., 2005; Pierce, Müller, Ambrose, Allen, & Courchesne, 2001; Schultz et al., 2003). For instance, Dalton and colleagues (2005) showed that autism and control participants scan and process images of faces differently, potentially leading to the hypoactivation of the fusiform gyrus commonly reported in studies of face processing in autism. Differences in activation between controls and participants with autism during social-emotional processing have also been found in less posterior areas, such as the amygdala and anterior DMPFC (Baron-Cohen et al., 1999; Critchley et al., 2000; Pierce, Haist, Sedaghat, & Courchesne, 2004; Pierce et al., 2001; Schultz et al., 2003; Wang, Lee, Sigman, & Dapretto, 2007).

In order to understand the implications of these impairments, consider a situation presented in a video in one of our experiments. When a man approaches a soda machine, he inserts his coins, checks the slot where the soda should come out, and finds no soda. He pushes some buttons, punches the machine, and tears off his shirt. Most witnesses to that scene would have similar perceptions and resulting cognitions: They would conclude that the man is angry, that the soda machine does not work, and that if they want a soda, they should choose a different machine. The neurotypical brain processes the social information automatically; focusing on non-social aspects of the scene (for example, what clothes he was wearing) requires effortful, top-down attentional modulation, while a person with autism may show the reverse pattern.

The processing of social or physical perceptual information hinges on mental models formed from intuitions or from deliberations. Intuitions involve the processing of information without conscious intention, and deliberations rely on explicit inductive and deductive reasoning. These models, when applied to emotional information, result in social learning, in which humans engage quite frequently to understand other people's intentions. Social learning is so important that, as indicated above, such processing usually occurs automatically, without conscious intent. Frontal areas of the brain control the attention of the more posterior visual and sensory areas, and behavioral decisions are influenced by intuitive or deliberative processes. Too much or not enough influence from either type of mental model can result in impaired functioning; consider a game of tennis, in which players have to use both logic and intuition to determine where they should stand in order to hit the tennis ball when it returns to them.

If any step in the social processing is flawed, information about emotions or intentionality will be absent, leading to an incomplete understanding of a scene. This can result in an exaggerated focus on information that is not socially pertinent or lead to behavior that is inappropriate in context of the scene (e.g., using the broken soda machine because one's processing of the information that it was not working was incomplete). People with autism often display a flattening of emotions and an inappropriate understanding of affect, which can be at least partially attributed to improper or incomplete emotional processing.

Research on emotional processing in people with autism has produced mixed results (see Schultz et al., 2003, for a review); overall, it appears that people with autism have limited access to emotional information, even when explicitly cued. A confounding variable is the type of stimulus used. Participants may be presented with black and white photographs that can be inspected and closely studied, but are not as true to life as dynamic, naturalistic videos that may present more of a challenge (Kilts, Egan, Gideon, Ely, & Hoffman, 2003).

Our lab set out to investigate emotional processing in autism by testing implicit and explicit emotional processing of naturalistic social stimuli.

Ultimately, we wanted to delve more deeply into the issue of underconnectivity of the emotional processing network by applying effective connectivity modeling to functional magnetic resonance imaging (fMRI) data.

The first study we conducted aimed to discover how people with autism spectrum disorders (ASD) comprehend and utilize emotional information without explicitly being asked to do so. We created point-light movies of an actor performing 10 physical actions (e.g., hopping), demonstrating five subjective actions (e.g., being tired), and demonstrating five emotional actions (e.g., being angry), as well as five videos of objects moving (e.g., a dustpan and brush sweeping). We played the 5 sec videos for control children and children with ASD, asking them to identify and describe what was happening. Responses were rated as "correct" if they accurately identified the action of the point-light displays. For the emotional condition, a response was considered correct if the participants used terms that captured the emotional experience, even though they were not prompted to use emotional words. The control and ASD participants performed comparably in identifying the physical action, subjective action, and object point-light displays, but the ASD group performed significantly worse than controls in the emotional actions condition (ASD: mean percentage of correct responses = 31.42; control: mean = 77.14; $p < .05$). This difference was not attributable to perceptual deficits, a misunderstanding of task demands, or an inability to perceive point-light videos as meaningful representations of people or objects by the people with autism, because their performance in the other conditions was similar to that of controls. Further, even in the emotional conditions, ASD participants were able to correctly identify the physical movements displayed by the actors (a participant might say, "The man is walking back and forth and then tapping his foot up and down," but would not call him angry). The conclusion we drew from this study is that, relative to controls, people with ASD have less of a tendency to think of situations in an emotional framework when not explicitly prompted to do so (Parron et al., 2008). The ASD participants were not apparently performing the emotional processing that the control participants did automatically; this conclusion prompted us to design imaging studies to compare the implicit and explicit emotional processing of people with ASD.

While much of the research on emotional cognition in ASD focuses on face processing, this experiment using full-body point-light displays began to investigate the comprehension of emotions conveyed by body movement. Over time, high-functioning individuals with autism may learn to associate particular facial expressions with certain emotional terms, but it is possible that their understanding of emotions is not deep enough to generalize that associative skill to body movements. Therefore, we developed another experiment to explore whether emotional processing deficits include problems with understanding body language in which we showed participants videos containing either one or two actors and with certain areas of the scene masked with a solid black circle. The four conditions were: (1) an emotional scene with one actor's face masked, for which the participants were asked to identify the emotion of the actor; (2) an emotional scene with an object masked, and again the participants had to identify the emotion; (3) an emotional scene with an object masked, for which the participant were asked to identify the masked object (e.g., a black circle located around the actor's feet masked shoes); and (4) a neutral scene with no mask and no interaction between the actors, only movement (for those videos with a single actor, we attempted to strip the video of emotional or social content), for which the participants pressed a button when the video finished. In the face-masked condition, participants did not have access to facial information and thus had to identify the emotion using body language and movements.

Behavioral performance was equivalent across groups: All the participants were able to identify the actor's emotion or the masked object. The brains of the controls responded to the movies as expected. In each of the emotion recognition conditions (conditions 1, 2, and 3), relative to the neutral condition, controls showed activation throughout the social-emotional brain in response to the facial expressions or the contextual information (i.e., body language). In contrast, the object identification condition (condition 3) elicited activation in the controls in all the areas of the social-emotional brain except the DMPFC. Note that, in this condition—viewing an emotional scene and identifying a masked object—emotional processing still would have occurred for the controls because, as described above, humans typically process any available emotional information, subconsciously, before other types of information. Therefore the areas of the social-emotional brain that activated in this task (i.e., fusiform gyrus, parietal cortex, STS, lateral PFC) can be considered the base network for implicit emotional processing, while DMPFC is specific to the explicit recognition of emotion. A final result for controls was increased STS activity in movies with two actors relative to one, presumably because of increased movement and interaction in the scene.

The ASD participants showed similar results, with the only major exception being a lack of significant response in the DMPFC in all of the conditions relative to the neutral condition. Remember that the ASD participants had equivalent behavioral performance to the controls. These two results indicate that ASD participants did not have explicit access to the same emotional information as controls, but they successfully used a different mechanism to identify emotions. Further investigation using percent signal change found that ASD participants had higher activation in DMPFC and precuneus during the neutral condition than the controls did. In contrast, the DMPFC deactivated for controls during the neutral condition. (The percent signal change analysis replicated the finding of increased activation for the typical subjects in DMPFC, and lack of increased activation for participants with autism, during the emotional conditions.)

The mystery of the brain functioning in autism during the emotional conditions prompted us to design an experiment on which we would model effective connectivity. Again, effective connectivity shows the influence of one brain region on another during a task. We recorded videos of neutral faces transitioning to either angry or happy expressions and asked participants to identify either the actor's age or the actor's emotion. (Another manipulation was in the direction of gaze, towards or away from the participant, but as it had no significant impact on the results, we collapsed the conditions across gaze direction.) Identifying the emotion of the actor involved explicit emotional processing, while identifying the age of the actor tapped implicit emotional processing. We analyzed implicit and explicit emotional processing with behavioral measures, skin conductance rate (SCR), fMRI, and effective connectivity. (For full results and more details, see Wicker et al., 2008.)

Behavioral performance was equivalent in the control ($n = 12$) and ASD ($n = 12$) groups across conditions. SCR amplitudes were found to differ in controls but not in ASD participants for the explicit versus implicit tasks. That is, the ASD group did not have differentiable responses to the explicit emotional processing relative to the implicit processing, as did controls. The fMRI analyses showed no between-groups differences in activation in primary visual areas, STS, or amygdala, indicating that the perceptual processing of the emotional information was intact in ASD, contrary to results from previous studies (e.g., Schultz et al., 2003). This finding could be due to the fact that we used more naturalistic stimuli than did previous studies—that is, colored videos of dynamic, naturalistic facial expressions as opposed to black and white photographs of people with no hair. Further, the fMRI data found that both groups had significant activation in the social brain (STS, lateral PFC, DMPFC, amygdala, temporal pole) in the explicit minus implicit contrast, but the activation was greater for controls than ASD participants in DMPFC (BA 9 and 10), right lateral PFC (BA 44 and 45), right parietal junction, and angular gyrus.

The next step was to model effective connectivity using structural equation modeling in order to explore group-level differences in cortical inter-region relationships. The structural model indicates the number and direction of connections between nodes, outputting path coefficients whose predicted variance-covariance most closely matches the observed variance-covariance. Path coefficients specify the degree of influence one node has on another. They fall between -1 and $+1$ such that $+1$ indicates that, with each unit change in activation (in units of SD) in the source node, there is a positive unit change in activation in the target node.

Our structural model was constructed based on previous functional connectivity analyses (Castelli et al., 2002; Just et al., 2004; Villalobos et al., 2005) and anatomical data in primates (Barbas, 2000; Ghashghaei, Hilgetag, & Barbas, 2007; McDonald, 1998), as well as the results of the explicit minus implicit emotional processing contrast in the current experiment. The nodes were seven regions of interest: a primary visual (occipital) area, fusiform gyrus, STS, amygdala, DMPFC, dorsolateral prefrontal cortex (dLPFC), and ventrolateral prefrontal cortex (vLPFC). For simplicity, and in order to preserve the model's stability, we only used activity observed in the right hemisphere and posited unidirectional connections. Connections between regions are generally reciprocal, but because this experiment intended to address the flow of information between posterior and frontal areas, the simplified model was considered sufficient.

In the model we constructed, information flowed from the occipital cortex (V1/V2) to fusiform gyrus and STS. It is difficult to know exactly which areas are connected to STS, so we chose not to have outputs coming from it. In addition to the perceptual pathways, we included connections between frontal areas that have a top-down influence on posterior areas (Büchel & Friston, 1997; Chaminade & Fonlupt, 2003). Because of its known role in interpreting emotional information, empathy, and Theory of Mind, amygdala was connected to DMPFC, which connected to dLPFC and then vLPFC. Thus we hypothesized an a priori model of explicit emotional processing (Figure 10.1, see plate section). Figure 10.1 depicts the strength and significance of correlations between brain areas. Five connections were impaired in autism (red arrows), one connection showed overconnectivity in autism (blue arrow), and the rest of the connections had no between-group significant differences (* = $p < .05$; ** = $p < .01$; *** = $p < .001$).

The mean adjusted signal from each of these regions was extracted separately for each participant. The maximum likelihood approach was used to calculate path coefficients that minimized the difference between the observed inter-regional correlation matrix and the correlation matrix created by the model. The model could be created in one of two ways: (1) by concatenating the time series data from all the subjects, assuming that variation among subjects was small, random, and well-behaved (Mechelli, Penny, Price, Gitelman, & Friston, 2002); or (2) by calculating the path coefficients separately for each participant and then using a second-level one-sample t-test to investigate the consistency of the inter-regional couplings, with the null hypothesis that the path coefficient was zero. We employed the latter method and calculated the path coefficients separately for each group, ultimately conducting a two-sample t-test to test the null hypothesis that path coefficients were identical between groups.

We evaluated separate models for the control and the ASD participants based on the activation data in the explicit emotional processing condition. (We did not model the connectivity using the implicit condition, since previous research (see above) finds that the same brain areas are involved in both explicit and implicit emotional processing, with the exception of DMPFC.) The most striking primary finding was that the variance-covariance structure of the activation elicited by the explicit emotional processing task was markedly different for the two groups. The path coefficients usually indicated similar pathways of information flow, but the relative efficiency of the connections was different. The between-groups significant differences are indicated in Table 10.1 and in Figure 10.1.

TABLE 10.1 Path Coefficients

Connection			Path Coefficient		Significance of Difference
			Controls	ASD	
Amygdala	→	DMPFC	0.29*	0.16	Trend
DMPFC	→	Dlpfc	0.48**	0.25	*
dLPFC	→	Occipital cortex	0.50***	0.50***	NS
Amygdala	→	Occipital cortex	0.23*	0.16	NS
Occipital cortex	→	Fusiform gyrus	0.66***	0.32**	**
dLPFC	→	Fusiform gyrus	–0.14	0.29**	***
Fusiform gyrus	→	STS	0.20	0.23	NS
Amygdala	→	STS	0.11	0.15	NS
vLPFC	→	STS	0.45**	0.31*	Trend
dLPFC	→	vLPFC	0.60***	0.37*	***
			(within-group difference from 0.0)		(between-group difference)

Note
Standardized path coefficients between regions of interest in controls and participants with autism spectrum disorder (ASD) in an explicit emotional processing task show different patterns of long-range connectivity. NS = not significant; Trend = significant at $p < .01$, uncorrected; * = $p < .05$, ** = $p < .01$, *** = $p < .001$, Bonferroni corrected.

Within the posterior areas, most of the connections were equivalent for ASD participants and control participants. Therefore, it can be concluded that the perceptual level of information processing was intact, consistent with the fMRI results discussed earlier. However, the connection between V1/V2 and fusiform gyrus was impaired (red arrow in Figure 10.1), implying that information is not sent from V1/V2 to fusiform gyrus as rapidly or as easily for ASD participants as it is for control participants.

In contrast, there were several significantly reduced path coefficients in ASD in the frontal lobe, indicating a lowered influence of particular frontal regions upon other regions when compared to the patterns seen within control brains. These differences (indicated by the red arrows in Figure 10.1) include (1) reduced influence of the amygdala on DMPFC ($p < .01$, uncorrected); (2) reduced influence of DMPFC on dLPFC ($p < .05$, with Bonferroni correction); (3) reduced influence of dLPFC on vLPFC ($p < .001$, corrected); and (4) reduced influence of vLPFC on STS ($p < .05$, corrected).

Also in the frontal lobe, one connection was found to be stronger for ASD participants than for controls: the influence of dLPFC on fusiform gyrus ($p < .001$, corrected). In fact, the path coefficient was –.14 for controls and .29 for ASD; the coefficients were so different they involved a change in the direction of the correlation.

At the most abstract level, these results indicate that participants with ASD experienced preserved perceptual processing but impaired higher-order processing. Because ASD subjects had behavioral performance equivalent to controls, it is likely that these individuals accurately perceive and categorize facial expressions of happiness and anger. The impairment seen in DMPFC and vLPFC (areas associated with the higher-order understanding of perceived emotional information), coupled with a recent finding of abnormal mid-vLPFC activation in emotion processing in children with autism (Dapretto et al., 2006), suggests that the strategies adopted by the groups differ such that individuals with autism fail to associate emotional features of the face with their social meanings. The autistic brain sees and identifies the same information as a control brain, but experiences it differently.

Intact perceptual processing contradicts previous research finding impairments in those processes (Pierce et al., 2001; Schultz et al., 2003; but see Hadjikhani et al., 2004; Pierce et al., 2004). The only impairment in the perceptual areas seen in this analysis is in the connection between V1/V2 and fusiform gyrus; this finding is consistent with a study by Bird and colleagues (2006) showing a lack of regulation of V1 on fusiform gyrus activity for autism participants during a face processing task. This result of the current study can be interpreted with reference to the role of fusiform gyrus and its intricate connectivity with other areas in the social-emotional processing network. A dysfunction at such an early stage in processing (but not the earliest stage, i.e., processing in occipital cortex) could contribute to the general impairment in social communication seen in autism.

The finding of reduced communication among areas in the frontal lobe in ASD relative to controls is consistent with previous studies that have found a circumscribed neural network used by people with autism during emotional (see Phan, Wager, Taylor, & Liberzon, 2002, for a review) and social (e.g., Pelphrey, Adolphs, & Morris, 2004) tasks. These differences in connectivity are reified by findings across methodologies; abnormal connectivity is seen in autism when it is investigated using each method that enables us to measure it.

Each of the abnormal pathways found in the effective connectivity analysis merits further investigation and sheds light on the nature of neural dysfunction in autism during emotional processing. The connection between the amygdala and DMPFC is perhaps the initial cause of emotional deficits in autism, as three instances of reduced connectivity are seen that follow this step in the circuitry we defined. The amygdala can act to amplify the signal to representational sites of emotional stimuli; in this model, the amygdala sends information to DMPFC, which has been shown to integrate information from areas throughout the brain when disparate regions are required for processing, such as in emotional processing. The ASD group's reduced correlation of the activity between these areas could indicate a disruption to the neural circuit that colors experience with emotion. Potentially, this could explain the flattened and/or inappropriate affect observed in autism.

The pathways among the prefrontal cortex regions (DMPFC, dLPFC, and vLPFC) were found to be significantly impaired in the ASD group. These highly interconnected areas control executive priorities and the distribution of processing resources (Barceló, Suwazono, & Knight, 2000), including top-down regulation of cognition and behavior (e.g., Dove et al., 2008). The DMPFC carries emotional information from limbic to executive areas (i.e., dLPFC and vLPFC), underpinning the interpretation of emotional and neutral events (Ghashghaei & Barbas, 2002; Ghashghaei et al., 2007). These prefrontal areas are phylogenetically and ontogenically late-developing regions (Giedd, 2004), supporting the hypothesis that they are particularly vulnerable to neurological and psychiatric disorders, including autism, that may not begin to affect brain function until slightly later in development. Important for the current analysis, activity among the areas of the prefrontal cortex is responsible for conscious processing guided by the subject and is not necessarily used in automatic encoding and retrieval (Petrides, 2005). This model was constructed using data from a task requiring explicit identification of emotion, thereby necessitating conscious retrieval and planned cognition. This task requires posterior input into a prefrontal network, but the abnormal activity and connectivity seen in dLPFC and vLPFC suggest that the participants with ASD did not adequately complete these processes.

The abnormally high influence of dLPFC on fusiform gyrus seen in ASD participants relative to controls could potentially explain the equivalent behavioral performance between groups. Although the activity in the prefrontal areas indicated that the groups were performing the task differently, the ASD group performed just as well as controls. This could be because dLPFC sustains emotional information while attention is directed towards goals (Taylor & Fragopanagos, 2005). People with autism have been found to scan and process faces differently than controls do, including an underutilization of the fusiform gyrus (Dalton et al., 2005). The difference in scanning and processing faces could explain the increase in effective connectivity between these areas seen in the current study if ASD participants supplement their understanding of facial expressions with concentrated, dLPFC-controlled fusiform gyrus activity, resulting in similar behavioral performance. The compensatory cognitive process supporting explicit recognition of emotions could thus be indicated by the high dLPFC control of fusiform gyrus. In the experimental context, this control mechanism resulted in satisfactory performance, but it is likely that in everyday social-emotional processing, this connection could fail to update or perform quickly enough and could lead to the behavioral impairments in emotional situations observed in individuals with an ASD. Underconnectivity between frontal and posterior temporal areas has been found in autism in executive tasks (Just, Cherkassky, Keller, Kana, & Minshew, 2007) and face memory tests (Koshino et al., 2008), implying that the ASD participants might not use an affective or social strategy to complete the task. However, individuals with ASD can be taught to explicitly decode facial information, including emotional cues, as seen in the current study.

By illuminating effective connectivity in emotional processing in autism, our results provide evidence for abnormal long-range neural connectivity during relevant tasks. The theory of reduced long-range (i.e., anterior to posterior) connectivity (Courchesne, Redcay, & Kennedy, 2004; Just et al., 2004) helps to explain many of the cognitive dysfunctions seen in autism, particularly those seen in tasks relying on frontal areas to integrate information from diverse brain areas/networks and to provide feedback, guidance, and control to lower-level systems (Taylor & Fragopanagos, 2005). The effective connectivity patterns seen in this study indicate that the dysfunction in emotional processing in autism may result from deficits in the dorsomedial, dorsolateral, and ventrolateral prefrontal cortices. Controls have a parallel attention processing system with privileged pathways allowing rapid comprehension of highly complex visual scenes, including emotional information; this system relies on prefrontal modulation of posterior areas, a collaboration shown to be weak in ASD. Dysfunction in the prefrontal cortices, as seen in participants with autism, results in a lack of top-down modulation, suggesting an alternative processing, possibly sequential, that results in an imperfect understanding of complex visual and emotional information. Deficits in the functioning of the prefrontal cortices are supported by recent histopathological, voxel-based morphometry, MRI volumetric analysis, and diffusion tenor imaging studies that find abnormal development and abnormal local connectivity in these areas (Courchesne et al., 2004; Waiter et al., 2004, 2005).

Currently it is unknown whether abnormalities in effective connectivity result from or give rise to the social-emotional deficits seen in autism. People with autism have been found to have enlarged head sizes, leading to an abnormal development of connectivity (see White, O'Reilly, & Frith, 2009), yet experience shapes the establishment and maintenance of neural connections (Blakemore, den Ouden, Choudhury, & Frith, 2007), especially in social-emotional domains. The theory of autism as a dysfunction of the mirror neuron system maintains that a person with autism is unable to conceive of their own experience in terms of someone else's. As such, differences in the mirror neuron system result in different experiences, and therefore different neural connections, possibly eventually resulting in an inability to interpret another's emotional experiences correctly. Maturation of the brain continues long after birth (e.g., Giedd, 2004), so postnatal experiences influence the formation of brain areas. Anterior STS and lateral PFC do not finish forming until age 10 to 12, the stage in development that coincides with an increased emphasis on correct social behavior. Differences in these critical areas between controls and people with ASD could include different maturation patterns and/or reduced plasticity. All these factors influence the formation of whole brain areas and the connections between them, which in turn affects the experiences we will have in the future, resulting in a complex interplay between anatomy and functioning of the brain.

Effective connectivity analysis offers a unique perspective on the strength and direction of connections among brain areas during a particular cognitive process. Its limitations, however, include the simplicity of its inputs; as stated above, the model used in the current analysis was constrained to the right hemisphere and utilized only unidirectional connections, while we can be sure that the brain's actual processes for comprehending emotion are more complex than that. Such constraints were necessary for the stability of the model, but significant differences in such a basic model lend credence to the theory of abnormal long-range connectivity in ASD. Future research should involve more complex investigations of effective connectivity, especially in brain areas known to be involved in social cognition. However, this method of effective connectivity modeling provides a template of analysis that can be tested in other fMRI studies. If the same impairments in effective connectivity are found for different kinds of processing, then we can more confidently assert that the main problems in autism are dysfunction in frontal areas and abnormal long-range effective connectivity between frontal and posterior brain areas.

REFERENCES

Barbas, H. (2000). Connections underlying the synthesis of cognition, memory, and emotion in primate prefrontal cortices. *Brain Research Bulletin, 52*, 319–330.

Barceló, F., Suwazono, S., & Knight, R. T. (2000). Prefrontal modulation of visual processing in humans. *Nature Neuroscience, 3*, 399–403.

Barnea-Goraly, N., Kwon, H., Menon, V., Eliez, S., Lotspeich, L., & Reiss, A. L. (2004). White matter structure in autism: Preliminary evidence from diffusion tensor imaging. *Biological Psychiatry, 55*, 323–326.

Baron-Cohen, S., Ring, H. A., Wheelwright, S., Bullmore, E. T., Brammer, M. J., Simmons, A., & Williams, S. C. (1999). Social intelligence in the normal and autistic brain: An fMRI study. *European Journal of Neuroscience, 11*, 1891–1898.

Belmonte, M. K., Allen, G., Beckel-Mitchener, A., Boulanger, L. M., Carper, R. A., & Webb, S. J. (2004). Autism and abnormal development of brain connectivity. *Journal of Neuroscience, 24*, 9228–9231.

Bird, G., Catmur, C., Silani, G., Frith, C., & Frith, U. (2006). Attention does not modulate neural responses to social stimuli in autism spectrum disorders. *NeuroImage, 31*, 1614–1624.

Blakemore, S. J., den Ouden, H., Choudhury, S., & Frith, C. (2007). Adolescent development of the neural circuitry for thinking about intentions. *Social, Cognitive, and Affective Neuroscience, 2*, 130–139.

Büchel, C., & Friston, K. J. (1997). Modulation of connectivity in visual pathways by attention: Cortical interactions evaluated with structural equation modeling and fMRI. *Cerebral Cortex, 7*, 768–778.

Büchel, C., & Friston, K. (2000). Assessing interactions among neuronal systems using functional neuroimaging. *Neural Networks, 12*, 871–882.

Casanova, M. (2004). White matter volume increase and minicolumns in autism. *Annals of Neurology, 56*, 453.

Castelli, F., Frith, C., Happé, F., & Frith, U. (2002). Autism, Asperger syndrome, and brain mechanisms for the attribution of mental states to animated shapes. *Brain, 125*, 1839–1849.

Chaminade, T., & Fonlupt, P. (2003). Changes of effective connectivity between the lateral and medial parts of the prefrontal cortex during a visual task. *European Journal of Neuroscience, 18*, 675–679.

Cherkassky, V. L., Kana, R. K., Keller, T. A., & Just, M. A. (2006). Functional connectivity in a baseline resting-state network in autism. *Neuroreport, 17*, 1687–1690.

Courchesne, E., & Pierce, K. (2005). Why the frontal cortex in autism might be talking only to itself: Local over-connectivity but long-distance disconnection. *Current Opinion in Neurobiology, 15*, 225–230.

Courchesne, E., Redcay, E., & Kennedy, D. P. (2004). The autistic brain: Birth through adulthood. *Current Opinions in Neurology, 17*, 489–496.

Critchley, H. D., Daly, E. M., Bullmore, E. T., Williams, S. C., Van Amelsvoort, T., Robertson, D. M., . . . Murphy, D. G. (2000). The functional neuroanatomy of social behaviour: Changes in cerebral blood flow when people with autistic disorder process facial expressions. *Brain, 123*, 2203–2212.

Dalton, K. M., Nacewicz, B. M., Johnstone, T., Schaefer, H. S., Gernsbacher, M. A., Goldsmith, H. H., . . . Davidson, R. J. (2005). Gaze fixation and the neural circuitry of face processing in autism. *Nature Neuroscience, 8*, 519–526.

Dapretto, M., Davies, M. S., Pfeifer, J. H., Scott, A. A., Sigman, M., Bookheimer, S. Y., & Iacoboni, M. (2006). Understanding emotions in others: Mirror neuron dysfunction in children with autism spectrum disorders. *Nature Neuroscience, 9*, 28–30.

Dove, A., Manley, T., Epstein, R., & Owen, A. M. (2008). The engagement of mid-ventrolateral prefrontal cortex and posterior brain regions in intentional cognitive activity. *Human Brain Mapping, 29*, 107–117.

Ghashghaei, H. T., & Barbas, H. (2002). Pathways for emotion: Interactions of prefrontal and anterior temporal pathways in the amygdala of the rhesus monkey. *Neuroscience, 115*, 1261–1279.

Ghashghaei, H. T., Hilgetag, C. C., & Barbas, H. (2007). Sequence of information processing for emotions based on the anatomic dialogue between prefrontal cortex and amygdala. *NeuroImage, 34*, 905–923.

Giedd, J. N. (2004). Structural magnetic resonance imaging of the adolescent brain. *Annals of the New York Academy of Sciences, 1021*, 77–85.

Hadjikhani, N., Joseph, R. M., Snyder, J., Chabris, C. F., Clark, J., Steele, S., . . . Tager-Flusberg, H. (2004). Activation of the fusiform gyrus when individuals with autism spectrum disorder view faces. *NeuroImage, 22*, 1141–1150.

Happé, F. (2003). Theory of mind and the self. *Annals of the New York Academy of Sciences, 1001*, 134–144.

Herbert, M. R., Ziegler, D. A., Makris, N., Filipek, P. A., Kemper, T. L., Normandin, J. J., . . . Caviness, V. S. Jr. (2004). Localization of white matter volume increase in autism and developmental language disorder. *Annals of Neurology, 55*, 530–540.

Hobson, R. P. (1986). The autistic child's appraisal of expressions of emotion. *Journal of Child Psychology and Psychiatry, 27*, 321–342.

Just, M. A., Cherkassky, V. L., Keller, T. A., Kana, R. K., & Minshew, N. J. (2007). Functional and anatomical cortical underconnectivity in autism: Evidence from an fMRI study of an executive function task and corpus callosum morphometry. *Cerebral Cortex, 17*, 951–961.

Just, M. A., Cherkassky, V. L., Keller, T. A., & Minshew, N. J. (2004). Cortical activation and synchronization during sentence comprehension in high-functioning autism: Evidence of underconnectivity. *Brain, 127*, 1811–1821.

Kana, R. K., Keller, T. A., Minshew, N. J., & Just, M. A. (2007). Inhibitory control in high-functioning autism: Decreased activation and underconnectivity in inhibition networks. *Biological Psychiatry, 62*, 198–206.

Keller, T. A., Kana, R. K., & Just, M. A. (2007). A developmental study of the structural integrity of white matter in autism. *Neuroreport, 18*, 23–27.

Kilts, C. D., Egan, G., Gideon, D. A., Ely, T. D., & Hoffman, J. M. (2003). Dissociable neural pathways are involved in the recognition of emotion in static and dynamic facial expressions. *NeuroImage, 18*, 156–168.

Koshino, H., Kana, R. K., Keller, T. A., Cherkassky, V. L., Minshew, N. J., & Just, M. A. (2008). fMRI investigation of working memory for faces in autism: Visual coding and underconnectivity with frontal areas. *Cerebral Cortex, 18*, 289–300.

McDonald, A. J. (1998). Cortical pathways to the mammalian amygdala. *Progress in Neurobiology, 55*, 257–332.

Mechelli, A., Penny, W. D., Price, C. J., Gitelman, D. R., & Friston, K. J. (2002). Effective connectivity and intersubject variability: Using a multisubject network to test differences and commonalities. *NeuroImage, 17*, 1459–1469.

Parron, C., Da Fonesca, D., Santos, A., Moore, D. G., Monfardini, E., & Deruelle, C. (2008). Recognition of biological motion in children with autism spectrum disorders. *Autism, 12*, 261–274.

Pelphrey, K., Adolphs, R., & Morris, J. P. (2004). Neuroanatomical substrates of social cognition dysfunction in autism. *Mental Retardation and Developmental Disabilities Research Reviews, 10*, 259–271.

Petrides, M. (2005). Lateral prefrontal cortex: Architectonic and functional organization. *Philosophical Transactions of the Royal Society of London. Series B, Biological Sciences, 360*, 781–795.

Phan, K. L., Wager, T., Taylor, S. F., & Liberzon, I. (2002). Functional neuroanatomy of emotion: A meta-analysis of emotion activation studies in PET and fMRI. *NeuroImage, 16*, 331–348.

Phelps, E. A., & LeDoux, J. E. (2005). Contributions of the amygdala to emotion processing: From animal models to human behavior. *Neuron, 48*, 175–187.

Pierce, K., Haist, F., Sedaghat, F., & Courchesne, E. (2004). The brain response to personally familiar faces in autism: Findings of fusiform activity and beyond. *Brain, 127*, 2703–2716.

Pierce, K., Müller, R. A., Ambrose, J., Allen, G., & Courchesne, E. (2001). Face processing occurs outside the fusiform "face area" in autism: Evidence from functional MRI. *Brain, 124*, 2059–2073.

Schultz, R. T., Grelotti, D. J., Klin, A., Kleinman, J., Van der Gaag, C., Marois, R., & Skudlarski, P. (2003). The role of the fusiform face area in social cognition: Implications for the pathobiology of autism. *Philosophical Transactions of the Royal Society of London. Series B, Biological Sciences, 358*, 415–427.

Taylor, J. G., & Fragopanagos, N. F. (2005). The interaction of attention and emotion. *Neural Networks, 18*, 353–369.

Villalobos, M. E., Mizuno, A., Dahl, B. C., Kemmotsu, N., & Müller, R. A. (2005). Reduced functional connectivity between V1 and inferior frontal cortex associated with visuomotor performance in autism. *NeuroImage, 25*, 916–925.

Vogeley, K., Bussfeld, P., Newen, A., Herrmann, S., Happé, F., Falkai, P.,… Zilles, K. (2001). Mind reading: Neural mechanisms of theory of mind and self-perspective. *NeuroImage, 14*, 170–181.

Waiter, G. D., Williams, J. H., Murray, A. D., Gilchrist, A., Perrett, D. I., & Whiten, A. (2004). A voxel-based investigation of brain structure in male adolescents with autism spectrum disorder. *NeuroImage, 22*, 619–625.

Waiter, G. D., Williams, J. H., Murray, A. D., Gilchrist, A., Perrett, D. I., & Whiten, A. (2005). Structural white matter deficits in high-functioning individuals with autism spectrum disorder: A voxel-based investigation. *NeuroImage, 24*, 455–461.

Wang, A. T., Lee, S. S., Sigman, M., & Dapretto, M. (2007). Reading affect in the face and voice: Neural correlates of interpreting communicative intent in children and adolescents with autism spectrum disorders. *Archives of General Psychiatry, 64*, 698–708.

White, S., O'Reilly, H., & Frith, U. (2009). Big heads, small details, and autism. *Neuropsychologia, 47*, 1274–1281.

Wickelgren, I. (2005). Autistic brains out of synch? *Science, 308*, 1856–1858.

Wicker, B., Fonlupt, P., Hubert, B., Tardif, C., Gepner, B., & Deruelle, C. (2008). Abnormal cerebral effective connectivity during explicit emotional processing in adults with autism spectrum disorder. *Social, Cognitive, and Affective Neuroscience, 3*, 135–143.

Section V
Overview

11

Organizing Principles for Autism Research

Where Do We Go From Here?

NANCY J. MINSHEW
CARLA A. MAZEFSKY
University of Pittsburgh, School of Medicine, Pittsburgh, PA

This chapter provides some historical perspective on autism research and discusses some of the key challenges facing autism research as we move forward. These challenges include difficulty in synthesizing highly technical and specialized findings from various methods and problems in appropriately communicating the scientific advances to the public. The challenges also include the need to translate understanding of autism's developmental neurobiology into treatments that can produce more rapid changes in the lives of affected individuals. There are also challenges related to the dissemination and implementation of new practices that arise from research findings. We attempt to underscore some of the common threads, such as underconnectivity theory, from this research that demonstrate the growing consensus across different methods, investigators, and topics. In order to do so, we also address some of the key concepts, such as different meanings of "cause" and understanding of the clinical syndrome, that aid in understanding how the different perspectives fit together to describe a central theme. The remainder of this chapter highlights key aspects of the preceding chapters.

FROM THEORIES TO AN EVIDENCE BASE

A mere 25 years ago, very little was known about autism, and so much of what was "known" had minimal objective evidence to support it. In the absence of valid scientific evidence, there had emerged an exuberance of "plausible sounding" theories about the cause of autism. It took a very long time for scientists to accumulate the evidence to rigorously test those original theories and separate what was scientifically valid from what was conjecture to arrive at a core of reproducible and valid findings that would provide the basis for forward progress. Until the evidence was in, and sometimes long after, the field would not give up the compelling early suppositions for the scientifically grounded findings. This attraction to the relatively simple theories that sounded so plausible is worth pondering because it put the emphasis on what was not known in favor of what needed to be known, thereby delaying scientific progress. It is important to recognize that science is a process, not a result. Theories are individuals' best efforts to make scientific sense of what is known in order to frame the best question to investigate next. It is also a team sport in which research groups all over the world pursue what they think is the best question and gradually a body of evidence evolves, is verified, and evolves again.

Technology has grown at an exponential rate during the latter part of the twentieth century, providing the foundation for the major advances in science and medicine that we hear about every day. It was major advances in technology that were responsible for the remarkable advances in the understanding of autism that have taken place over the past 10–15 years. The growth of technology continues at an exponential pace. Thus, the findings reported in this volume constitute big steps forward compared to what was known three to five years ago. The continued growth in technology also bodes extremely well for the future of advances in identifying mechanisms responsible for autism across all levels. With this understanding will come new and innovative interventions that are mechanistically based and thus progressively more efficacious and individually specific.

THE CHALLENGES FACING FORWARD PROGRESS

Synthesizing Technical Findings

One of the challenges of rapid, high technology-based scientific progress is that the findings become progressively more complex and "obscure," requiring increasingly more specialized scientific knowledge to understand even isolated findings. This complexity tends to promote silos of knowledge even among autism "experts." The full meaning or implications of findings are not apparent until the silos are integrated into a whole, because each piece informs the understanding of related pieces. The silos also mean that most people interested in autism, including professionals at all levels, parents, and the public, are unaware of the actual progress that has been made and what that portends for the near future. The "language" engendered by the technology is too specialized for those not doing the work to comprehend. There is therefore a growing challenge to not only disseminate new discoveries in comprehensible but accurate terms, but integrate them so that the larger picture of "what it all means" is apparent to all. Only then will there be a real appreciation for the scientific achievements and discoveries attained in the past 10 years especially, and for what is rapidly playing out. Never has so much been known about autism, but by so few people, with even fewer understanding how it all fits together.

Communicating Findings to the Public

For knowledge to become societal wisdom, it must be distributed widely and implemented to improve quality of life. At the moment, society is largely dependent on the media to be informed of scientific advances. However, the media is primarily a form of entertainment and thus relies on ratings, not on factual accuracy. Media's goal is *not* to disseminate knowledge (accurate verifiable facts and information with a critical appraisal). To be entertaining, "news" items must be brief (a minute in length), dramatic enough to grab viewers' attention, and simplistic enough to make superficial sense in that minute. Sadly, not much is conveyed about any science once it is put through this blender. In fact, it is far more likely not to be conveyed at all, thus depriving the public of the opportunity of being informed about what is going on in science.

No parent can or would want to describe "autism" in one minute, and no scientist will be able to describe discoveries about autism in one minute either. Autism is a neurologic disorder—a result of altered brain function that reflects altered brain structure, albeit at the "microscopic level," and not the ordinary microscope. It is furthermore a disorder of brain development. The brain is the most complex, most intricate structure on earth; its capabilities are unmatched. Furthermore, all the information or code needed for the brain to develop comes from the egg and sperm that form an embryo and is contained in the DNA of the embryo.

It is therefore not surprising that scientific research in autism—both the process and the results—would be at least as complex as the brain and all that transpires during its development. Science is far from reaching the end or the beginning of that complexity, but scientists are steadily engaged in advancing the frontline of knowledge. There is an all-out, exuberant, international hunt to discover the pieces. The hunt is well underway and, thanks to technologic advances, moving fast. But it is silent progress if people do not know about it. There is cause for great celebration, for hope, and for great expectations for the advances that have been made and those that are yet to come. Unfortunately, few people are able to enjoy and take comfort in events because of obstacles to communication and because of societal attitudes that have been shaped by the media to expect the instant minute.

It is therefore vital that new methods be developed to support communication about advances in science and medicine, so that all non-experts in an area can understand what is being done, why, how, what the current results are, what they mean for today, and where the hunt is going next. We need the best of information technology and the best of Hollywood animation working together to apply their remarkable skills for communicating the complex and the fantastic. Their skills are greatly needed to create new, audience-specific, multi-media vehicles that will effectively communicate scientific advances to all.

Translating the Science into Treatments

Another major challenge we are facing in science and in society is how the many new discoveries in autism, some of which are described in this volume, will be translated into new interventions and services. This aspect of science is called translational science. Every advance in the understanding of autism has the potential to improve assessment, intervention, services, and quality of daily life, if only applications and systems could be developed to implement them universally. This aspect of science is the "sleeping beauty"—greatly wanted but still "on ice." Translational efforts are not yet the conscious focus of intention and action in society that they need to be. It is almost as though there is a shared delusion that once a discovery is made "in the laboratory" or "in the scanner" or "in the DNA" that it automatically shows up as improvements in the office tomorrow to produce immediate improvements in people's quality of life. This impression is reinforced by news stories reporting a discovery only after a dramatic community impact is achieved, which is long after the original work and reflects little of what it took to achieve that result. In fact, scientific discoveries are far too complex and specialized today to move directly from the "laboratory" to office practice or daily life, as they did a few generations ago. Once the basic research is done, there are now equally complicated and lengthy research steps to translate scientific discoveries into new assessments and treatments that must in turn be tested for reliability in delivering the expected outcome and then compared to existing interventions for relative efficacy. Translational science needs to be an integral part of research in autism, and ways must be found to accelerate it so that the promise of science pays off in the lives of people today.

Disseminating New Practices

The dissemination and implementation of new practices is yet another major challenge. Even now, most medical practices and services available to the public are determined locally and vary widely in quality and availability. Until recently, advances in practice standards were largely implemented through changes at the time of education of the next generation of providers, be they physicians, teachers, or psychologists. Because science is now advancing much, much faster than the lifespan of providers, and because changes are much more complex than can be effectively conveyed through lectures and books (single exposures over a short time typically out of the context of daily practice), a new model for collating, translating, disseminating, and implementing scientific advances must be developed to meet this challenge.

One step in this process has already been taken in the form of "practice guidelines." The centralized development of "practice guidelines" or "best practices" under the auspices of academic medical specialty organizations provides a mechanism for the experts in an area to carry the responsibility and burden of interpreting and synthesizing new research findings, assessing the strength of the evidence for changes in practices stemming from new findings, and formulating their considerations into a consensus report that makes recommendations for standards of care that reflect the latest science has to offer. These guidelines are revised on a regular basis to reflect further advances. However, there is little awareness by health care policy makers of the existence and potential global beneficial role such guidelines can play in producing and sustaining widespread and uniform quality of care standards. Another obstacle to implementing practice advances is the limited human and information technology systems for systematically and rapidly disseminating and implementing guidelines or standards of care in a manner that automatically links them to individual cases, provides the training needed to use them, and offers the information technology support for checking fidelity of delivery and tracking outcome. The information technology exists to accomplish these tasks, but the human systems and software and hardware infrastructure do not.

The information technology and systems are beginning to emerge, as evidenced by the computerization of medical records and the recent introduction of programs that directly connect providers' records in the office with pharmacies to deliver prescriptions with built-in feedback about medication purchase and refills to monitor compliance. There are now elaborate software and hardware systems for remotely viewing patients in classrooms and homes, distributing the recording to all providers involved in care for analysis, and linking this information to all other existing records on the individuals. These systems are evolving rapidly but are still far too expensive to implement in non-research settings. These early efforts are the leading edge of the technological revolution that must proceed to revolutionize medicine and services.

GOALS FOR THE FUTURE

The purpose of science is to define and explain phenomena in reliable and scientifically sound ways (consistent with known scientific principles about how things work), so that the outcomes reported will replicate, when others faithfully follow all the same methods. This process has been responsible for changing childhood leukemia from a disease with a 15% survival rate to one with 90% survival. Childhood leukemia has become a disease that children live with rather than die from. There is no reason that the same scientific process cannot be applied to autism, with equivalent improvements in intervention. Recent surveys show that the majority of people throughout the world believe in and have confidence in science and scientists. In contrast, the media has produced an urban legend that people do not trust science or scientists. If the upside of media is instant awareness of what is going on, the downside of media is that every event that they focus on becomes part of society's sense of reality; but out of context, such reports distort reality.

While the internet has made more knowledge available to more people than ever before, wisdom or what it all means has moved far beyond the point at which a search of the internet, formerly the encyclopedia, can provide what people need to know to understand many issues. The way in which research is done today by widely distributed multi-site teams is far different from the lone scientist of the past. The changes in technology used in research are not only phenomenal and constantly evolving, but incredibly expensive at the beginning, limiting it, and rightly so for cost containment and public safety, to large institutions. How are people to know what to do in the face of so much knowledge from sources that they cannot assess? Again, like scientists, people will need to depend in the future on the analyses and interpretations of the experts available to them and their providers. The media will need to stop treating every source of information as valid or equally valid to what the true experts know. If a plane crashes, who do you want to go to for the answer—people on the street or the outcome of the careful examination of evidence by known experts with no bias? The explosion of information, fact or not, needs to come with an increase in sophistication for judging it.

The transition to the world of the future is thus full of new challenges, particularly the need to find new ways of thinking about and doing things. It will likely be very costly to build the infrastructure to realize these advances and will take a long time to implement. Attitudes, in addition to financing, will be major factors in speed of change and cost. It is up to everyone to embrace these changes to smooth and speed our entrance into the future and all the marvels it can bring. I see the above issues as the current societal challenges to converting discoveries into a better life. The responsibility for solving these challenges resides with every single person. This challenge has been embraced by many individuals and we are clearly making progress in our understanding of autism, as the next section of this chapter demonstrates.

THE SCIENCE IN THIS VOLUME

The previous chapters review the latest progress in understanding autism from behavior to genetics. The result has been a remarkably integrated set of findings. It was readily apparent that all of these contributions fit together, defining a consistent central theme. It is truly a landmark in the history of autism research that the evidence is now sufficient to define a neurobiologically sensible sequence of mechanisms from gene to behavior.

Cause: Etiology, Pathophysiology, and Context-Related Behavior

In order to understand how the different perspectives in this volume fit together, it is necessary to understand the various scientific and medical meanings of cause. Questions about the "cause" of autism are among the most commonly asked. However, "cause" has many different meanings and rarely do people distinguish which specific phenomenon they are referring to, which has contributed substantially to confusion. From a medical perspective, "cause" refers to pathophysiology (see Figure 11.1) and "etiology" refers to known specific initiating factors. In autism spectrum disorder (ASD), etiology may refer to tuberous sclerosis, maternal rubella or thalidomide during the first trimester of pregnancy, or the recently discovered gene mutations such as neuroligin 3 (Abrahams & Geschwind, 2008). The etiology of the autism syndrome is known in about 30% of cases but the proportion depends on how broadly the clinical definition is extended.

These two meanings of cause need to be distinguished from the instances when "cause" is used to refer to specific instances of behavior, as in "What caused the individual to act like that yesterday?" In this instance, "cause" is

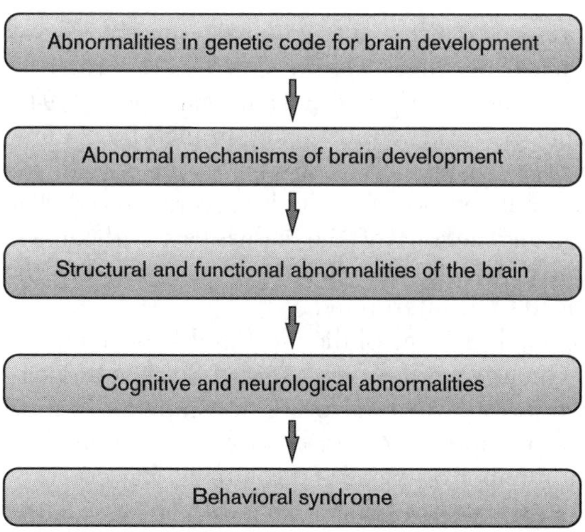

Figure 11.1 From DNA to behavior: A connected sequence of mechanisms at all levels.

about the interplay between the individual as he is currently and the demands of the circumstances; "cause" is then investigated by a functional analysis of behavior. The more general question may be "What causes people with autism to collect things?" In this instance, "cause" may refer to the cognitive basis of this behavior or to the pathophysiology in the brain that produces the cognitive pattern associated with autism.

Autism: The Clinical Syndrome

Having a uniform understanding of what is intended by various terms is relevant and important not only related to "cause," but also to defining the boundaries of the autism syndrome behaviorally for both clinical and research purposes. After decades of debate, research has recently demonstrated that the clinical distinctions among autism, Asperger's disorder, and pervasive developmental disorder not otherwise specified are neither clinically reliable nor neurobiologically valid. DSM-V therefore proposes to collapse all of the clinical syndromes under the single diagnosis of autism spectrum disorder (ASD). Although this diagnostic reduction is appropriate for community diagnosis, the distinctions made at autism research centers between "autism and not autism" and "autism and autism spectrum disorder" (Asperger's disorder, pervasive developmental disorder not otherwise specified) based on shared use of structured research instruments (*Autism Diagnostic Interview, Autism Diagnostic Observation Schedule*) and expert clinical opinion have played a vital role in scientific advances over the past two decades and will likely continue to be used in research studies to establish consistency in group assignment across sites.

There is also historical importance with regard to understanding the varying ways in which behaviors that make up the ASDs present. Dr. Kathrin Hippler's chapter provided a remarkable description of Hans Asperger's (1944) children as adults, extending the spectrum of functioning in high-functioning autism to Asperger's disorder. Her chapter also emphasized the role of the culture at the time and world events on how the children were viewed. The experiences, feelings, thinking, and actions of the individuals with autism define the questions that science seeks to understand and thus remains the context within which findings need to be interpreted.

The volume appropriately opened with one of the most well-known individuals with autism, Dr. Temple Grandin, Professor of Animal Science at Colorado State University and world-renowned advocate for humane animal treatment. Based on a lifetime of experience and careful observations, Dr. Temple Grandin emphasized a number of issues and solutions that everyone needs to seriously consider. First, she stressed that people with autism see and experience a different world than neurotypicals (those without autism). They also think differently about what they experience and have different feelings and reactions. No matter how much progress a child with autism makes, these differences persist to at least some degree, as they do in Dr. Grandin. Next, Dr. Grandin defined three types of thinking among those with ASD: visual thinkers, word masters, and pattern thinkers. Each of these thinking types has special aptitudes and particular limitations. For example, Dr. Grandin is a visual thinker and relies on visualization of everything in order to understand meaning; the extension of this is that she has the equivalent of 3-D software system in her brain for visualizing. The downside is that visualization does not explain abstract meanings. The word masters, in contrast, have a great deal of language (lots of words with varying degrees of comprehension) but do not think visually. Dr. Grandin emphasized that each type of thinker needs to be approached in the way that he or she can optimally learn. The thinking patterns she described in autism are similar to the variations in all children and that teachers learn about in their preparation to teach. The difference of course is the twist that autism adds to each of these types of thinker. The book *You're Going to Love This Kid! Teaching Students With Autism in the Inclusive Classroom* (Kluth, 2010) and many other such books may help teachers better understand the needs of children with autism.

Dr. Grandin has previously emphasized the importance of her mother's 1950s manners. These cultural expectations were uniform throughout her community and enforced by adults in every setting. Family meals, guests, and community activities became opportunities to practice these rules and build skills. She has commented on how important it was that her mother had made statements like "Ask your sister to pass the salt, Temple" when Temple would reach over her sister at the table. This teaching style specified the appropriate behavior in a non-judgmental way and omitted criticism. This culture, in terms of the caring and consistent manner of explicitly stating expectations, is just as important for the success of children and adults with and without autism today.

Once she was an adult, Dr. Grandin was able to combine her own extraordinary thinking abilities, visual memory, and imagery to *explicitly discover* basic principles of adult human interactions in society (secondary socialization). Her metacognitive approach (monitoring her own behavior and its impact on others to guide/shape her ongoing behavior) and concept identification abilities enabled her to make substantial social gains throughout her adult life. Many of the newer interventions for verbal teens and adults with ASD rely heavily on secondary social learning and fostering metacognitive awareness (e.g., Minshew & Eack, 2010).

Elucidation of Social Behavior and Early Manifestations in ASD

Advances in treatment are likely to come from both the insights gained from individuals with autism themselves and the critical research being done to illuminate the mechanisms underlying the manifestations of autism symptoms and how these symptoms unfold over time. Many of the authors presented findings on the neural bases of social function in autism, including Drs. Ami Klin, Warren Jones, Kevin Pelphrey, Susan Perlman, and Brent Vander Wyk. Drs. Jones and Klin described their fascinating work on gaze in toddlers at risk for autism. They showed evidence that toddlers later diagnosed with autism spent less time gazing at peers and more time looking at motion in the environment than neurotypical peers. This work demonstrates that an impairment seen at older ages is actually present considerably before the diagnosis of autism is made. This research is akin to the first birthday videotape studies that documented the existence of signs of autism long before a diagnosis of autism was entertained, and certainly before many pediatricians and often parents appreciated any abnormality in the children. Studies such as these have led to the now-established research strategy of studying infants at risk for developing autism by virtue of having a sibling diagnosed with autism. Dr. Bryson described her work with this method, which has demonstrated the roles of ascending motivational and descending attention control mechanisms in the first year and a half in autism.

Rogers (2009) published a summary of the findings that included this work integrated with all of the other "infant sibling" studies. I have included these findings here because they clear up many questions raised by several of the chapters. Rogers reported that the earliest manifestations of autism are not until nine months of age and involve unusual motor movements, unusual responses to sensory stimuli, and unusual visual regard (unusual interests). These signs are subtle at nine months but refute the long-held hypothesis that the syndrome of autism is caused (pathophysiology) by an early deficit in social motivation that then leads to a downstream cascade of events culminating in all the other manifestations.

Second, Rogers reported that development decelerated, and sometimes very rapidly, between 12 and 24 months of life in the infants later diagnosed with autism. In some cases, intellectual capacity dropped by 50% during this year. This observation makes it clear that intellectual disability is part and parcel of autism and the consequence of the same biological processes that cause the other manifestations of autism.

Between 12 and 24 months of age, the social and gaze abnormalities emerged; preoccupations became more intense. Along with these, regulatory impairments in temperament, inattention, activity, and mood emerged together as part of the same fabric of unfolding neurological dysfunction. These findings reveal the fallacy of thinking of autism as three core symptoms, with associated signs and symptoms, and with a number of co-morbidities. In fact, all of these manifestations are related to the same underlying neurobiologic disturbance. This is consistent with principles governing how neurologic disorders of brain development present in childhood with disruption of neuronal organizational events (Volpe, 2008).

Neural Mechanisms of Gaze and Motion Processing

The above infant research reminds us that signs and symptoms manifest when development reaches the point at which the defective mechanism is called into operation to support brain development and/or function (Volpe, 2008). Additionally, it is important to remember how neural circuitry becomes specialized in order to understand how symptoms in autism manifest. Drs. Pelphrey, Perlman, and Vander Wyk presented their interesting findings on the discovery of specialized neural circuitry for the detection of motion processing and of gaze. This study also considered the differences between biologic motion detection and the motion of inanimate objects. The identification of specialized cortical circuitry for motion detection is a reminder that typical brain development leads to a considerable amount of cortical specialization, and research is steadily demonstrating that this specialization of circuitry is not developing in those diagnosed with autism. In her chapter, Dr. Grandin discussed how we are doing a much better job understanding the mechanisms underlying behavior in autism; and, indeed, this is a good example of that.

Reward Processing in Adults with Autism

In addition to understanding the neural circuitry (pathophysiology cause), understanding of the mechanisms underlying behavior also requires consideration of motivational systems (cause related to functional analysis of behavior). Drs. Ashley Scott-Van Zeeland and Susan Bookheimer talked about social motivation mechanisms in individuals with autism. This harkened back to what Dr. Grandin wrote about how important it is to find out what motivates a person, and to use that motivator. Dr. Fred Volkmar once described a nine-year-old boy with Asperger's who loved snakes and was motivated only by this love for snakes. He was supposed to study the Civil War, but he would not, until Dr. Volkmar asked him to figure out what snakes the soldiers would have encountered when they went across the Gettysburg battlefield. Dr. Volkmar used what this boy was interested in, snakes, in order to help him complete a task that may not have otherwise been completed.

Drs. Ashley Scott-Van Zeeland and Susan Bookheimer discussed their work on abnormalities in the brain mechanisms for reward processing in autism (Scott-Van Zeeland, Dapretto, Ghahremani, Poldrack, & Bookheimer, 2010). This fMRI study demonstrated less brain activation in response to social rewards (smiling faces) than to monetary rewards (dollar signs) in those individuals with autism compared to typical peers. This finding is reminiscent of earlier studies reporting the lack of a differential fMRI response to the mother's face compared to a stranger's. Both of these findings appear to reflect a reduction in the connectivity of the amygdala with other cortical structures which would provide additional integration of related information. These investigators interpreted the results of this study as evidence that reduced social motivation causes (functional analysis of current behavior) the social disturbance in autism. The question left unanswered was what would be seen when the stimuli were the objects of their obsession? This question was answered in their later study, which reports an excessive response in the reward system. Hence, the reward system per se operates but its response depends on what is of most interest to the individual; and in autism it is their special interests as opposed to people's faces.

Implicit Learning and Automatic Processes

Drs. Scott-Van Zeeland and Bookheimer's study reported a second finding and that was a deficit in rewarded learning. The individuals with autism showed no evidence of implicit learning (e.g., learning something without knowing you are learning it, without conscious awareness). Impairments in implicit learning may be one of the most significant recent findings in autism, as the brain relies on these processes for its "thinking" or "information processing." These processes are automatic, nonconscious, and very fast. In contrast, verbally mediated processing, or explicit processing, typically is slow and involves conscious effort. Impaired implicit learning provides an excellent potential explanation for why individuals with autism do not know things that other children automatically know, and do not learn from experience and improve their performance at a second event like typical people do. Defining deficits in automatic processes in ASD may be the next major frontier in cognitive mechanisms and in intervention research. The recently described default network and the emerging description of other levels of brain organization that regulate function and information processing may well provide a neural basis for these automatic abilities.

Drs. Kana, Klein, Klinger, Travers, and Klinger also talked about abnormalities in implicit learning and in automatic processes for categorization, respectively. In typical individuals, the brain automatically integrates details to provide the meaning of the whole. This can range from integrating the details of a face to be able to remember it or discern its expression, or it can apply to the capacity to recognize that the people in the room are an audience listening to a speaker or the children are playing a game and the game is it-tag. In autism, extensive research has documented the unusual predilection of those with autism for details and for not seeing the whole. The deficits in implicit learning and automatic processes documented in autism represent yet another example of the lack of typical development of specialization in forebrain circuitry. These deficits also demonstrate that the neurobiology of autism involves not only abilities under voluntary control but also automatic thinking, feeling, and knowing. This relates back to the long ago words of Kanner, who said in 1972 that these children come into the world without the innately provided abilities to make social-emotional contact with others (Kanner, Rodriquez, & Ashenden, 1972).

In her discussion of how she determined the difference between cats and dogs, Dr. Grandin described a very slow, meticulous examination of all the details of both types of animals in order to ascertain that cats had retractable claws and meowed while dogs had a distinctively different nose and barked. She relies on slow, intentional, verbally mediated deductive logic. The processes she describes demonstrate the absence of the typical automatic learning processes present even in infants and toddlers, who typically learn to distinguish dogs and cats after exposure to a finite number of exemplars that are not usually photo realistic. A lot of social processes are also automatic and very rapid, which they must be if they are to keep pace with human thinking and interactions.

Affective Contact in Autism

Another rapid and often automatic process that significantly impacts interactions in autism (and everyone) is emotion processing and regulation. A number of the authors referred to the affective disturbance in autism. Autism was originally characterized by Kanner in 1943 as "a disorder of affective contact." Despite this, diagnostic criteria for autism have not included problems with emotion regulation as a feature. The seriousness of emotional explosions, in the form of either a verbal or a physical meltdown, or tantrum, increases substantially as the individual gets older. Typically, these individuals with ASD are given medication number one, followed by number two, three, four, then five, etc.; when those fail, they are sent to the hospital. Medications can be helpful to individuals with autism when they are used for a specific purpose and there is some empirical basis to support their use. However, when used as described above, in a nonspecific manner, without a clear plan or understanding of the mechanism contributing to the emotion dysregulation, there is diminished efficacy. It is therefore very important for research to focus on understanding emotions and emotion dysregulation in autism so that more effective interventions can be developed and the role of medications as a last resort can be much diminished.

Many of the packaged intervention programs include an affective component, promoting positive emotional exchanges during interactions and the acquisition of conscious understanding about emotions, emotion expression, and response to the emotions of others. For example, several interventions, from Greenspan's Floortime (Greenspan & Wieder, 2001) to Gutstein's Relationship Development Intervention (Gutstein, 2009) to the most recent adaptation of the Denver Start Early Intervention Model (Dawson et al., 2010), have included major efforts to promote behavioral changes in emotional connections. These interventions are designed to explicitly teach emotion skills that are usually naturally acquired.

Emotional competence is socially embedded and develops within peer and family contexts in typical development (Zeman, Klimes-Dougan,

Cassano, & Adrian, 2007). When typical children of (the mythical) normal parents become distressed, their parents come and embrace them to help contain the emotion. The parents label it: "Did that scare you?" or "Did that make you feel sad?" Parents also go on and provide language and concepts about how to deal with the emotion so that the child feels OK again: "That's not going to hurt you." "That dog surprised you but he did not hurt you. You are okay." Through such experiences, adults teach young children the language of emotion, how to regulate it, and acceptable ways to express it. Adults also teach children that the "rush" they are experiencing is emotion, that they will live through it if they pause, and that it is their responsibility to manage their own emotions. It is this process that the emerging secondary socialization and metacognitive-based neurocognitive interventions are attempting to introduce at an older age in verbal individuals with autism, with evidence of success.

Interventions are likely to be more successful, and could be more specific, with greater understanding of the underlying mechanisms. Impairments in emotional maturity are not the same as the social cognition and verbal and nonverbal communication deficits traditionally described in autism. The affective impairments have their own neural circuitry and neurological mechanisms—the "emotional brain"—that are different though overlapping with those of the "social brain." The importance of "affective disturbances" took on new meaning when structural MRI studies documented that the amygdala was one of the brain structures selectively increased in size along with total brain volume by two-to-three-year-olds with autism. The specific role of this structure in affective manifestations became an active area of investigation when fMRI studies then found alterations in amygdala reactivity in autism and underconnectivity of this structure with the cortex. Recent studies have reported alterations in frontostriatal connectivity with the amygdala in relation to emotion dysregulation. These studies have provided evidence that alterations in the experience, comprehension, and regulation of emotions in autism all have a basis in alterations in neural circuitry. The field of affective neuroscience has already defined a neural circuitry for automatic emotion regulation processes in typical individuals and disturbances in those with affective disorder. Although not yet reported in autism, it seems highly likely that disturbances in the automatic mechanisms for regulation of emotion are centrally affected in autism, particularly in individuals who get angry and explode before they can even think about the fact that they are angry, let alone why and what should be done about it.

Ms. Moss and Dr. Wicker reported the results of the fMRI study on explicit emotion processing in adults with high-functioning autism and Asperger's documenting a reduction in effective connectivity in neural networks engaged during emotion processing (Wicker et al., 2008). Structural equation models provided evidence that the abnormalities in effective connectivity particularly involved the connectivity with prefrontal cortex. They interpreted this as further evidence that the neurobiology of autism impacts the development of "long-range" cerebral connections.

Genetics of Autism

As we continue to make connections between neural circuitry and observed behavior, as Ms. Moss and Dr. Wicker's conclusions do, we need to also remember the basis of all brain differences is in an individual's genes (see Figure 11.1). Dr. Geschwind provided an excellent overview of the progress in genetic research in autism, thus closing the loop between behavior and gene (Abrahams & Geschwind, 2008). About 15–20 genes have been identified that each account for 1–3% of cases each (see Table 11.1). All of the genes implicated in ASD thus far guide some aspect of the development of cortical connections between neurons to produce the altered neural systems. Seeing the clustering of these gene effects together at a molecular level explains why they can all produce a fundamentally similar clinical syndrome.

Because there are many genes rather than one identified in autism, Dr. Geschwind proposed that there are a lot of "autisms." My view is that these genes all impact the same thing, neuronal connectivity. Because at this point science has not provided any clinically meaningful implications of the different genes, I would not divide autism into autisms. Once future research is able to document phenotypic or endophenotypic differences between cases arising from different developmental neurobiologic mechanisms, then cases will be divided into those that are axonal pathfinding disorders and those that are disorders of synaptic formation/maintenance, etc. It is likely to be difficult to differentiate phenotypically between etiologically different axonal pathfinding genes, for example.

It is important to understand that DNA contains the instructions for building humans from the first cell to the end of life. Every human being starts out in the very beginning as one cell. It is amazing that the error rate is as low as it is. However, the detection of copy number variations in the nucleotides of the DNA in autism has provided a new genetic mechanism for the emergence of spontaneous cases in families without another member with autism. With regard to the etiology and pathophysiology of autism, Dr. Geschwind said, "You can't get much more genetic, not in the traditional sense, but in the new sense."

CALLING IT A DAY OR THE SUMMARY

The cause of autism is no longer a great mystery to autism researchers. It is really a disservice to everyone to continue to say that very little is known about the cause of autism. As this volume has demonstrated, the cause of autism is not going to be found at the behavioral or cognitive level but it will be found at the genetic and developmental neurobiologic levels. The ultimate answers will

TABLE 11.1 Evidence Scores for ASD Gene Candidates

Gene	Syndrome or Mutation(s)	Replicated Association	Analysis of Variant	Mouse Model	Other Evidence	Total Score
Promising						
AVPR1A	0	0	0	1	0	1
DISC1	0	0	0	1	0	1
ITGB3	0	1	0	0	0	1
AHI1	2	0	0	0	0	2
EN2	0	1	0	1	0	2
GRIK2	0	1	0	0	1: homozygous mutation results in non-syndromic mental retardation	2
NRXN1	2	0	0	0	0	2
SLC25A12	0	1	0	0	1: associated with neurite outgrowth, expression is upregulated in ASD brain	2
Probable						
CACNA1C	2	0	1	0	0	3
CNTNAP2	2	1	0	0	0	3
MET	0	1	1	0	1: expression reduced in brains of cases versus controls	3
OXTR	0	1	0	0	1: expression reduced in blood of cases versus controls	3
SHANK3	2	0	0	0	1: modulates glutamate-dependent reconfiguration of dendritic spines	3
SLC6A4	0	1	1	0	1: clinical benefit from inhibitors, variation linked to gray-matter volume	3
CADPS2	2	0	1	1	0	4
DHCR7	2	0	1	0	1: hypocholesterolaemia in a proportion of probands	4
FMR1	2	0	1	1	0	4

TABLE 11.1 Continued

NLGN3	2	0	1	1	0	4
NLGN4X	2	0	1	1	0	4
PTEN	2	0	0	1	1: mutations result in abnormal structure and function of the synapse	4
TSC2	2	0	1	0	1: regulates dendrite morphology and function of glutamatergic synapses	4
GABRB3	2	1	0	1	1: expression is dysregulated in pervasive developmental disorders	5
MECP2	2	0	1	1	1: *MECP2* deficiency causes reduced expression of *UBE3A* and *GABRB3*	5
TSC1	2	0	1	1	1: regulates dendrite morphology and function of glutamatergic synapses	5
UBE3A	2	0	1	1	1: expression is dysregulated in pervasive developmental disorders	5
RELN	2	1	1	1	1: levels reduced in brains of cases versus controls	6

Notes
Reprinted with permission from Abrahams & Geschwind (2008).
Because the relationship to disease is most clear for rare variants, we biased our scoring accordingly. Genes associated with an autism spectrum disorder (ASD)-linked syndrome or mutation resulted in 2 points, whereas other lines of evidence resulted in 1 point. To qualify as a mouse model, 2 out of 3 core features were required to be present. The mean and standard deviation for evidence scores are 3.3 and 1.4, respectively. We assigned genes with scores greater than 3 as probable. Although we have done our best to systematically and comprehensively evaluate available data for each of the different molecules discussed, we recognize that these evidence scores are largely arbitrary. Together with unintended omissions of genes that are likely to be important in the ASDs, we hope that this table might serve as a useful starting point for discussion. AHI1, Abelson helper intergration site 1; AVPR1A, arginine vasopressin receptor 1A; CACNA1C, calcium channel voltage-dependent L type alpha 1C subunit; CADPS2, Ca2+-dependent activator protein for secretion 2; CNTNAP2, contactin associated proteinlike 2; DHCR7, 7-dehydrocholesterol reductase; DISC1, disrupted in schizophrenia 1; EN2, engrailed homeobox 2; FMR1, fragile X mental retardation 1; GABRB3, gamma-aminobutyric acid (GABA) A receptor beta 3; GRIK2, glutamate receptor ionotropic kainate 2 precursor; ITGB3, integrin beta 3; MECP2, methyl CpG binding protein 2; MET, met proto-oncogene; NLGN3, neuroligin 3; NLGN4X, neuroligin 4 X-linked; NRXN1, neurexin 1; OXTR, oxytocin receptor; PTEN, phosphatase and tensin homologue; RELN, reelin; SHANK3, SH3 and multiple ankyrin repeat domains 3; SLC25A12, solute carrier family 25 (mitochondrial carrier, Aralar) member 12; SLC6A4, solute carrier family 6 (neurotransmitter transporter, serotonin) member 4; TSC1, tuberous sclerosis 1; TSC2, tuberous sclerosis 2; UBE3A, ubiquitin protein ligase E3A.

be in terms of the molecular events that guide the development of cortical connectivity. What I recommend is to use Dr. Grandin's guideline: nothing but the facts. Follow the scientific evidence. Someone at NIH once said, "When God speaks, we listen, but from everybody else, we expect data." At the FDA, the saying is that "The plural of *anecdote* is not *evidence*." Both of these statements highlight the tantamount importance of the scientific process in discerning reliably associated events. Data (evidence) are the outcome of rigorous procedures that have a high likelihood of producing the same results if the same procedures are used. The data presented in this volume came from very, very careful studies. They are not the final word because the process of science also includes replication and verification by other scientific methods. Science is dynamic and is constantly evolving. However, what science has accomplished in autism in the last decade or more is a core of reliable findings that define a scientifically credible and validated view of the cause of autism. Surely there is much more to learn but this is an accomplishment. It is an accomplishment which comes from large-scale cooperation between scientists, clinicians, and individuals with ASD.

The brain is remarkably complex, and we are continuing to learn about both the brain in general and the brain in autism as research moves forward. A number of the authors stated that finding the same behavior and the same performance in people with autism and in controls does not necessarily mean that their brains are working the same way. The importance of this distinction is that, depending on the task, the "autism" way may be an asset, or it may mean that the "bootstrap" mechanism may not stand up to challenges. The other important ramification of these findings is that inferences about brain localization cannot be drawn from test performance. Rather to detect abnormality in brain function, a neurophysiologic or functional imaging technique must be used.

Neuroimaging methods have led to some consensus regarding underconnectivity as a central feature of the pathophysiology of autism. The overarching theme that cut across all of the chapters was how the development of neural connectivity makes it possible to be social, communicate, and detect biologic motion, among other skills. The genes implicated in autism are coding for events of neuronal organization and neuron pathfinding, all related to connectivity. The most commonly replicated imaging pattern involves underdevelopment of connectivity with frontal cortex and increased local activation posteriorly in visual, parietal, or temporal cortex. The alteration is typically characterized as (functional) underconnectivity of cortical systems (cortico-cortical intra-hemispheric connectivity) and (functional) over-connectivity of local cortical connections (e.g., Just, Cherkassy, Keller, Kana, & Minshew, 2007; Kana, Keller, Cherkassky, Minshew, & Just, 2009).

Underconnectivity also provides a neurobiologic explanation for the cognitive profile of enhanced visual perception and impaired higher-order processing. There is a pattern of increasing impairment with tasks that have higher dependence on the integration of information. While many basic abilities can remain intact or enhanced in autism, there are impairments in higher-order abilities of the same domain (Minshew, Goldstein, & Siegel, 1997; Williams, Goldstein, & Minshew, 2006). Thus, ASD not only affects the social, communication, and reasoning domains (highest information processing demands) but also higher cortical sensory and motor abilities, balance, and memory domains as well.

Moreover, not only does autism impact individuals across multiple domains, but there is remarkable variability between individuals with autism. Many authors brought up the challenge of individual variability. Striking amounts of variability is one of the most universal characteristics of research on autism, with significant differences found in everything from brain structures and function to cognitive characteristics, learning style, behavior, and emotional lability between participants with autism. After reading about the genetics findings, it is apparent that the observed heterogeneity is likely to reflect the genetic heterogeneity of ASD superimposed on familial inheritance.

Recently, Tony Charman (2010) published the results of a survey of verbal adults with autism about what, to them, were the most defining and most bothersome symptoms of autism. The symptoms they described were unusual perceptions and information processing, and difficulty with emotion. This volume has demonstrated that autism has come a very long way in understanding the origin of these manifestations and why there is variability in them among individuals with autism, and in so doing is bringing the capacity for far more effective, mechanistically based interventions. The brass ring hanging at the end will be the capacity to add brain function in those who desire it.

REFERENCES

Abrahams, B. S., & Geschwind, D. H. (2008). Advances in autism genetics: On the threshold of a new neurobiology. *Nature Reviews Genetics, 9*, 341–355.

Asperger, H. (1944). Die "Autistischen Psychopathen" im Kindesalter. *Archiv für Psychiatrie und Nervenkrankheiten, 177*, 76–136.

Charman, T. (2010). Developmental approaches to understanding and treating autism. *Folia Phoniatrica et Logopaedica, 62*(4), 166–177.

Dawson, G., Rogers, S., Munson, J., Smith, M., Winter, J., Greenson, J.,... Varley, J. (2010). Randomized, controlled trial of an intervention for toddlers with autism: the Early Start Denver Model. *Pediatrics, 125*(1): e17–23.

Greenspan, S. I., & Wieder, S. (2001). The DIR (developmental, individual-difference, relationship-based) approach to assessment and intervention planning. *Zero to Three, 21*(4), 11–19.

Gutstein, S. E. (2009). Empowering families through Relationship Development Intervention: An important part of the biopsychosocial management of autism spectrum disorders. *Annals of Clinical Psychiatry, 21*(3), 174–182.

Just M. A., Cherkassky V. L., Keller T. A., Kana R. K., & Minshew N. J. (2007). Functional and anatomical cortical underconnectivity in autism: Evidence from an fMRI

study of an executive function task and corpus callosum morphometry. *Cerebral Cortex, 17*, 951–961.
Kana, R. K., Keller, T. A., Cherkassky, V. L., Minshew, N. J., & Just, M. A. (2009). Atypical frontal-posterior synchronization of Theory of Mind regions in autism during mental state attribution. *Social Neuroscience, 4*, 135–152.
Kanner, L. (1943). Autistic disturbances of affective contact. *Nervous Child, 2*, 217–250.
Kanner, L., Rodriguez, A., & Ashenden, B. (1972). How far can autistic children go in matters of social adaptation? *Journal of Autism and Childhood Schizophrenia, 2*, 9–33.
Kluth, P. (2010). *You're Going to Love This Kid!: Teaching Students With Autism in the Inclusive Classroom* (2nd ed.).Baltimore, MD: Brookes Publishing Co.
Minshew, N. J., & Eack, S. M. (2010). Adapting cognitive enhancement therapy for autism spectrum disorders. NIH Grant MH-85851.
Minshew, N. J., Goldstein, G., & Siegel, D. J. (1997). Neuropsychologic functioning in autism: Profile of a complex information processing disorder. *Journal of the International Neuropsychological Society, 3*, 303–316.
Rogers, S. J. (2009). What are infant siblings teaching us about autism in infancy? *Autism Research, 2*, 125–137.
Scott-Van Zeeland, A. A., Dapretto, M., Ghahremani, D. G., Poldrack, R. A., & Bookheimer, S. Y. (2010). Reward processing in autism. *Autism Research, 3*(2), 53–67.
Volpe, J. J. (2008). Neural tube formation and prosencephalic development. In *Neurology of the Newborn* (5th ed.) (pp. 3–43). Philadelphia, PA: Elsevier Health Sciences.
Wicker, B., Fonlupt, P., Hubert, B., Tardif, C., Gepner, B., & Deruelle, C. (2008). Abnormal cerebral effective connectivity during explicit emotional processing in adults with autism spectrum disorder. *Social Cognitive and Affective Neuroscience, 3*(2), 135–143.
Williams, D. L., Goldstein, G., & Minshew N. J. (2006). Neuropsychologic functioning in children with autism: Further evidence for disordered complex information-processing. *Child Neuropsychology, 12*, 279–298.
Zeman, J., Klimes-Dougan, B., Cassano, M., & Adrian, M. (2007). Measurement issues in emotion research with children and adolescents. *Clinical Psychology: Science and Practice, 14*, 377–401.

Index

Page numbers in *italics* denote tables, those in **bold** denote figures.